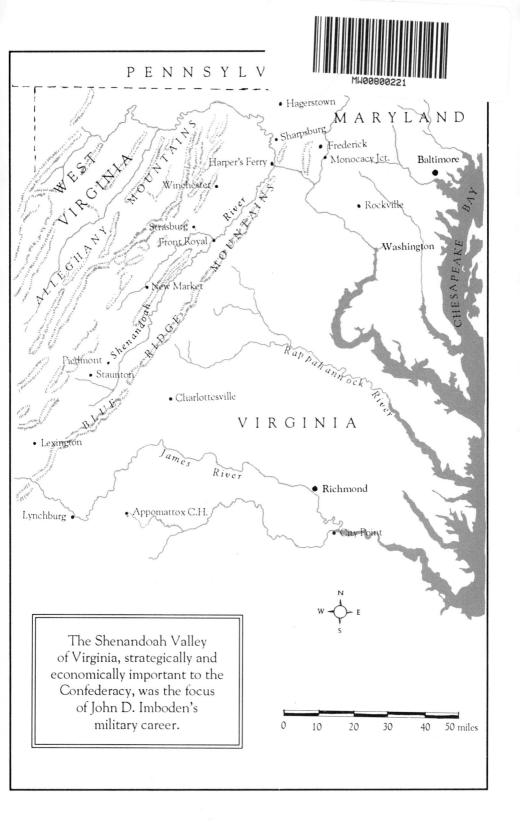

PENNSYLV

MW00800221

MARYLAND

WEST VIRGINIA

ALLEGHANY MOUNTAINS

BLUE RIDGE MOUNTAINS

Hagerstown

Sharpsburg

Frederick

Monocacy Jct.

Baltimore

Harper's Ferry

Winchester

Rockville

Strasburg

Front Royal

Washington

New Market

Shenandoah River

CHESAPEAKE BAY

Piedmont

Staunton

Rappahannock River

Charlottesville

VIRGINIA

Lexington

James River

Richmond

Lynchburg

Appomattox C.H.

City Point

N
W—E
S

The Shenandoah Valley
of Virginia, strategically and
economically important to the
Confederacy, was the focus
of John D. Imboden's
military career.

0   10   20   30   40   50 miles

DEFENDER OF THE VALLEY

Brigadier General
John Daniel Imboden
C.S.A.

DEFENDER OF THE VALLEY

Brigadier General
John Daniel Imboden
C.S.A.

Harold R. Woodward, Jr.

*To Norma Landes,
with my thanks and very
best wishes ...*

Harold R. Woodward Jr.

This book is dedicated to my parents, Harold Ross and Phyllis Ann Rice Woodward of Rochelle, Virginia. Without their help, encouragement and the education they provided, this book would not have been possible.

Published by

Rockbridge Publishing Company
Post Office Box 351
Berryville, VA 22611

Library of Congress Cataloging–in–Publication Data

Woodward, Harold R.
    Defender of the valley : Brigadier General John Daniel Imboden, C.S.A.
/ Harold R. Woodward, Jr.
      p.   cm.
    Includes bibliographical references and index.
    ISBN 1-883522-09-9
    1. Imboden, John D. (John Daniel), 1823-1895. 2. Confederate States
of America. Army. Staunton Artillery—History. 3. Confederate
States of America. Army. Virginia Partisan Rangers, 1st—Biography.
4. Shenandoah River Valley (Va. and W. Va.)—History—Civil War,
1861-1865. 5. Generals—Confederate States of America—Biography.
6. Industrialists—Virginia—Biography.
I. Title.
E467.1.I42W66   1996
973.7'3'092—dc20   95-26121
[B]   CIP

10 9 8 7 6 5 4 3 2 1
First Edition

Contents

Acknowledgements

Anytime one sets out to write a book such as this, he can't expect to be able to complete his work without help from many sources. Many people and institutions have helped in numerous ways to bring to completion this biography. In a way it is partly their book as well as mine. In naming those who have helped it is always a fear that someone's contribution will fail to be noted. I hope that has not happened in this instance, for everyone's assistance has been greatly appreciated.

As always I wish to thank my publisher, Kathie Tennery, for her help, confidence and guidance. I also would like to thank my good friend and compatriot, John Hightower, for his advice. Some relatives of the general have been very helpful: T. Gibson Hobbs, Mrs. John R. (Nancy) Garrett, Jim Moyer and Joseph Moyer. My thanks to Staunton genealogist Katherine G. Bushman, Dr. Owen Graves, Winston Wine, Fred Long, William Hamilton Long, Sr., Ed Hughes, Bob Ward, Miss Sarah F. Johnston and John Heatwole, and my travelling companions, Max Brandt, Jack Adams, Lloyd Powell, and Robert Lee Blankenbaker. I would like also to express my sincere appreciation to Major James J. Rumpler, U.S. Army (ret.), whose expertise, a result of his experience in the saddle, was of tremendous help.

Many libraries and institutions have made available their resources for the good of this project. My gratitude goes to: Alderman Library at the University of Virginia, the University of Kentucky Library, Madison County Public Library, Handley Library in Winchester, James Madison University Library, Mary B. Blount Library at Averett College in Danville, Washington and Lee University Library, the Virginia Military Institute and the Virginia State Library and Archives.

Also of great help were the Staunton/Augusta County Visitor Center,

John Bracken at the New Market Battlefield Military Museum, Clarke County Historical Association, Jefferson County (W.Va.) Historical Society, Fayette County (W.Va.) Historical Society, Lexington Visitor Center, Prince William Public Library, Lynchburg Visitor Center, the National Archives, Library of Congress, West Virginia University Library, Augusta County Clerk's Office, Grand Lodge of Virginia, A.F. & A.M., the New Market Battlefield Park, and the Genealogical Department of the Church of Jesus Christ of Latter-day Saints.

And I would like to express my sincere thanks to Teresa Aylor Jones for an excellent job of typing my manuscript and preparing it for the publisher.

Introduction

When offered a promotion to major general by Robert E. Lee in 1864, John D. Imboden replied, "I really feel that I have as high military rank as I am qualified for." Through this simple statement, one can truly see the essence of a great man.

Imboden was a man of great character. Tall, dark and handsome, the native-born Virginian was a natural leader of men. Highly intelligent and capable, Imboden possessed a rare quality, one that is seldom seen in men in his position—he knew his own limitations.

Born in the Shenandoah Valley of Virginia, Imboden's story is the history of the Valley during his lifetime. His extensive knowledge of the geography and people of the region made him a natural choice to lead troops there during the War Between the States. The prewar lawyer and educator was a logical successor to his good friend Stonewall Jackson as commander of the unique Valley District. Here the dashing, brave and daring Imboden showed his greatest ability as an independent commander. His record as district commander is unblemished, his valuable contribution to the Confederacy's war effort unquestionably immeasurable.

An undeniable factor in Imboden's successful career as a Confederate general was the calibre of men in his command. It was the fiercely devoted, intensely independent and stubborn troops who closely identified with their leader who won the battles and caused their enemies untold headaches. They followed Imboden everywhere, and their exploits on behalf of the South were immense. However, because of their stubbornness, undisciplined ways and fierce devotion to Imboden, trained generals from West Point often levied unwarranted and vicious attacks upon them. But when the chips were down and the cause depended on them, they came through in grand style with Imboden at the front, leading them where they would follow no other officer.

Robert E. Lee and Stonewall Jackson, two of the South's greatest leaders, had high regard for Imboden and his men. Although Imboden's accomplishments and contributions to history were of no small measure, he has largely been overlooked. When I completed a biography of his classmate and friend, James L. Kemper, in 1993, I determined to see that Imboden, who played such an important role in the history of Virginia, the Confederacy and the South, no longer remain just a footnote in history books. The postwar industrialist was, fortunately for the biographer, an accomplished author, leaving behind a wealth of personal recollections of his wartime experiences. Therefore, wherever possible, I have allowed the general to tell his own story, and what a story it is—that of a great and trying time in our history and of the great men who molded it.

The location for most of this story is the great Shenandoah Valley of Virginia, which lies between the Blue Ridge Mountains to the east and the Appalachian Mountains to the west. It takes its name from the Shenandoah River, which bears an Indian name meaning Daughter of the Stars. The river is unique in North America in that it runs from south to north.[1]

Before the war this great valley was a melting pot of nationalities and ideas, a fertile ground for both agricultural crops and independent thought. During the war it was the breadbasket of the Confederacy and the battleground of a nation. After the war it was a place of development and natural resource exploration.

Before, during and after the War Between the States, John Daniel Imboden was the Defender of the Valley.

Harold R. Woodward, Jr.
Rochelle, Virginia

Defender of the Valley
Brigadier General John D. Imboden, C.S.A

The Son of Immigrants

John Sweigert Imboden, born to Diel and Elizabeth Imboden on October 23, 1733, in Henau, Switzerland, ran away from home at age nineteen and immigrated to America aboard the ship *Two Brothers* from Rotterdam, Holland. He arrived in Philadelphia on September 15, 1752, and the ship's captain, Thomas Arnot, having the right to dispose of his services for a fixed number of years to pay for his passage, apprenticed him to a rich farmer in Lebanon County, Pennsylvania, named Diller, his future father-in-law.[1]

John Sweigert served as a private in the 1st Company, Second Battalion, of the Lancaster County (Pennsylvania) Militia during the American Revolution. He died on July 20, 1819, six years after his wife Eleanor's death on July 16, 1813. Both are buried in Hill Church Cemetery in Annville Township, Lancaster County.[2]

One of their seven sons, John Henry Imboden, born October 12, 1765, in Lancaster County, Pennsylvania, was married to Catharine Williams Fernsler (Faunceier) in 1786, had four children in Pennsylvania and emigrated with his family to the Shenandoah Valley of Virginia in 1793.

The first Europeans to view the Shenandoah Valley had come in a party with Virginia's colonial governor, Alexander Spotswood, in 1716. Before long the first settlers arrived in this beautiful agricultural region of sparkling rivers, limestone caverns and fertile soils with waist-high luxuriant grasses, and soon a flood of Scotch-Irish and German immigrants poured down from Pennsylvania, peopling the region with thousands of sturdy, hard working farmers.[3]

The officially recognized religion of the Virginia colony was the Anglican Church of England, yet the Lutheran Germans and their Calvinist Scotch-Irish neighbors continued their religious practices. The Lutherans met in homes until resident pastors could be had and formal churches established; the Scotch-Irish built houses of worship and assigned ministers from the start.[4]

Small villages and towns grew upon the landscape. About five miles east of one of the most prosperous of these towns, Staunton, there meanders a small stream called Christian's Creek, named for one of the earliest white settlers, Gilbert Christian. It runs from Port Republic in the north to South River, near Greenville, entirely within the borders of rolling, pastoral Augusta County.

On October 5, 1793, Gilbert Christian and his wife, Lucy, deeded a hundred ninety-five acres to Cornelius Ruddall and his wife Ingobo. Three years later the Ruddalls sold their property to John Henry Imboden and his wife.[5]

The Imboden farm was near the village of Fishersville and the Old Tinkling Springs Church, the oldest house of worship in the area, in a pastoral setting along a meandering stream. Their land adjoined that of Patrick Christian's, which had in earlier days been the location of Christian's Fort, the oldest defensive outpost in the area, erected by the early pioneers for protection against Indians.[6] John Henry and Catharine's son George William was born December 25, 1793, the fifth of eleven children and the first one born in Virginia.

The Imbodens were farmers, tillers of the soil. They were pleased with their new home and lived simply, determined to provide a good life for their family through hard work and thrift.

The families in the area were close. The children played together and enjoyed the pleasures of life on the farm and also worked together, coping with the hardships of rural life along with their parents. There was a daily routine of seemingly never-ending chores. Always far from easy, their life was at times made harder by the lack of medical facilities, the absence of social life and a constant lack of money.

Close neighbors along Christian's Creek were John Daniel Wunderlich (1765–1845) and his wife Susanna Saunders (1765–1850). Wunderlich's forefathers had come to America from Wurtenburg, Germany, also aboard the *Two Brothers*, but on a different voyage.[7] Wunderlich, Susanna and

John Henry Imboden are all buried in the old Lutheran cemetery about five miles from their homes.

The close proximity of the two families, their German heritage and their Lutheran faith brought George Imboden and the Wunderlich's daughter, Isabella (January 30, 1803–January 10, 1887), together, and on May 15, 1822, they were married in Staunton.

On Sunday morning, February 16, 1823, in the farmhouse of John Henry Imboden on Christian's Creek, George and Isabella's first child was born. A son, he was named John Daniel after his maternal grandfather.[8]

Childhood on the Farm

John Daniel Imboden was born while his parents lived with his grandparents. Over the next three years the family increased in size with the births of his sisters, Susan B., born in 1824, and Polly Jane, born in 1826.[1] By 1827 George and Isabella had saved money enough to buy John Wunderlich's three-hundred-acre farm, and soon the family welcomed Benjamin Franklin, born in 1828.[2]

John Daniel appears to have been a well-adjusted youngster, happy and playful. Besides his parents and siblings, his maternal grandparents lived with them in the spacious two–story brick farmhouse.[3]

As currency was always in short supply, the barter system prevailed in Augusta County at that time. Most purchases were paid for with farm products. Smaller farmers shared farm implements, even horses and oxen. No bank existed in Augusta County until 1847, when one was established in Staunton.[4]

Augusta County is a thousand square miles in size, but the population in 1820 was only 16,742, more than twelve hundred of whom lived in Staunton.[5] People lived at considerable distances from one another. Families were generally large, as children were necessary to keep a farm running. Church provided a weekly opportunity for social life between family and neighbors. Recreational activities consisted of picnics, hay rides, swimming and shooting matches. The Imbodens were healthy and industrious, and although they were not particularly wealthy, the children never lacked for food or clothing.

In the nineteenth century, public education in Virginia was virtually nonexistent. There were a few private schools and academies for those children whose parents were fortunate enough to be able to afford them. The Literary Fund of Virginia was established in 1810, but it was limited in 1818 to support only institutions of higher learning, particularly the state university. There was no provision for intermediate schools, where students could work their way to college or the university.

Basic educational needs for families who were less well-endowed were provided by the old field schools, which were established in a haphazard fashion. Teachers were paid from a common fund. Tuition was usually set at $1.25 per month, and attendance was generally very low. The typical field school was a building of rough-hewn logs with mortar made from creek sand to chink the gaps. The floor was made of puncheon, the roof of chestnut shingles. A raised platform with a pulpit at one end of the single room usually served as the teacher's desk. The pupils' desks were fashioned from wide boards coupled with crude, backless benches. Children of all ages attended the field schools, and no records were kept.

John Daniel's first educational experience came in one such school where he developed an early interest in learning. He was an avid reader, reading every book to which he could gain access, mostly by borrowing from friends and neighbors. This interest was spurred by school and the family's involvement in the Lutheran Church, which always had a learned ministry.

John Daniel was a strong, well-built, healthy, intelligent youngster. As he grew older and stronger he assumed more responsibilities on the farm. His family had built a water-powered sawmill beside the creek, and he performed his share of the work there, including feeding the mill. His father expected him to keep it at maximum efficiency, but the boy devised a scheme that would slow the machinery and allow him to read while working. His father noticed that the mill's output had diminished considerably and quickly determined the cause. John was given a sound whipping and warned that his father did not want him spoiled with book learning.[6]

When John Daniel was nine years old the family suffered the tragic loss of his sisters Susan and Polly and his youngest brother Henry (born in 1831). They were all stricken with scarlet fever, which reached epidemic proportions in the community. Since virtually no medical treatment was available, anyone who contracted the disease was given little hope of recovery. John Daniel, his brother Benjamin and both parents somehow managed to survive.

In the years to follow, six more children were born to the Imbodens. The first, Eliza Catherine (Kate), was born in 1832. She married John Thomas Gibson (1831–1862) in 1857 and died in 1892. After her birth came five boys: George William, born in 1836; David, born in 1838 (died in 1851); Francis Marion (Frank), born in 1841; James Adam (Jim), born in 1843; and Jacob Peck (Jake), born in 1846.

Despite their father's admonition against being spoiled by book learning, all but Jim received a higher education. John Daniel led the way in the autumn of 1841 when he left the farm and enrolled at Washington College in Lexington. Kate attended the Augusta Female Seminary (now Mary Baldwin College) in Staunton; George went to the Staunton Academy; and Frank and Jake attended Virginia Military Institute in Lexington.[7]

The Learning Years

The school that would one day become Washington College was founded in 1749 by early Presbyterian settlers. By 1776 it was known as Liberty Hall Academy, and in 1782 was granted a charter by the state of Virginia.

George Washington believed that education was worthy of philanthropy. In 1796 he gave the school a hundred shares of stock in the James River Canal Company valued at $20,000, which had been conferred upon him by the state legislature. The name of the school was then changed to honor its benefactor. By 1841 Washington College had become one of the more prestigious institutions of higher learning in the state, offering a four-year curriculum leading to a bachelor's degree and a two-year agricultural course designed "to qualify young men to become intelligent farmers."[1]

The sprawling red brick school buildings with their imposing white columns on a hill overlooking the town must have truly been impressive to the eighteen-year-old Imboden, who arrived at Lexington in late August to begin studies. Students were expected to adhere to very strict regulations against drinking, gambling, profanity and dancing. Classes began on September 1 and lasted through the end of June. Tuition was forty dollars per year, with room, board, laundry, firewood and candles costing an additional hundred and fifty. Classes were small in size, began with chapel services at 5:00 A.M. and lasted until dusk.

The first year's curriculum included mathematical and rhetorical studies and the second year was devoted to physical and natural sciences. In addition to the required courses, Imboden studied chemistry, natural philosophy (physics), ethics, French and ancient history.[2]

He also studied civil engineering at nearby Virginia Military Institute.

The state-run V.M.I. had been founded in 1839, and to increase enrollment the legislature had decreed that courses should be offered to Washington College students.[3] As a student at V.M.I., Imboden was a member of the Corps of Cadets, who wore military uniforms and were trained in the use of military equipment. They held dress parades and drilled daily from noon until 1:00 P.M.

Among Imboden's classmates were John Howard McCue, called Howard, of Fishersville, whose family would greatly influence Imboden's life; John Letcher of Lexington, who would become the wartime governor of Virginia; and James Lawson Kemper of Madison County, a future Confederate general and governor of Virginia.[4]

While in Lexington he met Francis H. Smith, a graduate of the military academy at West Point and a former mathematics professor at Hampden-Sidney College, who served as superintendent of V.M.I. for more than fifty years. Smith and Imboden formed a lifelong friendship built on mutual trust and respect.

Another notable person living in Lexington at the time was Claudius Crozet, a native of France, a graduate of Ecole Polytechnic, a soldier under Napoleon and a former professor of engineering at West Point. A man of great vision and talent, in 1823 he was appointed chief engineer for the state of Virginia. In that capacity he had a major influence on the development of education and transportation in the state for more than forty years. Contact with Crozet and the knowledge of his engineering accomplishments left Imboden with an abiding interest in engineering, especially as it applied to railroading and mining.

Four months after his twentieth birthday in June 1843, Imboden graduated from Washington College.[5] Intelligent, handsome and well over six feet tall, Imboden embarked on a career in education.

Choosing a Career

Imboden obtained a position as a teacher at the Virginia Institute for the Education of the Deaf, Dumb and Blind in Staunton.[1] He was an excellent teacher, and so strong was his interest in the welfare of his students that he became a member of the governing body of that institution, a position that he held for many years.

The town of Staunton, settled primarily by Scotch-Irish and German settlers, had become a seedbed for democratic and liberal thought, generously intermingled with the conservative philosophy of the

Episcopalian English. The growing town had recently emerged from a wilderness state into an interesting mixture of social and national elements.

Although a competent teacher, Imboden quickly realized that he was more interested in becoming a lawyer. A great majority of lawyers in that day did not attend law school, the accepted practice being to read law, usually in the office of an established attorney under his direct supervision. They studied *Commentaries on the Laws of England* by Sir William Blackstone and *Commentaries on American Law* by Chancellor James Kent. There were no small number of legal precedents with which to become acquainted, as lawyers of that age relied heavily on the common law of England.

Imboden read law for the better part of a year with William Frazier, after which he satisfied his mentor and other experienced attorneys of the area as to the level of his knowledge. He was then presented with his credentials before the presiding judge of Augusta County and admitted to the bar, fully qualified to counsel clients and represent them in court.[2] In October of 1844 he formed a partnership in Staunton with Frazier.[3]

A small town lawyer was expected to handle all sorts of matters. Imboden handled only a small amount of trial work, as he was involved primarily in business and property law, finance, debt collection and estate settlements. He also represented some corporate clients.[4]

He became well known in the community and interested in the Masonic fraternity. He was admitted to the Staunton Lodge, Number 13, A.F. & A.M., as an Entered Apprentice on December 21, 1844. He passed on to the degree of Fellowcraft on January 9, 1845, and to the sublime degree of Master Mason on January 14. His ardent interest in the Craft and his keen mind enabled him to assimilate the requisite and extensive memory work in a short period of time. His leadership qualities and determination led to his election as Worshipful Master in 1848 and again in 1849. Later he was appointed District Deputy Grand Master for Staunton District Number 11, a high honor bestowed by the Grand Master of all the lodges in Virginia. From 1850 to 1869 he was a member of the Union Royal Arch Chapter Number 2, R.A.M. of Staunton.[5]

The partnership with Frazier continued for several years, until Frazier left the practice to pursue an interest in commercial activities at Rockbridge Alum Springs, a health resort in Rockbridge County, seventeen miles from Lexington.[6] In 1854 Imboden became the junior partner of his college classmate and very good friend, Howard McCue.[7]

The McCue family was an old, well-established and highly esteemed family in Augusta County—Scotch-Irish Presbyterians, Whigs and Masons.

The Young Lawyer Settles Down

As Imboden's law practice grew, he became involved in other business ventures. He invested in Staunton real estate, purchasing building sites and erecting houses on North Market and West Main streets. He built a home for himself at the top of Market Street.[1]

The McCue family played important roles in Imboden's life. He practiced law with McCue and met and courted his cousin, Eliza Allen McCue, the daughter of Col. Franklin McCue. Known as "Dice," she was not yet twenty-one years old when they were married on June 26, 1845. Their first child, Jane Crawford, or "Jennie," was born on November 28, 1847. She was the joy of their lives.[2]

The McCue-Imboden law partnership continued until 1860, when McCue and his wife, the former Signora Willis, moved to her native Nelson County.[3] Imboden built a new office on Lawyer's Row in downtown Staunton in close proximity to the courthouse. It was completed in 1860 but would eventually be taken over by Harrison May, Esq.[4] The war would interrupt Imboden's plans to practice there.

Entrance into Politics

Imboden became interested in politics during the administration of President John Tyler, a staunch Jeffersonian and the first vice president to succeed to the presidency. As he followed politics closely on both a state and national level, he came to feel that he was adequately qualified to enter the political arena. Youthful and full of enthusiasm, he welcomed a challenge and felt the Whig party and its espoused principles to be the party that best represented him and his ideas.

The Whigs, the party of Kentucky's Henry Clay, with their roots in the old National Republican and Anti-Masonic parties, had been formed in opposition to President Andrew Jackson's Democratic party. Deriving their name from its use in England, the Whigs were said to prefer liberty over tyranny, privilege over prerogative and the Constitution and laws over the executive branch. The Whigs embraced the party principles of Madison and Monroe and included in their number a majority of the

Southern slaveholders. Southerners had a deep-seated hatred of Jackson because of his proclamation against South Carolina's nullification of federal laws. The Southerners believed strongly in free trade.[1]

The Whigs' first success in Virginia came in 1834 with the election of Littleton Waller Tazewell as governor, followed by Whigs David Campbell, Thomas Walker Gilmer and John Rutherford. The party suffered a major setback in Virginia in the election of 1842, however, when Democrat James McDowell was elected.

The election of 1844 pitted the Jacksonist Democrat James Knox Polk of Tennessee against Henry Clay, who was waging his third campaign for the nation's highest office. Imboden joined the Augusta County Whigs in their efforts to swing votes for Clay. Although Clay was extremely popular, Polk took a determined stand for the annexation of Texas and Oregon. The abolitionists fielded a candidate for the first time as well. Their candidate, James G. Birney of Kentucky, siphoned off 62,000 Whig votes to give Polk a victory by 38,181 votes.

This defeat did not sound the death knell of the Whigs, however, for in 1848 they succeeded in getting elected a Mexican War hero, Gen. Zachary "Old Rough and Ready" Taylor, the most popular man in the country. Taylor's political views were unknown, but the Democratic party was split over the slavery question, which signaled a huge victory for the Whigs.

Imboden, very active in Taylor's campaign, was making inroads into Whig politics. Although he had several prominent and influential Democratic friends—such as William "Extra Billy" Smith, John R. Floyd, Henry A. Wise and John Letcher—Imboden was a man of principle. He believed in a program of continuing internal improvements and was decidedly stubborn; also, the McCue family were staunch anti-Jackson Whigs.[2]

Imboden enthusiastically reaped the harvest of hard campaigning and travelled to Washington, D.C., to be at the inauguration in March 1849. He visited Baltimore and Philadelphia before returning to Staunton. The trip was more than just pleasure, however; it was a great educational jaunt as well. He had always been interested in railroads and wanted to experience firsthand the pleasures of riding the rails as well as studying their operation and management.[3]

Imboden had been appointed commissioner of schools in 1847, a continuing annual appointment that increased his standing and reputation, and had served as a presidential elector in 1848, a signal honor that greatly enhanced his status in the community. He was also given the responsibility of handling the funds doled out by Richmond for the operation of the Deaf, Dumb and Blind Institute, a capacity in which he continued until 1858.[4]

In April 1850 a statewide referendum was held to decide whether a convention should be called to change the Virginia Constitution of 1830. The western sections of the state responded enthusiastically to the chance for governmental reform since they felt that the power had been in the hands of the easterners for far too long. The contest became a battle between the conservatives and the reformers. Imboden's old classmate, John Letcher, joined the Whigs. Letcher, a leader of the Valley reformers, sought election as the convention delegate from the district that included Rockbridge, Highland and Augusta counties.

Imboden promised a majority in Augusta County despite rumors that Letcher was an abolitionist. He was able to convince solid Augusta County Whigs like John B. Baldwin and Alexander Hugh Holmes Stuart that Letcher was their man. Letcher himself took the bull by the horns and convinced the Valley people that he had their best interest at heart. When the election rolled around on August 22, 1850, the reformers won all five of the district seats at the convention.[5]

The convention held in Richmond drew up a new constitution which was presented to the people and ratified at the polls in 1851. It contained some radical changes, such as suffrage for all white male citizens without the condition of property holding and the popular election of judges and all county officials rather than appointment.

President Taylor, the second Whig president, died in office on July 9, 1850, and was succeeded by Millard Fillmore of New York, who would be the last of the Whig presidents.

Imboden ran for office himself and was elected in 1851 to his first two-year term in the Virginia House of Delegates.[6] That winter he travelled to Richmond to begin his career as an elected representative of the people.

Political Career

Transportation, especially railroads, would be a major issue for Imboden during most of his political career. On January 27, 1851, he wrote to Eliza of his first speech on the House floor, a half-hour presentation that advocated the extension of the Virginia Central Railroad from Richmond to the Ohio River.[1] On March 9 he made a second speech, twice as long, in which he supported a pending bill to provide the necessary funding for completion of the Virginia Central as far as Staunton.[2]

As a Whig, Imboden believed in the party's position of diversity of industry in the South. He saw industry as the key to wealth and independence and recognized the importance of providing local markets with a ready supply of manufactured materials. The expansion of the railroads could help to accomplish these goals.

During the period of 1851–1852 the Southern political parties reorganized. Mainstream Democrats sought to retrieve those who had strayed away into the Unionist faction. Southern Whigs no longer found any vital national issues on which to base their commitment to their Northern counterparts. Matters of internal improvement in the southern states were of the primary importance to them. On the national level the States Rights Whigs began to align themselves with the Democrats.[3] In August John Letcher wrote Imboden that "the continuing sectional crisis was exaggerating a few key differences and gradually destroying the traditional flexibility of the American political system."[4]

The Whigs still exhibited a penchant for military heroes in their candidate, Winfield Scott, who was the ranking general in the army and a bona fide hero of the Mexican War. But with the split in the Whig party Franklin Pierce, a New Hampshire Democrat, easily defeated Scott by carrying twenty-seven of the thirty-one states. The loss of the 1852 election, followed closely by the Kansas-Nebraska Act of 1854, put an end to the North-South confederation of the Whig party.

Caught up in the realignment of the political parties, Imboden failed to be returned to his seat in the House of Delegates for the 1853–1854 term, but he did not stay out of politics for long. By 1855 he was able to marshal sufficient votes from former Whigs to be returned to the General Assembly for his second term. There his colleagues recognized his abilities by making him chairman of the Census and Statistics Committee.[5]

Now in his early thirties, Imboden was a pleasant man, socially and politically mature, with a winning personality who had made many friends in the state capital. He was an interesting speaker, in much demand at various local functions.

The presidential election of 1856 saw the emergence of a new political party. The Republicans had as their only real issue the abolishment of slavery and put forth Gen. John C. Frémont as their first candidate. The Democrats nominated James Buchanan of Pennsylvania, and the remnants of the Whig party nominated former president Millard Fillmore.

Former president John Tyler of Virginia predicted that "if the Black Republicans won the election the Union would cease to exist."[6] Governor Henry A. Wise of Virginia stated that "the South would not submit to the sectional victory of a Free Soiler or a Black Republican." Buchanan won with 174 electoral votes over Frémont's 114. Fillmore carried only Maryland; southern Whigs had abandoned him in favor of Buchanan.[7]

The administration of President Buchanan was marred by a series of tragic events that widened the rift between the northern and southern sections of the country. In March 1857 the Supreme Court handed down the Dred Scott Decision, and in December 1857 the Le Compton Constitution was passed in Kansas. Those events, plus the split of the Democratic party in Congress, set the stage for the eventual and unavoidable split that would occur between the North and the South.

In 1857 Imboden was challenged by his old friend John Letcher in his bid for a fourth term in Congress. Imboden ran under the banner of the Distribution party, a local group of Whigs and Know-Nothings whose chief objective was to defeat Democrats. The Distribution party was confined to the local congressional district, principally Staunton. Imboden knew that he had no chance of winning but provided his supporters with a viable candidate nonetheless.[8] His opponent, a well-established diplomat and statesman, won by a three-to-one margin.[9] Although he lost the election, Imboden gained popularity among the old-line Whigs and received the wholehearted support of the Staunton *Spectator.*

After his ill-fated bid for Congress Imboden ran for the office of Augusta County Clerk, which was being vacated by Jefferson Kinney. He was easily elected for a six-year term starting on January 1, 1858.[10] He also became a trustee of the Augusta Female Seminary, a position in which he served for many years, well into the administration of the school's benefactress and future namesake, Mary Baldwin.

Imboden's family grew during this period. In 1847 he and Dice had built a comfortable home in Staunton that they named Ingleside Cottage. Their second daughter, whom they named Isabella, or "Bel," was born there on December 6, 1849. She died suddenly on July 27, 1852, leaving Imboden heartbroken. On March 29, 1852, their third daughter was born. Named Martha Russell but called "Russie" by her father, she was a happy, healthy little girl and the joy of her father's life. The couple's fourth child and first son, Frank Howard, was born on June 21, 1855, followed nineteen months later by another son on March 17, 1857, who was named George William, after his uncle.

Everything seemed to be going well for Imboden—he had a good career, political office, loving wife and children. Yet just two days before Christmas, on December 23, 1857, his wife of twelve years died from a lingering illness. He and Dice had been very close, sharing a mutual love and respect for one another, and her death left Imboden in a state of despondency. She was buried beside Bel at Tinkling Springs Church. It fell to ten-year-old Jennie to handle most of the domestic chores.

On May 12, 1859, Imboden married Mary Wilson McPhail, ten years his junior, the eldest daughter of John Blain McPhail and Nannie Carrington of Mulberry Hill in Charlotte County. He built a new home for her on Market Street in Staunton, called Green Hill. Mary proved to be a good stepmother to Imboden's children, as well as an excellent parent to their own. Nannie Carrington, "Nantsie," was born February 16, 1860; Mary Wilson was born November 12, 1860; and John Daniel, Jr., was born on July 21, 1863.[11]

Imboden spent a great deal of time in Richmond on political and business matters. He had become one of the most prominent and prosperous men from his section of the state.

Militia Service

Virginia had a long-standing militia system based on the citizen soldier's ability to protect his home, county and state when the need arose. The Virginia Militia had seen extensive service in the French and Indian War, Lord Dunmore's War and the American Revolution. Following the Revolution, each Virginia county was divided into districts, and each district was required to provide a company of militia, which was required to perform periodic drills and musters under the guidance of the county commander.

During the Mexican War, Imboden had seen militia service with the 32nd Regiment of Virginia Militia, later known as the 160th. In 1846, when President James Polk called for fifty thousand volunteers—twenty thousand from the South and West—Virginia supplied a regiment, in which Augusta County furnished one company. Maj. John Marshall McCue, adjutant of the 32nd Virginia who would serve in the Augusta Home Guard during the War Between the States, inquired of Imboden as to his interest in becoming the regimental adjutant.[1] Although he had no real military aspirations, Imboden wanted to do what was right and felt it was his patriotic duty to serve where needed. He accepted the appointment.[2] His brother Benjamin became a corporal in the Augusta

County company and was sent to Mexico; he died of typhoid fever at Buena Vista.[3] Imboden's militia service continued after the Mexican War.

In 1851 and 1853 changes were made in the law that abolished musters and discontinued training of militia officers, which effectively did away with the militia. Through the hard work and diligence of Imboden's classmate, James L. Kemper, who served in the General Assembly from Madison County in 1856 and again in 1858, the militia was restored to its former strength.[4]

When the system of drills, musters and training was reestablished, Imboden was commissioned a captain in the 160th Regt., 13th Brigade, 5th Division of the Virginia Militia by Governor Wise. On June 10, 1858, he took the oath of office at the courthouse in Staunton from the town's mayor.[5] He remained in active service with the West Augusta Guard until exempted from duty on August 25, 1858, because of his political office. Although not active, he remained on the company's rolls as an honorary member.[6]

Sectional differences in the country were heating up at this time. In October 1859 a fanatic madman by the name of John Brown captured the federal arsenal at Harpers Ferry with a small army of accomplices, intent on arming slaves for a massive revolt against their masters. Governor Wise ordered the state militia to the scene, and they, with the aid of a company of United States Marines under Col. Robert E. Lee and Lt. James Ewell Brown Stuart, captured the deranged abolitionist and his followers.

The residents of Virginia were shocked by the events, and a general call for a military buildup was issued. Then on November 19, 1859, a rumor circulated that a move was afoot to free Brown from the jail in Charles Town. The West Augusta Guard departed from Staunton by rail the next morning to stand guard until Brown and his accomplices could be brought to justice.[7]

Twelve new military units were formed in Staunton to supplement the militia—nine companies of infantry, two troops of cavalry and one battery of artillery.[8] Imboden was elected captain of the newly formed Staunton Artillery on November 28, 1859. Not surprisingly, he showed an inordinate talent for recruiting. His magnetic personality and natural leadership abilities enabled him to enroll a full complement of eighty artillerymen and subordinate officers in a relatively short time.[9]

On December 12, 1859, he wrote to Col. Francis H. Smith at V.M.I., requesting four mountain howitzers from the commonwealth for his battery.[10] When his request was denied, Imboden set out for Richmond to see Governor Wise, who personally approved the procurement of two brass six-pounder field guns, equipped. The elated captain visited the governor to thank him for his decision to overrule Adjt. Gen. William H. Richardson in awarding the guns to the Staunton Artillery. Wise replied,

> You could not have obtained them, sir, but for the confidence I have in you and your men to keep them in perfect order—ready for service—and all I ask in return is that whenever I call for these guns, and order you and your men to come with them, you will obey the call, whether I be in or out of office or the call be private or official.[11]

Imboden replied with the promise to "lacquer his guns, build them a shelter, drill his men, train his horses, and obey the call of the Governor, whether made on him Governor or not Governor." He also promised to furnish harness and accouterments for the cannon.[12]

The whole town of Staunton turned out to greet Imboden upon his return with the two guns. On Saturday, December 31, 1859, despite inclement weather, officers of all of Augusta County's volunteer companies met at the courthouse in Staunton to form themselves into a full regiment of volunteers. William H. Harman, brigadier general in the Virginia Militia and a veteran of the Mexican War, was invited to preside, and Imboden was appointed secretary. A second meeting was set for January 14, 1860, to finalize the plans and elect field officers.

On January 17, 1860, Col. William D. Anderson of the 160th Regiment ordered his captains to enroll all men eligible for military service. Boundary lines were established, and Imboden's brother George was elected captain of Co. A, 1st Battalion. His jurisdiction included "all of the Corporation of Staunton south of Beverley Street."[13] The officers set about to carry out their duties and prepare tables of organization.

True to his word to Governor Wise, Imboden immediately began to train his cannoneers. On the anniversary of George Washington's birthday, February 22, 1860, the Staunton Artillery made their first public appearance. Along with the West Augusta Guard, the artillerymen demonstrated the results of their training. About forty-five uniformed cannoneers had gained what the Staunton *Spectator* reported as "remarkable skill in a short time. The cannon were loaded and fired twenty-five or thirty times."[14]

Imboden contracted with a Richmond flagmaker to fabricate a banner for the Staunton Artillery. The beautiful and costly flag featured the state seal of Virginia on a bonny blue flag, along with the date on which the unit was organized, November 28, 1859. The flag was delivered in time for a ceremony to coincide with the annual three-day training period of the militia. The new cannoneers were reviewed by Gen. Harman, and the ceremonies concluded at the Central Railroad Depot, where the general, representing the ladies of Staunton and Augusta County, presented the flag to the battery.[15]

Imboden's battery and the West Augusta Guard greeted the arrival of John Letcher, the new governor, and other dignitaries from Richmond on July 5, 1860. Following a ceremony at the depot and speeches at the nearby Virginia Hotel, the guests and the militiamen moved to the homes of Lt. Thomas L. Harman of the artillery and Capt. William S.H. Baylor of the guards. There, according to the *Spectator,* "a thousand refreshments of the most substantial as well as delicate character" were served. The next day the governor inspected the Staunton Artillery and two infantry companies.

In August the artillery, the guard and Turner's cornet band journeyed by rail to Fishersville to attend a ceremony awarding a flag to the Augusta Rifles. Imboden's cannoneers fired the salute following a parade, with about fifteen hundred people in attendance. The *Spectator* boasted, "We challenge any town in the state to contrast its military companies with those of Staunton."[16]

As the nation moved closer to crisis, Imboden began to devote more and more time to military matters. He requested three copies of *Cavalry Tactics* from Secretary of War John B. Floyd, which were sent within two weeks.[17] When the time came, he and his men would be ready to stand the test.

The Secession Crisis

On April 23, 1860, in Charleston, South Carolina, the national Democratic party fell apart when dissension arose concerning the slavery question and the delegates from the Southern states walked out. The Northern wing of the Democrats, mostly supporters of Senator Stephen Douglas of Illinois, met two months later and nominated Douglas for president. The Southern wing of the party then met and nominated John C. Breckinridge of Kentucky.

The remnants of the old Whig party held a convention in Baltimore in May; calling themselves the Constitutional Union party, they nominated

John Bell of Tennessee for president. Later that month the Republicans, who publicly announced their opposition to slavery, particularly its expansion into the western territories, met in Chicago and nominated a virtual unknown from Illinois by the name of Abraham Lincoln.

Remembering the valuable service that Imboden had given the Whigs in the past, the Constitutional Union party actively sought his support.[1] Spokesmen from the party urged him to attend a grand rally in September, where he actively campaigned for Bell.

When the results of the November 6 election were in, the Republican Lincoln had won with one hundred eighty of the three hundred three electoral votes. The states of the deep South voted for Breckinridge, while Virginia and two other border states cast their electoral votes for Bell.

Almost immediately there was talk in the Southern states of seceding from the Union. Augusta County was largely pro-Union, and on November 26, 1860, a meeting was called in Staunton to proclaim the county's allegiance to the United States. A massive crowd gathered at the courthouse, and a citizens' committee was formed with Imboden as a member. Members of the committee presented resolutions that supported the constitution, respected the right of a state to secede, were sympathetic with the Southern states, recognized that the Republican administration was sectional and threatening, but stated bluntly that the "mere election of a citizen to the President. . .[is] not sufficient cause for breaking up the government."[2]

On December 20, 1860, an Ordinance of Secession was adopted by a convention held by the South Carolina legislature. South Carolina authorities immediately began to seize federal property.

As other Southern states followed South Carolina's lead and began to secede, Imboden shifted his position. He felt that the best course for Virginia to follow was to secede and maintain the stance of an independent state while acting as a mediator between the North and South. He hoped that finding a peaceful solution to the nation's troubles would lead to a new and better Union, with the slavery question settled by a convention called for that specific purpose.[3]

The Virginia legislature went into special session on January 7, 1861, to consider the commonwealth's course and agreed to hold a special convention to decide the issue. Delegates were to be elected by popular vote. Imboden ran for election favoring secession as the only peace measure Virginia could adopt.[4] Because of his openly secessionist views, he was overwhelmingly defeated by the Union candidate, Alexander H. Stuart.[5]

The largely pro-Union convention convened on February 13 and lasted for sixty-four days, with John Janney as president. Those raising voices for secession were former governor Henry Wise and former President John Tyler.

Imboden stayed in Staunton, where he divided his time between his law practice and his battery, watching with keen interest the happenings in Richmond and Charleston Harbor, where a drama was unfolding that would seal the fate of the nation. Fort Sumter, which guarded the harbor, was the last hold of federal authority that had not yet surrendered nor been seized by the South Carolinians.

In February 1861 Imboden considered speculating on lands in Florida and Louisiana. He was afraid that Virginia would not side with the South and seriously considered moving farther in that direction.

He owned eight hundred acres in Kentucky along the Cumberland River, mostly timberland worked by twenty to thirty hands. It was a profitable lumber business through which he anticipated an annual income of $10,000 for the next several years. His land was only twenty-four miles from free-soil Illinois, increasing his concern as to a war's effect on his business and the running off of his slaves.[6]

Once again on Washington's birthday, February 22, 1861, Imboden's battery, the guard and the cornet band paraded through Staunton and camped on the outskirts of town. The artillery fired a salute at noon, "shaking the earth with the loud reports of their cannon." That evening the troops marched to a fair at the depot. The *Spectator* reported:

> We never see these excellent companies, composed as they are of as good material as ever marched to martial tread, that we do not feel proud of them and regret there is a probability that they may be made food for powder.[7]

In April the convention in Richmond appointed a committee of twenty-one members, including former governor Wise, to report the best measure to keep Virginia out of a war. On April 12, after refusing to surrender, Fort Sumter was fired upon by Southern troops under Gen. Pierre G.T. Beauregard of Louisiana. Wise then moved for Virginia to adopt a plan of armed neutrality, a motion defeated by a vote of thirteen to eight.

The next day Imboden was summoned to Richmond.[8] He was about to embark on one of the most unusual and dangerous schemes of his career.

Raid on Harpers Ferry

On April 15, 1861, late in the day, Imboden received a telegram from Nat Tyler, editor of the Richmond *Enquirer*, summoning him to Richmond for a meeting at the Exchange Hotel. Imboden arrived in the capital city early the next morning.

Before reaching the hotel, Imboden met Henry Wise on the street.[1] According to Imboden, Wise appeared to be "worn down by overwork and anxiety." He despaired "of any fair adjustment or prompt action" for armed neutrality "between the Federal powers in Washington and the Confederate powers in Montgomery, and to fight in the Union against the invasion of either by the other, and to prevent the troops of either from crossing the territory of Virginia. . . . [He] spoke . . . of his impatience at the delay of the Convention and of the dark prospect of events."[2]

Wise inquired of Imboden, "Do you remember, sir, what passed between you and me when I was governor, at the moment you thanked me for the order permitting you to have two brass field pieces for your company of artillery in Staunton?"

Imboden replied, "Yes, I do, sir."

"What was a joke then is earnest now. I want those guns with which to aid in the immediate capture of the United States arsenal at Harpers Ferry; can they be had with all of the men you can raise?"

"They can. And, if you say so, the men shall be raised and the arsenal taken," responded Imboden.[3]

Wise then asked Imboden to find as many officers of armed volunteer companies from inland counties as he could and have them meet at the hotel by seven o'clock that evening. Imboden found brothers Turner and Richard Ashby of Fauquier County and Oliver R. Funsten of Clarke County, all captains of cavalry companies; Capt. John A. Harman of Staunton; and Alfred M. Barbour, the former civil superintendent of the government works at Harpers Ferry.[4]

They all joined Wise that evening and devised a plan for the capture of the arsenal. Turner Ashby, a wealthy landowner from Virginia's horse country, made his feelings known: "You have been the governor of Virginia, and we will take orders from you, sir, as if you were now governor; please draw your orders."[5]

No one in the room could deny the military importance of Harpers Ferry. Control of the Shenandoah Valley was vital to the safety of the South, and the little community at its northern end was the key to retaining it. Harpers Ferry was strategically located on the Baltimore and Ohio Railroad, which served as a lifeline to the federal government in Washington. Of equal import was the government arsenal there that contained machinery and arms which were sorely needed by Virginia.

Wise had no military experience himself, but he was committed to wresting control of Harpers Ferry from federal hands. He was comfortable with authority and would do whatever was necessary to get what he was after. A successful lawyer and farmer, Wise had served in Congress, the foreign service and as governor. Although no longer in office, he was still a power to be reckoned with in the state and had many loyal friends to call upon.

Near midnight the group was joined in their hotel room by Col. Edmund Fontaine, president of the Virginia Central Railroad, and John S. Barbour, president of the Orange and Alexandria and the Manassas Gap railroads. The two railroad tycoons had collaborated since 1855 in moving the mail between Washington and Richmond. Now they were about to agree on a different type of collaboration, something that had never been tried—conveying men and arms to battle via rail. It was Imboden's idea to use the railroads in the attack. He saw in their speed a way to obtain a vital military advantage—the element of surprise.[6] The idea conceived by Imboden that night would forever change the method of warfare.

A committee of three was chosen shortly after midnight to call on Governor Letcher, with Imboden as the chairman. They immediately proceeded to the governor's mansion, where they aroused him from his bed and laid their scheme before him[7] in the hope that he would "support, or countenance at least, an attempt to secure the arms and munitions at Harpers Ferry." Letcher declined even to consider the matter "as he was under some informal pledge not to do or promote any hostile action against the United States without apprising the Convention and conferring with it."[8] He was then asked if, contingent upon the passage of an ordinance of secession, he would order the raid by telegraph. To this Letcher consented. Imboden told him which companies would be under arms and ready to move at a moment's notice.[9]

Upon the committee's return with Letcher's reply, more questions were weighed. If the group were to wait for Virginia to secede, they would lose the element of surprise. They must, therefore, move no later than the next day, with or without the governor's approval. The railroad presidents pledged their full support and all the necessary rolling stock to accomplish the mission. Wise asked of those assembled, "Well, gentlemen, you have heard the report; are you willing and ready to act on your own responsibility?" Imboden later reported that they all agreed "to act without official authority."[10]

Wise drew up a three-pronged attack. At least two companies of infantry from Staunton and Augusta County would go directly down the Valley to Winchester, then by rail to Charles Town, six miles southwest of Harpers Ferry. Imboden would gather his artillery battery and board a train for Charlottesville, where he would attempt to organize more volunteers. From there he would head to Gordonsville, twenty miles out on the Virginia Central, gathering all the volunteers that he could along the way. At Gordonsville he would switch to the Orange and Alexandria and proceed to Manassas Junction, at which point he would transfer to the Manassas Gap railway and proceed to Strasburg, twenty miles south of Winchester.

The third prong of the attack would consist of the Ashby brothers and their mounted militiamen from Fauquier County, who would ride northwest across the Blue Ridge Mountains and await Imboden at a prearranged site near Harpers Ferry.[11]

It was decided to telegraph the captains of all volunteer companies along the way to be ready to march as soon as orders were received the next day. Imboden telegraphed his battery to assemble at the armory in Staunton by 4:00 P.M. on April 17. All of the telegrams designated Portsmouth Navy Yard as the destination, so as to deceive government officials in Washington should there be a leak.[12]

At that time Milton Cary came into the meeting, and he and Col. Fontaine set about arranging the railroad transportation. While they were in the midst of working out these details, Wise received a telegram from his son-in-law, Dr. Garnett in Washington, who had learned that a thousand–man regiment of Massachusetts troops had been dispatched to Harpers Ferry. The group in Richmond knew that a garrison of only forty-five troops were currently assigned to the arsenal; without being reinforced they could easily be captured or driven off, perhaps without shots being fired. The need for speed and secrecy was now heightened. The inexperienced Virginia militiamen would be tested against well trained and equipped federal troops.[13]

Imboden and the others remained awake all night. Making his way to the state armory, he roused the superintendent, Capt. Charles Dimmock. Although a Northerner by birth and a West Point graduate, Dimmock was loyal to the cause and in full sympathy with the conspirators. He filled Imboden's request for ammunition and had it moved to the railway station before sunrise, along with a hundred stand of arms for the Martinsburg Light Infantry, a new company just recently formed. All of this Imboden took receipt of and had placed on the train.

Just before it pulled out of the depot with Imboden and the other officers, Alfred Barbour made an unguarded remark in a loud voice which was overheard by a Northern traveler, who scribbled a hurried message to President Lincoln and paid a Negro on the station platform one dollar to take it to the telegraph office. Imboden had the man followed and the dispatch was taken from him, which prevented even more troops from being sent to head off the raiding party.[14]

Imboden's telegram to Staunton had touched off wild excitement which spread rapidly throughout the county and brought thousands of people to town to meet the train. Augusta was a strong pro-Union county, and it was doubted that Imboden was acting on the governor's orders. To satisfy the crowd, George Imboden sent a telegram to his brother in Gordonsville inquiring under whose authority he was acting. Capt. Harman received the message and replied, in John Imboden's name, that they were acting under the orders of Governor Letcher. Harman was sure that by the time the message got back to Staunton the state would have seceded and the governor would indeed have ordered out his troops.

Harman handed the dispatch to Imboden before the train reached Staunton and told him what had transpired. Imboden was annoyed until the train arrived at the station about 6 P.M. and the proud captain saw his battery drawn up in perfect formation. Imboden was met by Gen. William Harman and Maj. Gen. Kenton Harper of the Virginia Militia, another Mexican War veteran. As he stepped from the train, they handed Imboden a telegram from Letcher ordering them into service and referring them to Imboden for information and directions. Taking them aside, Imboden told them in confidence of the true destination—Harpers Ferry, not Portsmouth. Harper was to take command, and full written orders would reach them en route.[15]

At dark the troops pulled out, Harper with the infantry by team to Winchester and Harman in command of the train that pulled out amid great ceremony. The Staunton *Spectator* reported the scene as the most exciting ever witnessed in Staunton: "There was a general feeling that the crisis was a solemn one, united with a firm and universal determination to resist the scheme set on foot by President Lincoln to subjugate the South."[16]

The Secession of Virginia and the Capture of Harpers Ferry

While this revolutionary group was making their way from Richmond to Staunton a drama was unfolding in the state capital. Henry Wise arrived at the meeting of the convention on the morning of April 17. Delegate Waitman T. Willey recorded the events:

> The scenes witnessed within the walls of that room . . . have no parallel in the annals of ancient or modern times. . . . Mr. Wise rose in his seat and drawing a large Virginia horse-pistol from his bosom, laid it before him and proceeded to harangue the body in the most violent and denunciatory manner. He concluded by taking his watch from his pocket and, with glaring eyes and bated breath, declared that events were now transpiring which caused a hush to come over his soul.[1]

Wise told them of the proceedings of the secret meeting held the previous day and of the plans to seize Harpers Ferry and Norfolk, where he had sent troops with directives to sink Yankee vessels, obstruct the harbor and take the powder magazine.

At this disclosure, denunciations of Wise were swift and impassioned. John Baldwin of Augusta County wanted to know who was in charge and who the activists were. Wise replied that he assumed full responsibility and that the movement was already "on the march" to "aid the people who have waited on the convention too long in vain, in seizing arms for their own defense." Baldwin continued to protest, but Wise told him that the "patriotic volunteer revolutionists" were Baldwin's own constituents, "his friends and neighbors of Staunton . . . marching under my order to take their own arms for their own defense. . . ." Baldwin was "aghast" and sat down silenced. Willey reported that the delegates were

> thrown into bewildering excitement by Mr. Baylor, Baldwin's colleague, rushing by, almost over the seats, and down the aisles, making his way to Wise . . . to grasp his hand, with tears streaming down his cheeks and exclaiming "Let me grasp your hand; I don't agree with

you; I don't approve of your acts, but I love you, I love
you."[2]

In this atmosphere of emotion and passion the convention passed an
act entitled "An Ordinance to Repeal the Ratification of the Constitution
of the United States by the State of Virginia, and to Resume all the Rights
and Privileges Granted under said Constitution," an ordinance to be
ratified by a vote of the people. A military alliance was established with
the new Confederate States government in Montgomery, Alabama.

Imboden arrived in Charlottesville that night, where the Monticello
Guards under Capt. W.B. Mallory and the Albemarle Rifles under Capt.
R.T.W. Duke came aboard. At Culpeper the trains stopped and took on
another rifle company. As the trains puffed northward, cavalry troops
under the Ashby brothers were filling the gaps in the Blue Ridge. They
had already sent some troops to cut the telegraph lines between Manassas
Junction and Alexandria and had posted men to be sure the lines stayed
down.[3]

At sunup on the morning of April 18 three trains pulled into Manassas
Junction, startling the people of that quiet village. Resplendently
uniformed militiamen leaped from the cars and switched them from the
tracks of the Orange & Alexandria to the Manassas Gap Railroad. General
Harman at once impressed a locomotive of the Manassas Gap line to take
the lead toward Strasburg. It was commanded by Imboden.[4]

The three trains rolled westward under a canopy of gray smoke and a
shower of bright sparks. Not five miles out of the station Imboden noticed
that they were slowing down. He worked his way forward and discovered
that an engineer with Unionist sympathies had figured out their
destination and had allowed the boiler's fire to go down, thus bringing
them to a near standstill on a lightly ascending grade. Pulling out his Navy
Colt and cocking it, the captain placed it next to the engineer's head and
suggested that he pick up speed.[5] According to Imboden, "The weight of
that particular argument was enough to coax a speed of full forty miles per
hour."[6]

The trains reached Strasburg shortly before 10:00 A.M. Troops poured
from the cars, and before long the officers had the milling infantry formed
into units and on the march for Winchester.

The battery had a harder task. The four six-pounders were unloaded,
but there were no horses to pull them. No matter how hard Imboden
pleaded his case, most of the farmers refused to cooperate. The situation
being urgent, he took the needed animals by force and by noon had

acquired teams sufficient for the task at hand. The guns rumbled northward, with Imboden followed by threats of indictment by the next grand jury of the county. By nightfall on April 18, 1861, the battery rolled into Winchester. Afterward Imboden commented that the people had received them very coldly.

General Harper informed him that the infantry had already been dispatched by a short line railroad, the Winchester and Potomac, to Charles Town, just six miles from Harpers Ferry. A short time later the trains returned for the battery. The teams were unhitched and returned, unharmed, to the relieved farmers.

The infantry moved out of Charles Town around midnight. The train carried the artillery to Halltown, four miles from their destination. The cannons were rolled forward by hand to Bolivar Heights, just west of Harpers Ferry. At dawn they would be in position to rain shells down upon the town if necessary.[7]

Just before dawn the next morning the Virginians saw a brilliant light rising from the confluence of the Shenandoah and Potomac rivers. General Harper, up until that moment, had expected to confront the Massachusetts regiment that had reinforced the arsenal's defenses. He was in the midst of making his dispositions for an attack when this fiery light convinced him that the Federals had fired the arsenal and fled. Harper marched his troops in immediately and took possession, but was too late to extinguish the flames.[8]

The element of surprise had been lost. Soldiers, townspeople and arsenal employees set about to battle the flames. Nearly twenty thousand rifles and pistols were destroyed, but not all was lost. The buildings were gone, but the workshops and all the machinery were saved, along with five thousand finished and three thousand unfinished muskets.[9] The weapons were forwarded to Richmond, while the machinery was dismounted and shipped to Fayetteville, North Carolina.[10]

At first the militiamen were uncertain how the Federals had been warned of the impending raid, but the townspeople soon answered the question. Former superintendent Alfred Barbour had returned to Harpers Ferry following the meeting with Wise in Richmond. There he called a meeting with the employees and urged them to stay with Virginia, stressing to them the need for skilled labor and promising good wages for their services. Most decided to accept his advice; however, Lt. Roger Jones, commandant of the forty-five man guard force of regular soldiers in the 42nd Infantry, heard of the situation and sent for reinforcements. Unable to obtain assistance, he was ordered to destroy the rifle works and withdraw. Thousands of rifles were gathered into piles and covered with gunpowder, and powder trails were laid throughout the buildings.[11]

At 10:00 P.M. a panting messenger informed the garrison that the Virginia militia was only a mile away. The torch was applied, and while the armory and other arsenal buildings were engulfed in flames, the garrison escaped across the Potomac.[12] In the shops, workmen with Southern sympathies had managed to wet some of the powder, rendering it harmless.[13] Although the consequences could have been much worse, Barbour undoubtedly did the Southern cause no good through his carelessness. He was written off by many as a traitor, yet received credit from Jones for alerting the garrison.[14]

Despite Barbour's obvious treachery, the expedition was clearly a success. The Virginians had captured an important federal installation on the Maryland border and in doing so had, in effect, gained control of the vital B&O Railroad. Within a week small groups of Virginia volunteers began to trickle into Harpers Ferry, eventually swelling the militia force there to about thirteen hundred. The narrow streets of the town resounded with activity, and the town bustled as volunteers continued to arrive.[15]

Soldiering at Harpers Ferry

The patriotic farmers armed with flintlock muskets provided the greatest concentration of Virginia troops ever assembled in one place. They were gathered into companies, but little organization existed above company level. Two brigadier generals and a major general from the state militia were in command, but they had few effective staff. Nearly the whole force, from the commanders down to the farm boys in the ranks, were amateurs at soldiering.

This almost wholly untrained army had virtually no support structure. There were no hospital, ordinance or commissary departments. To further complicate matters, they had no telegraph link with the authorities in Richmond, and it was a two-day ride by courier. Nevertheless, there was no shortage of what Imboden termed "fuss and feathers." Every evening official displays consisting of assembled troops, speeches and music were presented.

Imboden, the senior artillery officer at Harpers Ferry, commanded three batteries, all without horses. Near the end of the first week of occupation, he was summoned to Gen. Harper's headquarters. The general had learned that a number of trains on the B&O would attempt to pass through during the night, transporting troops from the West to Washington.[1] Harper was determined to prevent their passage, even at the risk of battle. He ordered Imboden to post the cannons so as to command the railroad for a half mile or more. The guns were sighted on the track and manned day and night, ready to fire upon the trains if and when ordered. Infantry companies with orders to fire into the trains if the artillery failed to stop them were posted. Pickets were placed three miles out with orders to fire signal guns as soon as the first trains bearing troops approached.

About 1:00 A.M. the militiamen heard the rumble of an approaching train. An edgy cavalryman, thinking that he saw soldiers through the windows, mistook the regular mail train for a troop transport. He fired off the first signal, which caused the other sentries to fire as well. Their signals alerted the gunners. Primers were inserted into the guns and the lanyards held tight, ready to be pulled when the engine passed a specific point about four hundred yards distant.[2]

Col. William S.H. Baylor of the 5th Virginia Militia Regiment was with his men just a little ahead of the artillery. When the train passed, he saw no troops on board and signaled it to stop, which it did a mere hundred yards before the artillery would have fired upon it. Entering the train with his soldiers, Baylor captured "one old fellow in uniform asleep on the mailbags." It proved to be Brig. Gen. William A. Harney of the United States Army on his way to Washington to resign. He surrendered and was taken to Harper's headquarters, where he spent the night. The old soldier assured Harper that no troops were coming from the West, and Harper withdrew his troops. General Harney was paroled the next morning and sent to Richmond.[3]

The artillery still lacked harness and caissons for its guns. The resourceful Imboden sent for harness from Baltimore, purchasing it with his own credit, and also sent to Richmond for red flannel shirts and other clothing for his men, as their uniforms were considered "too fine for camp life."[4] The governor later ordered reimbursement by the state treasurer. In the armory he found a large number of horse carts, which the artisans and mechanics of the battery converted to good caissons.

Harper was having a difficult time obtaining the munitions and supplies. Around the end of April he sent Imboden to Richmond to see the governor with a list of necessities and a report on their defenseless condition should a federal force move against them. By the time Imboden reached Richmond, Gen. Robert E. Lee had been placed in command of all of the Virginia forces.

Imboden had hoped to channel some of the state's military resources to Harpers Ferry; instead he found that all militia officers above the rank of captain had been reduced in rank, and the governor and his advisors were to fill the vacancies. Imboden saw this as "a disastrous blow to the pomp and circumstance of glorious war at Harpers Ferry."[5]

The militia generals were replaced by Col. Thomas J. Jackson of the Virginia Military Institute, a West Point graduate and Mexican War veteran. The V.M.I. professor arrived at Harpers Ferry and took command on April 30. He and his small staff of tactical officers and cadets from V.M.I. immediately began to turn the untrained militia volunteers into an efficient fighting machine.

Imboden returned to Harpers Ferry in a few days and could hardly believe the changes that had occurred in such a short time. The militia generals were all gone, along with their staffs and all the trimmings. The new commanding colonel had taken quarters at a small wayside hotel near the railroad bridge. Imboden immediately sought an interview to deliver a letter and some papers that he had carried from General Lee. Jackson and his adjutant, Maj. James W. Massie, were at a small pine table poring over the rolls of the present troops.

Imboden described Jackson as being "dressed in well-worn, dingy uniform of professor in the Virginia Military Institute."[6] Jackson had issued a short and simple order taking command but had had no direct contact with the troops. He had taken a quick survey of the situation, and to him the outlook seemed depressing. All that the militia had accomplished was to occupy the town—no precautions had been taken against attack, and most of the captured machinery still needed to be shipped away.

The atmosphere was not pleasant; the men had liked the easygoing militia officers, and their removal was greatly resented. The volunteers had to be mustered into regular state service, but it was highly uncertain that the disgruntled men would join the army officially. To Imboden fell the responsibility of beginning the muster.

As he made his way to his battery's camp, he passed the camp of the 5th Virginia, also from Augusta County. They were deeply attached to their field officers and greatly excited about the state of things. On seeing Imboden they called for a speech, but he did not feel it appropriate to speak to them since he was not a member of their regiment. Instead, he ordered the Staunton Artillery to fall in. He told them that Jackson was requiring them to muster for either twelve months or for the war at their option and urged them to go for the duration of the war, hoping to set an example for the others watching from a distance.

They responded by shouting in unison, "For the war! For the war!" Before dismissing them, Imboden completed the mustering-in ceremony and proudly took the roll to Jackson with the remark, "There, colonel, is the roll of your first company mustered in for the war."[7] Jackson looked the roll over, rose and shook Imboden's hand, saying, "Thank you, captain, thank you; and, please thank your men for me."

Sufficiently impressed with Imboden's recruiting ability, Jackson asked him to serve as mustering officer for the other artillery companies,[8] thus solving a potentially troubling problem. Jackson lacked the talents and flair for the oratory of a stump politician. Imboden, on the other hand, was an accomplished speaker and could still any discontent that presented itself in the camps. Before sunset the rolls of the other artillery batteries were brought in, and the next day all of the other troops were mustered in.

With the muster completed, Jackson wasted no time in organizing his troops. Unassigned troops were assigned to companies, and companies were assigned to regiments. By early May the ranks had been swelled by volunteers from nearly every county in the state. The forces at Harpers Ferry numbered nearly eight thousand, and Jackson was confident that he could hold his position if attacked.

Jackson was a rigid disciplinarian who set his men to a daily drill routine, but a kindly man who took time with his untrained troops. He was universally respected by his officers and troops alike. Little by little he fashioned some semblance of an army. When he discovered that Imboden's battery was without horses, he did not trouble to untangle the knots of red tape in Richmond—he instead ordered his quartermaster, Maj. John Harman, to proceed to the Quaker settlements of Loudoun County, famous for their quality horses, and to buy or exact as many as were needed.[9]

In May Jackson sent Imboden and his battery to occupy Point of Rocks, Maryland, on the Potomac twelve miles below Harpers Ferry. Imboden took possession of the bridge and fortified the Virginia end. He also mined the bridge in case of attack—Gen. Benjamin F. Butler's federal army was nearby. Imboden began to stay up all night and sleep during the day, ready for any emergency. He sent reports twice daily, morning and night, to Jackson.

After remaining at this post for a week, Imboden was aroused from his nap on a Sunday afternoon by one of his men. Two men in blue uniforms were in camp, riding about and looking closely at everything. They were suspected to be spies. When Imboden approached the pair he found them to be Jackson and a member of his staff. Imboden supposed that Jackson was familiarizing himself with the situation, including the canal and railroad at that point. He congratulated Imboden on doing a fine job, asked that his presence not be revealed, and rode off.[10]

Within a few days, Imboden would learn the true purpose of Jackson's mysterious visit.

The Great Train Heist

From the very beginning of the war, the South was greatly in need of rolling stock for its railroads, particularly locomotives, but there was a lack of shops in which to build them. Well aware of this, Jackson devised a plan to obtain the badly needed locomotives from the B&O Railroad.

Approximately one hundred twenty miles of B&O track, between Point of Rocks and Cumberland, Maryland, lay within the area of his command. The railroad dipped southward into Virginia, then recrossed the Potomac just west of Martinsburg. Though sympathetic to the South, the B&O board of directors supported the federal government. The line became a lifeline to Washington, continuously shuttling troops and supplies between the Ohio River Valley and Baltimore.[1]

Not wishing to offend the state of Maryland, which, it was thought, might secede any day, Jackson continued to allow the many daily freight and passenger trains to pass Harpers Ferry unmolested, with the sole exception of Gen. Harney's arrest. The coal shipments increased daily as the federal government accumulated supplies for the ships being used to blockade the Southern coast.[2] Other trains, heavily laden with grain to feed the huge army organizing for an invasion of the South, lumbered past daily. Empty trains rumbled westward night and day.[3]

Jackson's plan would prove to be one of the boldest and most brilliant of the war. When he sent Imboden to Point of Rocks, he also sent Col. Harper with the 5th Virginia Infantry to Martinsburg. Complaining to B&O president John W. Garrett that the night trains disturbed the slumber of his troops, he requested that all eastbound trains should pass

Harpers Ferry only between 11:00 A.M. and 1:00 P.M. Mr. Garrett complied readily enough.

Jackson waited a few days, then complained that the empty trains that passed at night were continuing to interfere with the peace and quiet of his camps. Since the tracks were doubled from Point of Rocks to Martinsburg, a distance of nearly thirty miles, he proposed that these trains also be limited to the same time as the others.[4] Garrett, always eager to please, promptly complied; and for the next week, for two hours each day, there existed the busiest section of railroad in America. But as subsequent events would prove, Jackson was not nearly so concerned with his weary troops' sleep as he led Garrett to believe.

As soon as the schedule was working smoothly, Jackson sent Imboden across to the Maryland side of the river with orders to allow westbound trains to pass until noon, but to allow none to go east. At noon he was to obstruct the tracks in such a way that it would take several days to make repairs. Harper was to do the opposite at Martinsburg. The trains backed up for miles, and the railroad was completely shut down. Jackson had set a trap, and Garrett had guilelessly walked right into it.

Jackson's forces had captured fifty-six locomotives and three hundred eighty-six railway cars—the largest single haul of rolling stock taken intact during the entire war.[5]

His plan having worked to perfection, Jackson now had to carry off as much of his captured goods as possible. The only Southern-controlled railroad that connected with the B&O was the very short Winchester and Potomac. Some of the locomotives were sent south to safety at Winchester, where they were dismantled and hauled overland by teams of horses on the macadamized Valley Turnpike to Strasburg, for service on the Manassas Gap Railroad. Others were sent as far south as Staunton. Never had such a task as the movement of the captured engines and cars been undertaken anywhere in the world. In addition to the locomotives and cars, badly needed tools and machinery were captured at Martinsburg and also sent south.[6]

While Imboden held the Point of Rocks bridge, Lt. Col. J.E.B. Stuart, a native Virginian and West Point graduate, reported to Jackson for assignment to duty. Jackson ordered all of the cavalry companies to be consolidated into a single battalion under Stuart. This order offended Turner Ashby, who had led his own company in the raid on Harpers Ferry and had performed valuable service there. Ashby was older than Stuart and felt that he deserved a promotion.[7]

Ashby went to see Imboden and told him of the order and his intention to resign. Imboden urged Ashby to meet with Jackson before resigning, so Ashby rode his black Arabian stallion the twelve miles to Jackson's headquarters. Upon Ashby's explanation of his position, Jackson agreed to divide the cavalry companies between Stuart and Ashby and to seek Ashby's promotion.[8]

While this drama was unfolding in remote Harpers Ferry, Virginia adopted the Constitution of the Confederate States of America on May 2 and sent representatives to the Confederate Congress. On May 20 the congress adjourned in Alabama to reconvene in Richmond, and on May 29, President Jefferson Davis arrived there. By the terms of a treaty between Virginia and the Confederate government, all state troops were transferred to Confederate command. One of the first acts of the Confederate government in Richmond was to appoint a commander of higher rank and more experience to Harpers Ferry. Gen. Joseph E. Johnston, a native Virginian and West Point graduate, was selected to take over this command.[9]

When Johnston arrived at Harpers Ferry, several thousand men were assembled there from nearly all of the seceded states east of the Mississippi River. Johnston at once began the task of organizing these troops into brigades. Jackson was given command of an all-Virginia brigade and almost immediately promoted to brigadier general.[10]

Johnston was very aware of Washington's interest in the situation at Harpers Ferry. He was also aware of eight to ten thousand volunteers under Gen. Robert Patterson moving across western Maryland. Johnston felt that the position at Harpers Ferry could not be held if attacked and decided to move his army from there to Winchester.

The March to Manassas

The Confederate army under Joseph E. Johnston occupied Harpers Ferry until June 15, when the last of his regiments withdrew. Serving as rear guard during this retrograde movement, the Staunton Artillery finally withdrew on June 16, their horses toiling to pull the six-pounders in a cloud of dust.[1]

The next day Imboden was ordered to draw up in a line of battle at Bunker Hill, a few miles north of Winchester. There they waited for three days, anticipating an attack from Gen. Patterson, who had crossed the Potomac. When the cautious Patterson and his cumbersome army of raw recruits recrossed the Potomac without attacking, Imboden fell back to Winchester, and the battery went into camp just north of the town.[2]

The muster rolls for June 30 show one hundred seven officers and troops present for Imboden's battery. Imboden reported:

> This company entered the service with excellent cadet grey uniforms in good condition and which cost $20.50 each and had not been damaged by use more than $2.50 or $3.00 each. They have since been supplied by the County of Augusta with a suit around consisting of a grey cap, and flannel shirt, grey woolen pants, and woolen socks.
>
> The state has furnished no clothing.
>
> They have good tents purchased and paid for by the captain out of his private means costs $298.
>
> The public property and arms in their possession on the date of mustering into service consist of 4 bronze, 6 pr. field guns and 54 old fashioned heavy artillery sabres all in good condition.
>
> They are also having caissons constructed and will be supplied with harness and horses in a short time to equip them fully.
>
> This was the first or among the first companies called into service and the nature of its duties have been and was all the time owing to the fact of their separation into various detachments on duty at remote points they have not sooner been mustered into (Confederate) service.[3]

On July 2 Patterson crossed the river in force. Col. Stuart reported this movement to Johnston, who sent Jackson with one regiment and one field piece to feel out the enemy. Imboden was ordered to accompany the South Carolina brigade of Gen. Bernard E. Bee in support of Jackson. Bee's command reached Darkesville and formed a line of battle.

Jackson's 5th Virginia met two brigades of enemy troops at Falling Waters, a small country church five miles south of the Potomac, where a slight skirmish resulted in few casualties. The affair was a Confederate victory, with fifty of the enemy captured. Patterson reported that he had encountered thirty-five hundred Confederates—more than ten times the actual number. On July 5 Imboden's command was ordered back to Winchester, the crisis having passed.[4]

Imboden's battery was officially assigned to Bee's brigade on July 12, the same day that Imboden wrote home complaining of difficulties in procuring shoes and clothing for his men. During this period the battery spent every day arduously drilling at the guns, and the efficiency of the company greatly increased. Soon the outfit received better harness and additional horses and completed construction of the caissons.

Imboden wrote on July 17 that the men slept by the guns all night, expecting the enemy to advance at any time. "We are resolved to die rather than let these devils drive us back to our homes."[5]

Just after midnight that night Imboden accompanied Gen. Bee to headquarters, where several brigade commanders assembled with Johnston in a conference that lasted more than two hours. Johnston had received a telegram from Gen. Beauregard at Manassas begging for reinforcements, as his army had been attacked by advance troops from Union general Irvin McDowell's advancing army. The next day, July 18, Johnston's army began the fifty-seven mile trek from Winchester to Manassas.

The Staunton Artillery was again chosen to serve as rear guard, and they took up the line of march late in the afternoon. It was thought that Patterson would detect the movement and follow the army. Imboden held firm, expecting an attack, while Stuart and Ashby's cavalry provided a screen that so completely masked the army's departure that Gen. Patterson never suspected a thing.[6]

Although Imboden's unit was the last to leave the Valley, it soon overtook the main body of the army. The green troops wilted in the intense summer heat, travelling only fifteen miles the first day of the march. They camped that night just east of Millwood in Clarke County. The officers roused the exhausted men at dawn, and soon the army was climbing through Ashby Gap. By 8:00 A.M. they had trickled into Piedmont (now called Delaplane), a small village on the Manassas Gap Railroad, twenty-three miles from Winchester. There, locomotives waited under a full head of steam to expedite the movement by rail. By the afternoon of July 19 they were in Manassas, having covered the last thirty-four miles in eight hours.[7]

While the trains steamed eastward, Johnston ordered his artillery chief, Col. William Nelson Pendleton, to assemble the artillery in a column and use the country roads to reach Manassas. The artillery consisted of five batteries, one attached to each brigade and one held in reserve. As the guns rolled into Piedmont, Imboden sought out Pendleton; by nightfall only three of the five batteries had arrived. The exhausted cannoneers slept by the roadside, oblivious to the pouring rain. Rising before daylight, they started out in the dark and marched on, reaching Salem (now Marshall) in Fauquier County by eight o'clock that morning.[8]

At Salem the whole population turned out to greet them. Men, women and children brought them baskets, trays and plates loaded with breakfast. Being raw campaigners, the men had finished off three days' worth of rations the night before, so Imboden ordered a thirty minute halt to enjoy the feast. He later wrote, "I made special note of that breakfast because it was the last food any of us tasted till the first Bull Run had been fought and won, thirty-six hours later."[9] Forage for the horses was also obtained.[10]

The road to Manassas was slow, narrow, and rough. Although the men and horses, unaccustomed to the rigors of war, tired rapidly, Imboden saw the need for haste and drove his men and teams onward. Finally, at 11:30 that night, they rolled into Camp Walker just below Manassas Junction. The men threw themselves to the ground and fell asleep instantly. Despite the lateness of the hour, Imboden sought out Gen. Bee to announce the safe arrival of his artillery.[11]

Imboden arrived at Bee's headquarters about a mile northeast of Manassas around 1:00 A.M. and found the general in the small log cabin. After reporting his progress, Imboden was ordered to unharness the horses and bivouac for the night. "You will need all the rest you can get," Bee told him, "for a great battle will begin in the morning."[12]

The Battle of Manassas

Imboden and his men were aroused at daybreak by the loud report of a thirty-pound Parrott gun fired from about two miles away, on the other side of Bull Run. The sound was followed by the crash of a great shell through the treetops four hundred yards to their left. Every man in the battery sprang to his feet instantly, and in a very short while the horses were harnessed and hitched to the guns and their caissons.[1]

A courier arrived with a message requesting Imboden's presence at headquarters, where the captain found Bee standing on the porch of the cabin in his shirtsleeves. He greeted Imboden with news of a federal advance and rapidly informed him of the disposition of Johnston's troops. Bee was dissatisfied with the prospect of possibly missing the battle; his brigade and the battery had been ordered to a stone bridge over Bull Run, three miles away, on the extreme left of the army. As they listened to the sound of artillery in the distance, Bee asked Imboden if his battery could "stand that." Imboden replied, "Not if we can help it," explaining to Bee that his men and horses had been without food for twenty-four hours. "You will have plenty of time to cook and eat, to the music of a battle in which we shall probably take little or no part," Bee assured him.[2]

Union general McDowell led his army of thirty-five thousand men over the rough, broken country and through the second growth of pines, where he would face the combined Confederate forces of generals Beauregard and Johnston. Johnston's Army of the Shenandoah was more than eight thousand strong, while Beaureguard's Army of the Potomac had nearly ten thousand.[3]

After an hour on the march along Sudley Road, the Staunton Artillery ascended the hill leading to the Lewis house, Portici, where a courier brought news that the federal army seemed to be marching in a northwesterly direction on the other side of Bull Run. Halting the battery, Imboden rode to the top of the hill where he had full view of a long enemy column moving on the north side of the creek. Down the valley, he could see Bee's brigade advancing.

When Imboden galloped to meet the general with news of what he had seen, Bee quickly envisioned McDowell's plans. He and Imboden rode past the Lewis house, across a hollow, up the next hill, through the pines and onto a summit just east of the Henry house. "See the glistening bayonets of the enemy!" Bee exclaimed. "Here is the battlefield, and we are in for it! Bring up your guns as quickly as possible, and I'll look around for a good position."[4]

McDowell had decided late on the previous afternoon to try to turn the Confederate left rather than attempt a frontal assault. The ten miles of winding road led to the unguarded Sudley Ford, across which McDowell sent his troops to rain down on the Confederate left flank. Rather than being too far out to see any action as they had thought, Bee and Imboden were right in the path of the federal advance.

In less than twenty minutes Imboden was leading his battery past the Lewis house when he met Bee coming out of the pines. With his cap on the point of his sword, the general frantically urged the galloping battery forward to a depression a hundred yards northeast of the Henry house, where they unlimbered.[5]

Bee had chosen the best possible position for the battery. Imboden recalled,

> Our position commanded a beautiful open farm which

rose gently from the valley in front of us, back to the woods about 500 yards distant. In the edge of these woods a heavy column of the enemy was marching to the southward, while we were descending the hill to our position. At the moment we wheeled into line, I observed one of their batteries [Rickett's] of six guns do the same thing [beside the Sudley Road near the Matthew's house] and they unlimbered simultaneously with us. We immediately loaded with spherical-case shot, with fuse cut for 500 yards.[6]

Imboden's battery was in a depression, almost under cover due to a slight swell about fifty feet in front of them. Their first shot passed not six inches above the ground at this swell, and the recoil ran the guns back to an even lower area. As the guns were loaded, only the men's heads were visible to the enemy.[7] Whereas Imboden's four guns were brass, smoothbore six-pounders, his opponent was equipped with six ten-pound Parrott rifled guns.[8]

Bee ordered Imboden to wait until the 4th Alabama Infantry and one gun from another battery reached a position in a piece of woods within five hundred yards of the Federals. Recalled Imboden,

He had hardly uttered the order, however, when the enemy's battery opened on us with elongated cylindrical shells. They passed a few feet over our heads, and very near the general and his staff in our rear, and exploded near the top of the hill. We instantly returned the compliment. General Bee then directed me to hold my position until further orders, and observe the enemy's movements toward our left, and report to him anything I might discover of importance.[9]

When Bee realized that the Yankees were using conical-shaped projectiles, which simply buried themselves in the sloping ground upon impact, he directed Imboden and his troops to fire low and ricochet their shot on the hard smooth open field in front of the enemy. The Yankees' fire was relatively ineffective; Imboden's fire, however, was very destructive.[10] He described the action:

The firing of both batteries now became very rapid—they

at first overshot us and burst their shells in our rear, but at every round improved their aim and shortened their fuse.

In about fifteen minutes we received our first injury. A shell passed between two of our guns and exploded amongst the caissons, mangling the arm of private J. J. Points with a fragment in the most shocking manner. I ordered him to be carried off the field to the surgeon at once. He was scarcely gone when another shell exploded at the same place and killed a horse. About this time the enemy began to fire too low, striking the knoll in our front, from ten to twenty steps, from which the ricochet was sufficient to carry the projectiles over us; they discovered this, and again began to fire over us.

After we had been engaged for perhaps a half hour, the enemy brought another battery [Griffin's] of four guns into position about 400 yards south of the first and a little nearer to us, and commenced a very brisk fire upon us. A shell from the last battery soon plunged into our midst, instantly killing a horse and cutting off the leg of private W. A. Siders, just below the knee. He was immediately taken to the surgeon. A few minutes afterward another shell did its work by wounding 2nd Lieutenant A. W. Garber so severely in the wrist that I ordered him off the field for surgical aid. We now had ten guns at work upon us, with no artillery to aid us for more than an hour, except, I believe, three rounds fired by the gun with the Alabama regiment. It ceased to fire, I have heard, because the horses ran off with the limber and left the gun without ammunition.

During this time the enemy's infantry was assembling behind, between and to the right (our left) of their batteries in immense numbers, but beyond our reach, as we could only see their bayonets over the top of the hill. Two or three times they ventured in sight when the Alabamians turned them back on their left by a well-directed fire, and we gave them a few shots and shells on their right with the same results, as they amicably dropped back over the hill when we fired at them, as almost every shot made a gap in their ranks.[11]

The massing of federal troops to the Confederate front led to very heavy fighting. Col. Nathan G. "Shanks" Evans with his eleven hundred troops was the first to feel the brunt of the Union attack. Evans at first suspected that the action in his front was only a demonstration and it was some time before he fully realized the extent of the federal attack. Bee marched his twenty-seven hundred men to the hill just across the turnpike, where he judged by the sound of the musketry and roar of cannon that Evans was outnumbered and must be supported. He initially decided to form a new line but was begged by Evans to come to his immediate support. Bee reluctantly complied by pushing his own and Col. Francis S. Bartow's brigades across the turnpike.

At first Imboden's was the only artillery on that part of the field, held under a pitiless fire from the enemy batteries. Then two guns from Latham's Alexandria Artillery Battery joined the fray from a position on the north side of Young's Branch, across the turnpike. Together they supported the infantry in their front until about 11:00 A.M., when two brass twelve-pound Napoleons of the Washington Artillery of New Orleans unlimbered to Imboden's right.[12]

Wrote Imboden,

> My men were by this time so overcome with the intense heat and excessive labor that half of them fell upon the ground completely exhausted. The guns were so hot that it was dangerous to load them—one was temporarily spiked by the priming wire hanging in it, the vent having become foul. My teams were cut to pieces, five of the horses were killed out of one single piece, and other teams partially destroyed, so that, alone, we could not much longer have replied to the enemy's batteries as briskly as necessary.[13]

For at least an hour no Confederate soldier was visible from Imboden's position, the infantry having been completely driven across Young's Branch. To Imboden's complete surprise, no order came to withdraw his battery, which was alone, the Washington Artillery having pulled out. Since Bee's orders had been to "stay here till you are ordered away," Imboden stayed. He couldn't know that orders to withdraw had been sent forty-five minutes earlier with a staff officer named Maj. Howard, who had fallen, desperately wounded, before reaching his destination.[14]

Imboden wrote,

> We were now serving the guns with diminished numbers,
> lieutenants working at them as privates, [one] had the
> hand spike in his hands directing the piece, when one of
> its rings was shot off the trail by a piece of shell. The
> enemy advanced a third battery of four pieces down the
> hill directly in front of and about six hundred yards
> distant from us, upon which we opened fire immediately
> and crippled one of their guns by cutting off its trail,
> compelling them to dismount and send the piece away
> without its carriage.[15]

Infantry was now massing about five hundred yards away near a stone house on the turnpike to charge Imboden's position, and Imboden rode to a hilltop nearby to ascertain their identity. From there he ordered his battery to concentrate their fire, but in the noise of the mass confusion, his commands could not be heard. His sergeants chose this inopportune moment to inform him that their ammunition was almost completely exhausted.

Continued Imboden,

> My order to limber up the second section was understood
> as applying to the entire battery, so that the drivers had
> equalized the teams sufficiently to move all the guns and
> caissons, and the pieces were all limbered. On riding back
> a short distance, where I could see over the hill again, I
> discovered the enemy approaching rapidly, and so near
> that I doubted our ability to save the battery; but, by a
> rapid movement up the ravine, we avoided the shell of
> the batteries that were now directed at us, sufficient to
> escape with three guns and all caissons. The fourth gun
> was struck under the axle by an exploding shell, as it
> broke right in the middle, and dropped the gun in the
> field. We saved the team.[16]

Imboden's battery came under increased enemy fire, forcing the captain to choose a line of retreat concealed by the Henry house which, unbeknownst to all involved, was occupied by the elderly, bedridden Mrs. Judith Henry. For about four hundred yards the house sheltered Imboden's retreat. Enemy shells passed through the house, scattering shingles and boards and mortally wounding the woman inside.

The charging Union infantry advanced close enough to deliver one volley on Imboden's retreating battery. As the Staunton Artillery crossed the summit along the edge of the pines between the Henry and Robinson houses, Imboden met Gen. Jackson at the head of his brigade, marching at the double-quick. Johnston and Beauregard had also arrived on the field and were hurrying their troops into position. Imboden was very angry at what he regarded as bad treatment by Bee and expressed himself so with some profanity, which was displeasing to Jackson.[17] Jackson ordered the Staunton battery back into action. When Imboden requested that his caissons be permitted to go to the rear for ammunition, Jackson replied, "No, not now—wait till the other guns get here, and then you can withdraw your battery, as it has been so torn to pieces, and let your men rest."[18]

As Jackson had ordered, Imboden moved his battery back into action. He recounted,

> The caissons, except one, were empty, and many of the men were ready to faint from sheer exhaustion. We got into position 300 to 400 yards north of the ground we had first occupied, with full view of the enemy's heavy column of divisions advancing toward us. We opened fire at once, but slowly, as we had not over four or five men left able to work the guns, respectively, and ammunition had to be brought from a caisson left two hundred yards in the rear, because we were unable to get it up with the guns. Every shot here told with terrible effect, as we could see a lane opened through the enemy after almost every fire. Our first gun was worked, during this part of the action, by the captain, first lieutenant, and two privates. In the course of three quarters of an hour our supply of shot and shells were exhausted—the men could no longer work—we had nothing but canister left.[19]

Jackson rode up and reported that three or four batteries were rapidly approaching to relieve Imboden's fatigued soldiers. The exhausted captain wrote,

> I asked permission to fire the three rounds of shrapnel left to us, and he said, "Go ahead." I picked up a charge (the fuse was cut and ready) and rammed it home myself, remarking to Harman, "Tom, put in the primer and pull her off." I forgot to step back far enough from the muzzle, and, as I wanted to see the shell strike, I squatted to be

under the smoke, and gave the word, "Fire!" Heavens!
what a report. Finding myself full twenty feet away, I
thought the gun had burst. But it was only the pent-up
gas, that, escaping sideways as the shot cleared the
muzzle, had struck my side and head with great violence.
I recovered in time to see the shell explode in the
enemy's ranks.[20]

The blood gushed from Imboden's left ear, an injury that would leave
him totally deaf on that side for the rest of his life.[21] The other guns fired
the last two shells just as the Rockbridge Artillery arrived. Imboden's
battery had fired four hundred sixty rounds during the day. Of the
seventy-one horses which had gone into battle, ten were killed and
twenty-one others were wounded or injured. Most of the harness was
destroyed or lost, but the lost gun was recovered and soon back in service.[22]

Jackson ordered Imboden to inspect each individual battery to ensure
that the guns were being worked properly, an assignment which took only
a few minutes. Imboden soon requested permission to rejoin his own
battery. The battle was becoming very hot. Imboden wrote,

As he told me to go, he made this gesture (throwing up
his left hand with the open palm toward the person he
was addressing). The air was full of flying missiles, and as
he spoke he jerked down his hand, and I saw that blood
was streaming from it. I exclaimed, "General, you are
wounded." He replied, as he drew a handkerchief from
his breast-pocket, and began to bind it up, "Only a
scratch—a mere scratch," and galloped away along the
line.[23]

Imboden made his way to his horse, which he had tied in a ravine about
fifty yards to the rear for safety. To reach him he had to pass six hundred
infantrymen of the Hampton Legion of South Carolina, lying a short
distance from the front. While he was untying his horse, a shell exploded
in the middle of the infantry, killing several and stampeding others. In an
effort to rally them, the gallant captain was knocked down by a huge
soldier with his bayonet affixed, raking Imboden's left arm from wrist to
shoulder and allowing the fleeing soldier to escape. Imboden tore off the
dangling sleeve of his flannel shirt and returned to his battery bare-armed.

He found the remnants of his battery by the Lewis house, where Gen.
Johnston was observing the battle nearby. Imboden reported his

ammunition gone and requested the location of supply wagons to replenish his unit. Of Johnston's response Imboden recorded,

> Observing the sorry plight of the battery and the condition of the surviving men and horses, he directed me to remove them farther to the rear to a place of perfect safety, and return myself to the field, where I might be of some service. I took the battery back perhaps a mile, where we found a welcome little stream of water. Being greatly exhausted, I rested for perhaps an hour, and returned to the front with Sergeant Joseph Shumate.[24]

Upon their return to the Henry house hill, they found that the enemy had been swept from the field and was in full retreat. As J.E.B. Stuart's cavalry charged the fleeing Yankees across the stone bridge and disappeared into the distance, Imboden and Shumate made their way back to the battery.[25] The battle of Manassas was over.

Aftermath of Manassas

On their way back to the battery, Imboden and Sgt. Shumate met Gen. Johnston and his staff near the Lewis house. Imboden recalled,

> [They were] preceded a little by a gentleman on horseback, who was lifting his hat to everyone he met. From the likeness I had seen of President Jefferson Davis, I instantly recognized him and told Shumate who it was. With the impulsiveness of his nature, Shumate dashed up to the President, seized his hand, and hooraied at the top of his voice. I could see that Mr. Davis was greatly amused, and I was convulsed with laughter. When they came within twenty steps of me, where I had halted to let the group pass, Shumate exclaimed, to the great amusement of all who heard him: "Mr. President, there's my captain, and I want to introduce you to him." The President eyed me for a moment, as if he thought I was an odd-looking captain. I had on a battered slouch hat, a red flannel shirt with only one sleeve, corduroy trousers, and heavy cavalry boots, and was begrimed with burnt powder, dust, and the blood from my ear and arm, and must have been about as hard-looking a specimen of a

captain as was ever seen. Nevertheless, the President grasped my hand with a cordial salutation, and after a few words passed on.[1]

At last Imboden rejoined his battery. After eating a hurried but hearty meal of bacon and bread, the captain threw himself on a bag of oats and fell fast asleep. He slept through a pouring rain that beat down on him all night and was aroused long after daylight next morning by a messenger from former South Carolina governor Alston, who summoned him to the side of the dying Gen. Bee. Until that point he was unaware that Bee had been wounded and Col. Bartow instantly killed near the Henry house.

Imboden hurried to the cabin that Bee had used as his headquarters before the battle, where he found Bee unconscious. Within a few minutes, with Imboden holding his hand, Gen. Bee died. It grieved Imboden deeply that he had not arrived sooner. During the night, after learning of his battery commander's concern at being left unsupported, Bee had sent for Imboden. He wished to tell him with his own lips about Maj. Howard's death and his own wounding, just prior to which he rallied his troops with the line, "Rally behind the Virginians—there stands Jackson like a stone wall," thus giving Jackson the nickname by which he would be known from that time on.[2]

Three days after the battle Imboden learned that Jackson's wound had become inflamed and went to visit him. He arrived at the little farmhouse in Centreville where Jackson had his headquarters and later described what transpired.

> Although it was barely sunrise, he was out under the trees, bathing the hand with spring water. It was much swollen and very painful, but he bore himself stoically. His wife had arrived the night before. Of course, the battle was the only topic discussed at breakfast. I remarked, in Mrs. Jackson's hearing, "General, how is it that you can keep so cool, and appear so utterly insensible to danger in such a storm of shell and bullets as rained about you when your hand was hit?" He instantly became grave and reverential in his manner, and answered, in a low tone of earnestness: "Captain, my religious belief teaches me to feel as safe in battle as in bed. God has fixed the time for my death. I do not concern myself at that, but to be always ready, no matter when it may overtake me." He added, after a pause, looking me full in the face:

"Captain, that is the way all men should live, and then
all would be equally brave."[3]

Imboden took that last remark as a rebuke for his having cursed on the
battlefield when commenting on the abandonment of his battery and
apologized to Jackson. The general replied, "Nothing can justify
profanity."[4]

Imboden had fought bravely in the battle, assuming the task of
supporting the infantry despite facing superior enemy artillery. His green
volunteers had faced well-trained, regular army troops who were fully
equipped, and his service did not go unnoticed. Gen. Beauregard
mentioned Imboden and the Staunton Artillery no less than eleven times
in his official report on the battle,[5] noting that the Staunton Artillery "had
been handled with marked skill."[6] Jackson, in his report, recorded,

I met General Bee's forces falling back. I continued to
advance with the understanding that he would form in
my rear. His battery, under its dauntless commander,
Captain Imboden, reversed and advanced with my
brigade.[7]

Gen. Johnston also took note of Imboden's performance, writing,
"Imboden rendered excellent service with his battery in this difficult
operation."[8] Perhaps one of his enemy paid Imboden as great a
compliment as any when he penned, "Behind this hill the enemy had,
early in the day, some of his most annoying batteries planted."[9] Unknown
to this Yankee officer, he was facing only one battery—Imboden's.

The battle of Manassas was followed by a period of inactivity while the
army awaited orders to follow up on its great victory and advance on
Washington. Sharp disagreement erupted between the commanding
generals and the president and his secretary of war, Judah P. Benjamin.
Generals Johnston and Beauregard maintained that it was impossible to
move the army due to inadequacies in food and transportation. Although
the quartermaster's and commissary departments in Richmond tended to
disbelieve the destitution that existed in the army at that time, on the
battery's muster roll following the battle Imboden commented that "the
fatigue of that day together with privations and exposure to tremendous
rains cause the great amount of sickness."[10]

In order to ascertain the facts, Johnston organized a board of officers to
investigate and report on the conditions of the army's transportation and
commissary at Manassas both at the time of the battle and for two weeks

afterward. On the board were Lt. Col. Robert B. Lee (a cousin of Robert E. Lee), representing the commissary department; Maj. W.L. Cabell, representing the quartermaster's department; and Imboden, representing the line. Both of Imboden's associates were former United States Army officers with much experience in army matters. They met in early August and, after an exhaustive investigation into the issue, drafted a detailed report.

The board found that on the morning of the battle not one full day's rations existed for the combined army at Manassas, and for the next two weeks at no time was there as much as three days' rations available. The report also revealed that an insufficient number of wagons and teams were available for distribution should three days' worth of supplies be delivered by train. They noted that Beauregard had sent repeated urgent requests to Richmond for supplies for two weeks after the battle. The board decided unanimously that the commissary general, Col. Northrop, had not only failed to send the needed supplies, but had also interfered with efforts to secure supplies from the region around Manassas. They concurred, therefore, that a rapid pursuit of their defeated enemy had been impossible.

The report was signed and forwarded to Secretary Benjamin in Richmond, who returned it to the board stating that they had exceeded their powers and had no right to express an opinion as to what the facts proved or disproved. For reasons unknown, the report was suppressed and never seen again.[11]

During August Imboden wrote recommendations for his brother George and C.C. McPhail, an ordnance officer at Winchester, to be promoted to second lieutenants in the battery with the explanation that

> Gen. Johnston has increased my battery by the addition of two of the captured guns and directed me to enlarge my Company to 150 rank and file—Any regular officer will tell you that it is impossible to manage a six piece battery—especially of mixed guns—rifles—smooth and Howitzers—with less than 4 Lieuts. Indeed 150 men, 110 horses and six pieces, with necessary baggage and artificer's train would well employ 5 Lieuts. in the field—but 4 are absolutely required.[12]

The captain was successful in getting a promotion for his brother but not for McPhail.

At the end of July, Imboden had reported that his company had only sixty-eight horses; by the end of August, however, this number had increased to a hundred eight horses and mules. They were given a ten-inch howitzer and a ten-inch James rifle from the captured stocks taken at Manassas to supplement their armament and moved from Camp Pickens to Camp Jones at Bristoe Station.[13]

Finally, on September 18, the Staunton Artillery received orders to march to Dumfries in support of Gen. Isaac R. Trimble's forces at Evansport. While he and his battery busily prepared their winter quarters, Imboden took the opportunity to write home on several occasions. In a letter dated September 30 he requested a new uniform coat because "the weather is getting cool very fast" and complained that Gen. William H.C. Whiting, now in command of that sector, refused to grant him leave. He also commented on the condition of the battery:

> By recruits, increase of guns from 4 to 6 with proper caissons and harness, the company is now in more prosperous and efficient condition that it has ever been since its organization on 1 November 1859. It may be proper to add that this company has never received from state or Confederate governments whatever, nor blankets nor tents except one single Yankee tent captured property, nor anything except its arms, horses, harness and 100 knapsacks and canteens. . . . [14]

Later he reported that "on the 17th day of October the Batteries were unmasked, and this Company took part in the engagement with the enemy's flotilla, firing only 8 rounds from their rifle gun."

On November 2 he wrote home for shot to use in partridge hunting and sent money to buy a hundred pairs of trousers for his men, noting that color was not a concern so long as they were all the same and heavy enough for winter weather.[15]

The attorney-turned-soldier was adjusting well to army life, serving as topographical engineer for Gen. Whiting. Not quite a week later, on November 7, he wrote,

> All is quiet. The river is clear of Yankees for 5 miles, above and below the batteries. Gen. Whiting ordered me this morning to select a suitable position for another battery of 10 heavy guns some miles from the present batteries. I have found a magnificent position and will report in the morning. I think it is probable he will put

me in charge of the construction of the works. With 400
men I can have the guns in position in a week—and do
the work under cover in the day time.

We are all well. Unless some of my men, who I
understand are going about town [Staunton] as usual,
return here in a few days, I shall be compelled to have
them arrested for desertion—in which case the reward
for arrest is $30—will be taken from their pay and they
will be severely punished by court-martial besides. I have
had to report the names of all absentees to
Headquarters.[16]

Meanwhile, the company was busy building stables, cribs and harness
houses for the horses and equipment as well as working on cabins to house
the men. On November 30 Imboden wrote,

Here we are perfectly quiet. For a while in November our
Generals expected an attack would be made upon these
batteries and even now Gen. Whiting thinks we are to
have a fight here one of these days.

The mud in places for miles is to a horse's belly. God
only knows how we are to get our supplies a few weeks
hence. At this time it is a Herculean task. The provisions
of the neighborhood are exhausted. We must be supplied
by RR. It is 18 miles to Bristow—12 to Aquia. The road
to either is next to deplorable. There are about 20,000
troops in this neighborhood using about 52,000 lbs. of
food per diem. We are living hand to mouth having only
3 days ahead.[17]

A few days later, on December 3, a correspondent for the Richmond
Dispatch related,

Close by town, lying under "Rose Hill" and almost in the
shadow of the haunted house, is the camp of Capt.
Imboden, whose battery did such good service in the
battle of Manassas Plains. This gallant soldier is now very
busy with Gen. Wigfall in examining the country around
him, and in selecting locations where his guns could be
used should the enemy advance. I have spoken of the
erroneous map of the battlefield, upon which Gen. Ewell

has a false position. It is even worse with Capt. Imboden, for in places where he fought like a tiger and where the battery did the best services, the credit is given to another corps of artillery. Frequently on the 21st I saw his battery fight as well as the best General could wish, but until late did not know whose guns they were, or who the gallant officer who armed them. Capt. Imboden is now under Gen. Wigfall, and will have a prominent place in the fight by the Occoquan, should one occur.[18]

The Confederates were still alert for a Union advance on December 9 when Imboden noted, "Today the *Harriet Lane* shelled a piquet at Freestone Point, 4 miles above us, and burnt John Fairfax's house, barn, stables, and crib with about 400 bushels of wheat. The conflagration was visible from a hill above my camp." He complained that the horses' legs were "scalded by the mud."[19]

Thus the Confederate army settled down into winter quarters, the dull routine of camp life broken only by occasional snowball fights. Everyone in the army now realized that they were in for a long war.

Partisan Service

The Staunton Artillery encamped at Dumfries during the remainder of the winter of 1861–1862. According to the muster rolls for November-December, "No event of interest occurred to the company during the period . . . except two fake alarms from Occoquan in November resulting in a rapid march to Neabsco and a slow one back each time." Imboden reported that the health of the company was "excellent."[1]

Promotion was slow in the artillery, as that particular branch of the service possessed an abundance of West Point and V.M.I.-trained professional soldiers, and Imboden had seen no prospect for real action since Manassas other than the occasional picket skirmish or clash of foraging parties. Although recognized as a "gifted artilleryman,"[2] the once-reluctant soldier sought more exciting, active warfare.

In the border counties of western Virginia, Maryland, Missouri and eastern Tennessee, independent bands of Confederate fighters waged a ruthless type of war against Yankee invaders, assembling and striking at all hours in many places, frequently against the B&O Railroad. The

guerilla activity first occured in western Virginia around the time that
Johnston arrived at Harpers Ferry. It was an inexorable, taunting type of
warfare fought by self-centered, individualistic patriots. These clandestine
troops, mostly angered farmers, called themselves independents, irregulars or
partisans. Their Yankee enemies called them bushwackers.[3]

Guerilla warfare, dating back nearly to the beginning of time, was
primarily a resort of the overrun and outnumbered. By 1862, when the
first official inquiry as to its legal status was made by F. A. Briscoe, Esq.,
of Winchester, it had become a valuable tool that no military science was
prepared to handle. Within a week of Briscoe's query, Adjt. Gen. Samuel
Cooper replied, "Such a force, when organized, armed, and equipped, will
be received into service and commissions issued to the officers thereof."[4]

The cry for local service went up all over western Virginia but sounded
loudest in the area between Harpers Ferry and Wheeling. As regular
Confederate forces were already spread thin and unable to defend all
fronts, men began to raise their own companies for irregular or
independent service. Counties sent petitions to President Davis and
Governor Letcher, who was authorized by an act of the general assembly
to issue commissions for the organization of ten companies of partisan
rangers.[5] Virginia recruiters only winked at that restriction, however, since
more than ten companies were already positioned in the field.

Caught up in the fervor, on March 7 Imboden revealed, "I have written
the President about raising a legion for guerila service in the Mountains.
I will hear from him next week. If he authorizes it I shall go home at once
to raise the men in the mountain counties."[6]

His brother Frank was in partisan service already. He had been
commissioned a captain in Ben McCulloch's Rangers, a small band of
independents in Gen. Henry Wise's Legion,[7] and had fought gallantly
until captured at Roanoke Island, North Carolina. Now Imboden sought
his exchange, so that Frank could share his experiences.[8]

On March 8 Imboden's battery joined the rest of Whiting's command
as it abandoned its position along the Potomac and withdrew toward
Fredericksburg. Upon their arrival the Staunton Artillery was assigned to
Gen. Gustavus W. Smith's division. Their stay at Fredericksburg did not
last long, for on March 21 they took up the line of march for the Virginia
Peninsula, slogging through extremely inclement weather.

The battery was reorganized on April 22 after they reached Yorktown,
but Imboden declined reelection and resigned his commission to await
word on his request for partisan service.[9] Only the day before, after much

hot debate, the Confederate Congress had resolved the issue of guerilla warfare by passing the Partisan Ranger Act.[10]

Under the law, partisan troops could be organized as cavalry or infantry. Recruits were to be received regularly into the service with the same pay as other soldiers and subject to the same military regulations. Not accorded to regular soldiers was the act's inducement that for any arms and munitions of war captured and turned over to the government, the partisans would be paid the prevailing price.

Moreover, in an unprecedented action, the Confederate Congress had passed a Conscription Act on April 12 that provided for the possible conscription of all white males between eighteen and thirty-five years of age for three years of service. Not wanting to bear the stigma of having been drafted and wanting to serve close to home, young men were eager to join partisan groups. Thus was the attractiveness of partisan service increased by the first military draft law ever enacted on the American continent.[11]

Imboden sought Jackson's approval or assistance in organizing an independent command as well as the backing of John Harman and Turner Ashby.[12] On May 7, 1862, he received word from Secretary of War George W. Randolph authorizing him to raise a regiment in Jackson's military department for partisan service. Immediately upon completion of his regiment's organization Imboden would be commissioned a colonel.[13]

Broadsides announcing the formation of Imboden's Partisan Rangers appeared in stores and other meeting places in the counties of western Virginia. There was no doubt about the kind of warfare Imboden intended to pursue. One of the circulars spelled out the role of partisan rangers:

> My purpose is to wage the most active warfare against our brutal invaders and their domestic allies, to hang about their camps and shoot down every sentinel, picket, courier, and wagon driver we can find; to watch opportunities for attacking convoys and forage trains and thus render the country so unsafe that they will not dare to move except in large bodies.[14]

A broadside made clear the type of soldier for whom he was searching:

It is only *men* I want, men who will pull the trigger on a
Yankee with as much alacrity as they would on a mad
dog; men whose consciences won't be disturbed by the
sight of a vandal carcass.[15]

Imboden placed a notice in the Richmond *Dispatch* under the heading
"Active Service in the Mountains of Virginia," in which he stated that he
wanted ten companies of "picked men" to operate west of the Blue Ridge.
He described this branch of the service as one in which "individual prowess
is not swallowed up on the mere mechanism of great masses of men."[16]

Declaring that his plans "had the highest military approval," he asserted
that in carrying out his mission he would "rely on great celerity of
movement, sleepless vigilance, good marksmanship and plenty of
old-fashioned rough fighting and bushwacking, so as to make the country
too hot to permit a Yankee to show his head outside of camp."[17]

In response the *Dispatch* gave its editorial opinion that partisan warfare
was "beyond a doubt, the most attractive branch of the service (and would
attract the attention) of all young men of daring and adventurous natures."[18]

Although Imboden's most fervent desire had been to operate in his
native region of Virginia, this area had now become virtually a no-man's
land. It was extremely irritating to such an ardent believer in the right of
secession and states rights to see his area of the state slipping under the
control of the hated Yankees. He sincerely believed that a
semi-independent command raised in the region could regain all lost
territory for the Confederacy, and before long eager recruits began to cast
their lot with the South in response to Imboden's summons.

Men assembled from all over the disputed territory. In less than two
months, four complete companies had been raised, while four additional
units rapidly approached company strength. After all Imboden had
already accomplished for the young Confederate nation, it was only
natural and fitting that his should be the first ranger unit authorized under
the new law.[19]

The First Virginia Partisan Rangers

Imboden established his headquarters at Staunton. Scarcely had he settled in when he received a letter from a soldier in the Staunton Artillery, echoing the feelings of many in Imboden's former command: "I will never be satisfied to remain in the company under the present officers. . . . I have no confidence in them and now that you are gone, I wish to go also."[1] Imboden's cousin, John Alexandria Ruff Imboden, also wrote to request a position in the new command, stating that he had recently visited the battery and found many young men who wished to join as well.[2]

Imboden's command was to operate in Jackson's Valley District, west of the Blue Ridge and east of the Alleghenies where Stonewall Jackson was then waging his own war. Since mid-March he had detained large numbers of Union troops in the Valley and then engaged Union general James Shields at Kernstown, about four miles south of Winchester, on March 23. After several hours of intense fighting Jackson was repulsed, followed by an orderly retreat up the Valley to Swift Run Gap in Rockingham County. Jackson's presence caused great concern in Washington, and the federal government reversed the direction of several divisions on the road that were heading for a military buildup in the east.

Jackson's meager force was reinforced by Brig. Gen. Richard S. Ewell's division about May 1, bringing the total number of troops to approximately thirteen to fifteen thousand. As for the Federals, Union generals Robert Milroy with forty-one hundred troops at McDowell; Robert Schenck with twenty-five hundred at Franklin; John C. Frémont with twenty thousand near Franklin; Nathaniel P. Banks with another twenty thousand at Strasburg; Irvin McDowell with thirty-four thousand just east of the Blue Ridge; and Col. Miles with seven thousand at Harpers Ferry were all within striking distance. In all, about eighty thousand federal troops were near enough to keep Jackson concerned.

Banks followed Jackson slowly, taking nearly a month to reach Harrisonburg. Jackson then slipped out of the Valley, leaving Ewell to keep an eye on Banks, crossed the Blue Ridge at Brown's Gap and hurried to waiting railroad cars at Mechum's River, west of Charlottesville. His men clambered aboard the train and headed west to Staunton to face the advancing troops of Frémont.

Shortly after noon on May 5, to the great joy and excitement of the citizenry, Jackson and his troops arrived in Staunton with a small force under Brig. Gen. Edward "Allegheny" Johnson and the cadet battalion from V.M.I., which Jackson had called out for the emergency, to greet them.[3] Jackson sought Imboden but could not locate him. Desperately wanting Imboden with him in this campaign, Jackson wired Lee to determine the captain's whereabouts, to which Lee replied, "I have not seen Captain Imboden. If I can find him I will urge him to join you with such men as he can at once, as you desired."[4]

Jackson finally pushed westward without Imboden, who had been out in the surrounding countryside recruiting. On May 8, at the top of Bull Pasture Mountain, three miles east of McDowell, he encountered Milroy and Schenck, whom he drove from the field and chased all the way to Franklin. Jackson's important victory at McDowell saved Staunton and prevented the juncture of Frémont and Banks.[5]

On the morning after the battle of McDowell, Imboden met with Jackson at the residence of Col. George W. Hall and offered his services. Jackson dispatched him shortly with a telegram to President Davis, with orders to provide couriers in the days to come. The message to the president read simply, "Providence blessed our arms with victory at McDowell yesterday."[6]

After providing dispatch riders for Jackson, Imboden was left at Staunton with his embryonic force. The cadets were sent back to their studies in Lexington, and Johnson and Ewell joined Jackson in a push down the Valley. Together they won smashing victories at Front Royal and Winchester, then chased the retreating Banks across the Potomac into Maryland.

Imboden continued to organize and drill his new recruits at Staunton. From New Market, Jackson sent him orders to place as many of his men as possible into Brock's Gap west of Harrisonburg and into any other mountain gaps through which Frémont might pass to reach the Shenandoah Valley. Imboden fortified these passes with all the men he could arm, determined to defend their positions to the last man.[7]

As soon as Frémont heard of Banks's defeat, he put his army in motion to cut off Jackson's move up the Valley. Although Ashby's cavalry was ready to face him at McDowell, Frémont did not choose that route; instead, he moved toward Brock's Gap, where Imboden waited with about fifty men. The Confederates in the cliffs let the enemy troops get well into the gorge before pouring a deadly volley into the column. The barrage was completely unexpected. Not knowing the strength of the attackers, the Union force stopped dead in its tracks and hesitated to advance. A second volley followed by a rebel yell turned them back, and Frémont travelled the route to Moorefield and Strasburg, missing Jackson entirely.[8]

Jackson's withdrawal up the Valley drew two federal armies along with it. As he approached Staunton the general called Imboden out to guard the bridge over the North River at Mount Crawford to prevent enemy cavalry from passing on his rear. With a battalion of partisan rangers, four mountain howitzers and a rifled Parrott gun, Imboden successfully guarded Jackson's wagons against a flank attack during the battle of Cross Keys.

At ten o'clock that night a courier handed Imboden a note from Jackson. Scrawled in pencil on the margin of a newspaper, it was orders to report with his command at Port Republic before daybreak. At the bottom of the page, added as a postscript, Jackson had written, "Poor Ashby is dead. He fell gloriously. I know you will join with me in mourning the loss of our friend, one of the noblest men and soldiers in the Confederate Army." Imboden would later write that he carried that slip of paper until it was literally worn to tatters.[9]

Imboden reached Port Republic an hour before daylight on June 9 and sought Jackson's headquarters. Not wishing to disturb the general so early, he asked for Sandie Pendleton, Jackson's adjutant, but inadvertently came upon Jackson himself, sound asleep yet fully dressed with boots, sword and uniform. Although he tried to withdraw without waking the general, Jackson turned over, sat up and asked, "Who is that?" Upon Imboden's apology, Jackson replied, "That's all right. It's time to be up. I'm glad to see you. Were the men all up when you came through camp?" When Imboden replied that they were preparing their morning meal, Jackson answered, "That's right. We're to move at daybreak. Sit down. I want to talk to you."[10]

The captain sat down to await Jackson's instructions, but the general instead spoke of Ashby's untimely death and of the irreparable loss suffered by the army. When Imboden complimented Jackson on his recent victory, Jackson gave credit to God's blessing the army, with the hope that He would do so again. Then, by the dim light of a flickering candle, Jackson, who usually kept his plans to himself, outlined the day's plan. The plan included dividing Imboden's Rangers.[11]

Imboden had placed one of the first companies in his new command under his brother George. Although not fully equipped, the company did have four mountain howitzers and one Parrott gun.[12] Jackson directed Imboden to give "the big new rifle gun (the twelve-pound Parrott) to

[Capt. William T.] Poague [of the Rockbridge Artillery] and let your mounted men report to the cavalry." Then he laid before Imboden a plan for himself and the four howitzers:

> I want you in person to take your mountain howitzers to the field, in some safe position in rear of the line, keeping everything packed on the mules, ready at any moment to take to the mountainside. Three miles below Lewis's there is a defile on the Luray road. Shields may rally and make a stand there. If he does, I can't reach him with the field batteries on account of the woods. You can carry your 12-pounder howitzers on the mules up the mountainside, and at some good place unpack and shell the enemy out of the defile, and the cavalry will do the rest.[13]

Later that same morning, while Imboden led his "Jackass Artillery," brigadier generals Charles Winder with the Stonewall Brigade and Richard Taylor with his Louisiana Brigade attacked the enemy at different angles. Imboden carried out his assignment to the letter, placing his mule-borne battery in a ravine several hundred yards to the rear of the Rockbridge Artillery.

A few enemy shots aimed at Poague overshot their mark and burst in and around Imboden's gunners and their mules. Imboden recorded,

> The mules became frantic. They kicked, plunged, and squealed. It was impossible to quiet them, and it took three or four men to hold one mule from breaking away. Each mule had about three hundred pounds weight on him so securely fastened, that the load could not be dislodged by any of his capers. Several of them lay down and tried to wallow their loads off. The men held these down, and that suggested the idea of throwing them all down and holding them there. The ravine sheltered us so that we were in no danger from the shot or shell which passed over us.
>
> Just about the time our mule "circus" was at its height, news came up the line from the left that Winder's brigade near the river was giving away. Jackson rode down in that direction to see what it meant. As he passed on the brink of our ravine, his eye caught the scene, and, reining up a

moment, he accosted me with "Colonel, you seem to have trouble down there." I made some reply which drew forth a hearty laugh, and he said "Get your mules to the mountain as soon as you can and be ready to move." Then he dashed on.[14]

The general rallied his old brigade, led them back to their original line and, together with Taylor's brigade, shoved the enemy from the field. As the Yankees began a wild retreat, Jackson kept up a vigorous pursuit for more than eight miles. Upon his return Imboden accompanied him back to headquarters.

Thus, with Jackson's grand victories at Cross Keys and Port Republic, the Valley Campaign ended. The operation had covered three months, entailing six major battles and numerous skirmishes, and Jackson and his little army had marched up and down the Valley five times.

The next day Imboden returned to Staunton to continue recruiting and organizing his command, but not before performing a very unpleasant duty. Wrote Capt. John W. Wayland of the Mt. Crawford Cavalry,

Gen. Imboden, who was in command of the cavalry, detailed me and my company to gather up and bury the dead. At one place we buried 81 bodies, and at another 21. They were mostly foreigners from the looks of them.[15]

On July 3, 1862, George Imboden's company was officially sworn into Confederate service and designated as Co. B, 1st Virginia Partisan Rangers. Imboden also attempted, unsuccessfully, to have the Staunton Artillery transferred to his command.[16]

When Jackson left the Valley to join Lee in repelling the enemy invaders before Richmond, Imboden elected to stay in Staunton to build up his force. Petitions to join his service continued to pour in. In July Capt. John F. Harding requested a transfer of his entire company from the 31st Virginia to ranger service. He claimed that since his men were from Pocahontas and Randolph counties, they were familiar with the territory now occupied by Union forces and could entice many friends in the region to join them.[17]

Later, in mid-July, Imboden's command was joined by a bearded cattleman from Missouri named John Hanson McNeill. Hanse McNeill, born in Moorefield in 1815, was an ardent secessionist who had led a company of mounted volunteers in the pro-Southern Missouri State

Guard. Under Gen. Sterling Price's command, while fighting to keep Missouri from falling into Union hands, he was wounded and captured but had escaped and come east. After seeking authority from Richmond to raise a partisan ranger company to operate in western Virginia, he was given permission to recruit men from his native Hardy County with orders to report to Imboden.[18] He and Imboden would work well together in the years to come.

Imboden's command continued to grow as men armed with shotguns and rifles and the determination to drive the advancing Yankees from their midst—men who would become known for their conspicuous bravery—arrived at Staunton. Without any formal military training, they were destined to become some of the most formidable fighters on either side during the war.

Independent Command

The nature of partisan warfare required the use of tactics that many officers trained at West Point found to be outside their definition of legitimate warfare, since the guerilla mode of attack contrasted severely to the type of combat contained in military textbooks of the period. To many of the federal officers schooled in the Napoleonic tactics of Europe, partisan activity overstepped the bounds of civilized warfare. In fact, the hit-and-run tactics of the partisans kept the Union army off balance by forcing the deployment of sorely needed combat troops to guard vulnerable supply lines. Union officers, unable to cope successfully with such an effective mode of warfare, declared partisans to be outlaws.

The glamour of partisan service lay deeply rooted in Southern tradition and heritage. One of the best-known and well-respected of all Southern heroes was Francis Marion of Revolutionary War fame, a South Carolinian affectionately known as the Swamp Fox. Not only had a whole generation of Southerners been reared listening to stories about him, but many southern boys, including Colonel Imboden's brother Frank, had been named in his honor. To a Southerner, the term partisan evoked an image of a dashing cavalier fighting for freedom and justice, to which was added the inducement of operating near one's home with only a minimal amount of military discipline.

Imboden and his small band were to figure prominently in the Confederate strategy. Lee recognized the threat that Imboden could be to the B&O Railroad and directed him to launch a raid against the vital

Northern lifeline, striking at the railroad bridge at Rowlesburg, a hundred fifty miles northwest of Staunton. Although many efforts had been made at the B&O connection over the Cheat River, all had failed. In June of 1861 Gen. Robert S. Garnett had reached Huttonsville but could go no farther. Likewise, Col. Angus McDonald with a small party of independent cavalry never moved past Romney. Lee had taken to the field after Manassas but made no headway, and Gen. William W. Loring had failed to damage the railroad in his attempt in January 1862. In a message to President Davis, Lee remarked,

> I hope to hear every day of Imboden's success in his attempt on the B&O railroad. He started from Staunton sometime since with almost 600 men and by his own calculations would have reached the trestle work four or five days since. We must make allowance for delays and difficulties. I hope he will be in time to arrest troops from the west.[1]

This was not to be the case, however, as Imboden left Franklin, about a hundred miles southeast of the railroad bridge, on August 14. His six companies covered twelve to fifteen miles each day through the mountainous, heavily wooded terrain, often forced to hack their way through the forest. A small camp of Union troops at Parson's Mill on the Cheat River, about twenty-three miles south of Rowlesburg, was Imboden's first objective. After an all-night march the Confederates surrounded the camp, only to find that the Yankees had fled.[2]

Imboden's intended raid had been frustrated by a nineteen-year-old girl. On August 18 Mary Jane Snyder heard that Imboden was near her father's house and early the next morning rode through the wilderness to warn a company of western Virginia Unionists encamped at Parson's Mill, ten miles above St. George. Her warning came a mere four hours before Imboden's force reached the camp but provided ample time for the displaced soldiers to get word of Imboden's approach to other Federals in the area. They fortified the bridge, outnumbering Imboden's small force, and forced Imboden to abandon the raid and head for home.[3]

During the first week of September 1862 Lee crossed the Potomac with his Army of Northern Virginia, the first large-scale Confederate offensive into Union territory. While Jackson battled at Harpers Ferry and Lee confronted George McClellan along Antietam Creek near Sharpsburg, Maryland, Imboden made a second threatening move toward the B&O.

Union general Benjamin F. Kelley kept troops moving up and down the line in a frantic attempt to stave off the guerilla activity west of Harpers Ferry.[4]

Imboden tied down several thousand federal troops during and after the Sharpsburg Campaign—troops that could have threatened Lee's supply lines. With only infantry and artillery, Kelley was handicapped in his pursuit of Imboden's troops, moving first here, then there, wherever the guerillas struck. The colonel had no difficulty in eluding Kelley, who was aggravated by Imboden's freedom of movement west of the Alleghenies. A federal soldier wrote to Francis Pierpoint, the Unionist "governor" in Wheeling that "it is a burning shame that Imboden is permitted to stalk through this country as he pleases without being even annoyed by any of our men."[5] Kelley was finally given some New York cavalry, whom he ordered on the trail of Imboden in the last week of September. They were eminently unsuccessful, however, and one party was captured by McNeill, who was by then operating on his own.

Imboden returned to the business of recruiting and rapidly filled up his command. To encourage more men to join, he had moved his base of operations to Hampshire and Hardy counties[6] and by late September had enlisted more than the ten companies required by Confederate law to constitute a regiment.

His 1st Regiment, Virginia Partisan Rangers was a conglomeration of infantry, cavalry, and artillery. On September 24, Hanse McNeill arrived at Imboden's headquarters at Bloomery with his company, where McNeill's men were formally mustered into Confederate service as Company I.[7] Imboden continued to operate freely in western Virginia for the rest of September and into October, organizing and recruiting new troops from his base camp even as he anxiously awaited an active campaign.

The Army of Northern Virginia had now completely withdrawn from Maryland to the northern Shenandoah Valley, where Gen. J.E.B. Stuart proposed a cavalry raid that would encircle the part of Union general McClellan's army still remaining in Maryland. Stuart felt that he could safely ride around McClellan's right flank into Pennsylvania, then return to Virginia by taking a route between the enemy's left flank and Washington, D.C. Gen. Lee endorsed this plan with the provision that Imboden make a diversionary raid against the B&O. Imboden was to begin his assault before Stuart's departure and hopefully divert the attention of the federal army from Stuart's proposed route.

In compliance with Lee's orders, Imboden left his camp at Capon Bridge on October 2 and headed west for seven miles to a point near Hanging Rock, where he encountered a scouting party from the 1st New York Cavalry. In this brief engagement, Imboden's Confederates captured five men, fourteen horses, and a number of small arms. Turning northward, the command rode on to attack the B&O. Immediately upon reaching the railroad the Southerners began their mission of destruction by striking at the bridge that spanned the south branch of the Potomac. Unable to inflict total destruction of the iron structure with the means at their disposal, they turned to the east and followed the railroad right-of-way in search of more vulnerable targets.[8]

Continuing eastward on the morning of October 4, the Confederates arrived at an entrenched federal camp guarding the railroad bridge at the mouth of Little Cacapon River. At daybreak the Southerners charged under the cover of a dense fog, taking the Federals completely by surprise. Imboden's men took fifty-five prisoners and killed or wounded eight men of the 54th Pennsylvania Volunteers. They then burned the wooden railroad bridge, as well as all of the nearby railroad buildings and rolling stock.

Determined to further disrupt traffic on the railroad, Imboden continued eastward to the tunnel at Paw Paw, where the partisan infantry surrounded the camp of the federal bridge guard while the cavalry crossed the Potomac into Maryland to cut off any federal retreat. The Union garrison surrendered after offering only a token resistance. The Confederates not only took prisoner ninety men of Co. B, 54th Pennsylvania Volunteers, but also captured a hundred seventy-five Austrian rifles and eight thousand rounds of waterproof ammunition. While the men were collecting their spoils, his scouts informed Col. Imboden that two train loads of Union reinforcements were approaching rapidly from the east. Realizing that his force was too weak to face this new threat, Imboden ordered most of the captured stores to be burned and withdrew to the South.[9]

The eventful three-day raid had resulted in extensive damage to the track, bridges and rolling stock of the B&O railroad. In addition, several hundred badly needed arms were captured and more than a hundred fifty casualties inflicted on the enemy. All of this was accomplished without a single loss of life in Imboden's command, prompting Lee's praise for his success:

I have read with pleasure your report of the attack upon
the enemy's cavalry at Hanging Rock and the subsequent
surprise of the two companies of the enemy's infantry
stationed at the mouth of the Little Capon and at Paw
Paw Tunnel. The results accomplished, and the judicious
arrangements which enabled you to effect them without
loss of life on your part, are deserving of high
commendations.[10]

Imboden's railroad raid had accomplished the desired effect of diverting
federal attention from Stuart's route. Four days after Imboden's attack on
Paw Paw, Stuart set out on his raid into Pennsylvania. He completely
circled McClellan's army and safely returned to Virginia after eluding the
pursuing enemy by the slimmest of margins.

Yet, upon their return to the base camp, the jubilant Southern raiders
found that the enemy had taken advantage of their absence. On October
4, two companies of the 1st New York Cavalry had attacked the
understrength guard, approximately one hundred unarmed men under Lt.
Henderson Stone, at Capon Bridge. The Yankees had charged headlong
across the covered bridge into the Confederate camp before the surprised
defenders could fire the two mountain howitzers that guarded the bridge.
The fight was over in less than five minutes, but the Confederate partisans
suffered nearly two dozen casualties; the remainder of the guard escaped
by fleeing to the mountains. The invaders seized all of the Southerners'
supplies, including a half dozen wagons loaded with tents, blankets and
camp equipment, the two mountain howitzers, and the herd of horses and
mules.[11] All of Col. Imboden's personal and official papers were
confiscated.[12]

The other Confederates returned soon after the attack and took up the
pursuit of the Yankee raiders. Imboden's partisans pressed their enemy so
closely that the Federals were forced to abandon the captured wagons and
cut loose the horse herd. Most of the seized possessions were recovered, the
net loss amounting to one wagonload of supplies.

The ease with which the Federals had approached his camp while he
was gone convinced Imboden of his need to relocate to a more secure base.
In order to put more distance between themselves and the Federals,
Imboden moved his encampment in mid-October to a sheltered valley
between Petersburg and Moorefield.

His men prepared for the winter in this new location by building huts
and laying in supplies to see them through the harsh months ahead [13] while

Col. Imboden concentrated on organizing his raw troops into a consolidated strike force. His attempt to actively resupply his force was rewarded, as on November 6 they received a small supply of overcoats and blankets. [14]

The mood of the region greatly aided his recruitment effort, for the residents of western Virginia were living in a virtual no-man's land, with no escape from the ravages of war and no neutral ground. Each individual had to declare his allegiance, either North or South, and stand by that decision. When the opposing side was in control of the area, no mercy was shown on the lives or property of the other. It was a true guerilla war, involving such brutal tactics as raids, constant skirmishing, robbery, and murder.

In early November 1862 Milroy issued an order to assess known Confederate sympathizers for losses incurred by Union men from Confederate raids. The order read:

> If they fail to pay at the end of the time you have named, their houses will be burned and themselves shot and their property all seized; and be sure that you carry out this threat rigidly and show them that you are not trifling or to be trifled with. You will inform the inhabitants for ten or fifteen miles around your camp, on all the roads approaching the town upon which the enemy may approach, that they must dash in and give you notice, and that upon failure of any one to do so their houses will be burned and the men shot. [15]

The choice was clear: submit to the Union or fight.

It was under these conditions that Col. Imboden received men from western Virginia into his command. Of these new recruits Imboden commented, "The large majority of the men have but recently escaped Pierpoint's dominion and are brimful of fight."[16] Those in his command came primarily from Hampshire, Hardy, Pendleton, Tucker, Barbour, Upshire, Lewis, Randolph, Pocahontas, Webster, Braxton, Frederick, Shenandoah, Rockingham, Augusta, Highland and Bath counties. Many had previously served in various commands, primarily the 33rd, 25th and 52nd Virginia infantry regiments.[17]

Official notice of Milroy's program was brought to the attention of Imboden by Job Parsons, who went to Imboden for the purpose of joining the partisan rangers and showed the colonel the papers containing

Milroy's orders. Furious, Imboden passed them on to President Davis with this explanation:

> The pretext of "robberies of Union men by bands of guerrillas" is a falsehood. The fact is that Union men have conspired to run off each other's horses to Pennsylvania, where they are secretly sold, the owners afterward setting up a claim for reparation on the false ground that guerillas have robbed them.[18]

He mentioned the matter only as evidence of the "atrocity of General Milroy," and added that "this is only one of a thousand barbarities practiced here in these distant mountains of which I have heard for the last four months. Oh, for a day of retribution!"[19]

Imboden had completed the reorganization of his troops and was impatient to strike out at his enemy. Within twenty-four hours, he would lead his men on yet another raid against the B&O Railroad.

Winter of 1862-63

As the snow began to fall on November 7, Imboden assembled his command for inspection. He selected three hundred ten of his best armed and mounted troopers, and at 2:00 P.M. the Southerners rode out of camp headed due west, headed for a surprise attack on the vital B&O bridge across the Cheat River in far western Virginia. Their first objective was the small town of St. George in Tucker County, thirty-eight miles away, across the Allegheny Mountains.[1]

Imboden expected to reach St. George the following night, but his schedule was upset by a snowstorm so severe that the irregulars were forced to walk and lead their horses for miles on end. They reached St. George the next day, and his men surrounded the courthouse. The small Union garrison fell on November 9 when the outnumbered Federals gave up without a fight. The Confederates gladly took possession of their Enfield rifles, blankets, overcoats, and rations.

The horses were too worn to continue on to Rowlesburg, the storm had delayed them for far too long, and the citizens of St. George brought news of federal scouting parties nearby, as well as the approach of Milroy's force—about four thousand troops from Beverly. Prudently, Imboden turned back. After destroying all that was unsuitable for the journey, the partisans marched out of St. George and encamped ten miles east of

Beverly the next afternoon, where a civilian brought news that Milroy was in the field and that the Union baggage train was at Camp Bartow on the Greenbrier River—within striking distance.[2]

Imboden immediately altered his plans, resolving to attack the train, destroy it, and make good their escape through Pocahontas and Bath counties. Yet, despite a competent guide and a compass, a blinding snowstorm caused them to become completely lost. After several hours in the wilderness, Imboden learned that the Federals had sent three details galloping off in different directions in a desperate attempt to intercept him.

They stopped briefly at a friendly farmer's to feed the horses, the first grain the animals had eaten in days, and not long afterward came across the trail of one of the federal search parties. They covered their tracks by following in the wake of the Union troopers, mingling the hoofprints of their mounts with the Yankees', and eventually reached a gap in the mountains where they crossed to safety.

When Imboden reported the raid to Gen. Lee, he acknowledged that the results were less significant than anticipated. "Our escape, under all the circumstances without the loss of a man, is felt and acknowledged by all to be truly providential," he admitted.[3] Lee appreciated the extraordinary difficulties encountered on the raid and recognized the valuable results, expressing hope for future success.[4] The general wrote to Secretary of War Randolph,

> Colonel Imboden was unable to destroy the bridge at Cheat River in consequence of the strength of the enemy in that quarter, as is in position on the Shenandoah Mountains. He captured one company of the enemy, paroled the men and brought off their arms and equipment.[5]

Upon his return from St. George, Imboden again found his camp raided and this time burned by a force of eight hundred cavalrymen under Gen. Kelley. They had chased the majority of the defenders into the mountains; but fifty prisoners, a large quantity of arms, three hundred fifty fat hogs and a number of horses, cattle and wagons were captured.[6] For three weeks following the raid Col. Imboden spent the majority of his time reorganizing and resupplying his troops, while the men built huts and cabins for the winter.

This brief period of inactivity caused the Union high command to lower its guard in northwestern Virginia. The partisans took advantage of the weakened federal defenses by renewing their attacks on the scattered garrisons stationed in the area. Operating in small detachments or as single companies as the weather permitted, Imboden's troops relentlessly hammered at the Unionists in nearby counties.[7] Despite the coming of winter and the near halt of operations in the mountain district, there would be no respite for the Federals stationed in Imboden's region.

Imboden and his men were becoming quite adept at raiding the enemy. Not only were the soldiers wary of his threatening force, but the civilian population shuddered at the mention of his name as evidenced by a poem by a young Unionist lass, apparently written after the thwarted raid at Parson's Mill the previous August:

> I was awake that morning when someone came through the pass,
> Riding like mad down the road, 'twas Farmer Snyder's Lass;
> Bareback she rode, she had no hat, she hardly stopped to say:
> "Imboden's men are coming, they're marching down this way.
> I'm out to warn the neighbors, he isn't a mile behind,
> He seizes all the horses, every horse he can find.
> Imboden, Imboden the raider, and Imboden's terrible men
> With Bowie knives and pistols are marching down the glen."[8]

During a momentary lull in active fighting, a paper war began. Milroy's order concerning Confederate sympathizers had prompted Imboden for the past several months to send all prisoners of war to Richmond rather than parole them. The enemy was doing likewise, refusing to parole soldiers or partisan rangers. The Union commanders tended to label the partisans as outlaws, thereby distinguishing them from regular Confederate soldiers. The Federals often responded to Imboden's actions by hanging partisans immediately upon capture. The situation attracted the attention of Confederate authorities and resulted in a great deal of correspondence between Richmond and Washington.

The authorities in Richmond supported Imboden's policy of no parole. They notified their counterparts in Washington that prisoners taken by the partisan corps would not be exchanged until the Federals consented to the exchange of partisans. Within a few days the federal government distributed a circular which reclassified the role of partisan rangers, removing the distinction between them and regular prisoners in regard to their exchange.[9]

Reorganization

Although the issue of the parole of prisoners seemed to be somewhat resolved, Imboden's fight with Milroy intensified after the first of the year. In early January 1863 a few of Imboden's men captured the Unionist sheriff of Barlow County and sent him to the governor of Virginia. In retaliation, Union troops took into custody fifteen men and women of Southern sympathy and threatened to shoot them if the sheriff was not released in fifteen days.[1]

Imboden's response was to write Milroy a scorching communication as befitted an officer and a gentleman. He accused Milroy of encouraging atrocities, provided an explanation for the sheriff's capture and complained that the mules of two of his men had been found dead in the road. He claimed that federal troops had murdered two civilians near Phillippi for failure to comply with Milroy's order that civilians were to warn the Union garrison at the approach of Confederate forces. In conclusion, Imboden warned that if Milroy executed the arrested citizens, "I will hang two of your men for each one so executed."[2] Milroy's inflammatory reply warned the Southern commander that he had more Confederate prisoners than Imboden had Federals and "to beware of trifling with Federal humanity."[3]

Fortunately for the prisoners and civilians of both sides, the Imboden-Milroy feud remained a struggle of words rather than deeds. Imboden's intemperate remarks stayed the hand of the Northern general. Although the North still transgressed on the rights of citizens, neither side endorsed execution as official policy.

As the winter dragged on, small scale raids into Union-held territory became commonplace, and hit-and-run raids were the norm. One such raid was led by Hanse McNeill and a force of twenty-four men near Romney. Hiding in the woods alongside the road, McNeill sprang out and, as his men surrounded a Union forage train of wagons, yelled, "I don't want to hurt you. Throw down your arms!" Without firing a single shot, the Confederates captured twenty-seven wagons, a hundred six horses and seventy-two prisoners. Imboden reported the news of the raid to Lee, who in turn sent it on to Jefferson Davis with the comment: "These successes show the vigilance of the cavalry and do credit to their officers."[4]

Pvt. John O. Casler of the Stonewall Brigade described another example of partisan life. While on leave from Lee's army, Casler met up with Lt. Monroe Blue of Imboden's command with a squad of fifteen men. To escape dull camp life, they decided to go into Hampshire County and raid a Yankee camp. Each armed with a rifle and a six-shooter, they posted themselves halfway between the camp and the B&O, on which the Federals received their supplies. The raiders hid behind rail fences along both sides of the road and allowed several strong parties to pass before capturing a mail wagon, four extra horses and three prisoners.

Spurred on by their success, they attempted to seize a wagon train the second day. They captured one of three cavalry escorts, five wagons, twelve horses and four guards and wounded one Yankee; three wagons and two guards escaped. The marauders soon found themselves pursued by Union cavalry and galloped away in a hail of bullets. They lost one man and three horses, and the remaining raiders returned to Imboden's camp in Augusta County. In Casler's words, "[We] did not want to hurt anyone, nor get hurt ourselves, if we could avoid it. We had made a good capture and wanted to get away with our booty."[5]

A few weeks earlier, on December 23, Imboden had received a telegram from Adjt. Gen. Samuel Cooper informing him that the secretary of war invited his cooperation to "change your entire present organization from partisan rangers to a regular command for the war." He gave Imboden the authorization to fill his companies and regiments with conscripts and to recruit all the men he could from counties within the enemy's line. "From the energy and zeal you have displayed in the service, the department has no hesitation in committing to you this important undertaking."[6] But before this reorganization could occur, Imboden first had to obtain the consent of his men.

The proposition to change their status from partisan rangers to regular troops caused a furor in the ranks. Though most felt that they were of most service to the Confederacy as partisans, the thought was that so long as Imboden remained in command, the mere fact that they were transferred on paper to the regular army was inconsequential. All were given the chance for democratic expression in a vote on whether to stay with the command or resign. Imboden's powers of persuasion were effective, as all but seventeen of McNeill's men voted to sign on as regulars.[7] To make the offer more attractive to Imboden, Secretary of War James A. Seddon had nominated him for promotion to brigadier general on January 28, 1863, contingent upon him raising a brigade.[8] The announcement of Imboden's promotion to general brought praise from the Staunton newspaper: "We predict, from what we know of the man, and the material of which his command is composed, that General Imboden will accomplish whatever is possible in that section."[9]

While he was in the midst of reorganization and recruitment, Imboden's home territory was the scene of a raid launched by Brig. Gen. William E. "Grumble" Jones and his Confederates, accompanied by a few of Imboden's cavalry. After four days Jones returned, having failed to accomplish anything save the capture of five wagons by Imboden's men under Capt. Frank Imboden and forty-six horses and twenty-five prisoners by McNeill. The lackluster performance by Jones led Lee to conclude that the best hope for the recovery of northwestern Virginia lay with Imboden and his troops. Four days after Jones's return, Lee wrote to Imboden:

> I am anxious for you to proceed, as rapidly as possible, in the organization and increase of your command, so that you may bring a strong brigade into the field at an early period. I wish the enemy driven out of the valley entirely, both the South Branch and the Kanawha.[10]

Imboden aggressively enlarged his command to brigade strength. His infantry was officially designated as the 62nd Regt. Virginia Mounted Infantry under Col. George H. Smith; the cavalry became the 18th Regt. Virginia Cavalry under Col. George Imboden, the general's brother; and the horse artillery was organized into a battery under the command of Capt. John H. McClanahan. Reporting directly to Imboden were the independent commands of Lt. Col. Elijah White, Capt. Harry Gilmor of Baltimore and McNeill,[11] while the addition of four companies from the 25th Virginia Infantry in late January further increased their numbers.[12]

As Imboden organized his men into brigade structure, small groups of his rangers continued their raiding activities. By early April 1863 the brigade was ready for active field operations. Gen. John D. Imboden's Northwestern Brigade would strike fear into the hearts of the enemy and gain accolades for itself from Confederate authorities in the months to come.

The Jones-Imboden Raid

Throughout the severe winter of 1862–1863 and the following spring, the B&O Railroad remained a constant thorn in the side of the Confederacy. In late 1862 Governor John Letcher had declared:

> The Baltimore and Ohio Railroad has been a possible nuisance to this state, from the opening of this war to the present time; and unless its management shall hereafter be in friendly hands, and the government under which it exists be a part of our Confederacy, it must be abated.[1]

But the B&O was not in friendly hands. It continued to be the primary base for federal military operations in both the Trans-Allegheny and Lower Shenandoah Valley theaters of combat, providing the shortest route from the Ohio River to the Potomac. As such, over it were transported vast quantities of troops, materials and rations, not to mention most of the timber and coal used by the federal navy in its blockade of Southern ports.

In early March McNeill proposed a raid by six hundred cavalrymen on the Cheat River bridge in Tucker County to cripple the B&O. Imboden sent the proposal up the chain of command and wrote to Lee concerning the possible consequences of the assault.[2] He hoped that such a raid would bring recruits into the Confederate army; destroy bridges and trestles on the B&O from Oakton to Grafton; lead to the defeat and capture of the Union forces at Beverly, Phillippi and Buckhannon; overthrow the newly created Unionist government in the state of West Virginia at Wheeling; and replenish low supplies of horses, cattle and grain. For their part, the Confederate authorities hoped that Imboden could hold northwestern Virginia as well as destroy the greater portion of the railroad west of the Alleghenies. They believed that he could draw federal troops out of Winchester, thereby opening the lower Valley to Confederate quartermasters and recruiters.[3]

After many weather-related delays and changes in plans, a finalized strategy was settled upon, which called for the assistance of Grumble Jones. Imboden and Jones exchanged ideas regarding the coming expedition and, after conferring with Lee, agreed on a two-pronged attack. Imboden was to advance in a single column against Beverly, Philippi and Grafton, while Jones was to advance upon Moorefield, gain control of the Northwestern Turnpike and strike the railroad at Oakland and

Rowlesburg. The two brigades would then simultaneously attack the railroad at Oakland and Grafton.[4]

Lee felt this raid to be so significant that he sent Imboden two veteran regiments, the 25th and 31st Virginia, just nineteen days before the battle of Chancellorsville. Most of April was spent preparing the men and procuring the necessary supplies and equipment. On April 20, 1863, Imboden ordered his command westward.[5]

They left Shenandoah Mountain with just 1,825 men, but reinforcements who arrived the next day swelled his strength to 3,365—seven hundred of whom were mounted. The general led his troops at the head of the column, followed in order by the 62nd Mounted Infantry, his staff with a fife and drum corps and the 18th Cavalry. The 22nd Virginia under Col. George S. Patton marched next, followed by Col. William L. Jackson with the 19th Cavalry, Col. Dunn with his battalion of dismounted cavalry, Col. Joseph A. Higginbotham with the 25th Infantry, Col. Huffman with the 31st Infantry and McClanahan's battery. All began the journey with colors flying, accompanied by martial music.[6]

The march itself turned out to be a nightmare. What began as a drenching rain turned the roads to a quagmire before changing to sleet in the higher elevations. They spent the first night at Camp Bartow, twenty-five miles from Hightown, and awoke to find that the weather had worsened. The rain and sleet had turned to snow, accumulating up to twenty inches on Cheat Mountain. That night the battered troops—wet, cold, and hungry—entered Huttonsville. They had marched seventy miles in four days.[7]

As Imboden's force climbed the rugged, steep, and treacherous snow-covered mountains, endured the pouring rain and forded swollen streams, Jones departed from Lacey Springs with about thirty-five hundred men on a path that led them through Brock's Gap to Moorefield and then to the railroad at Oakton. High water at Moorefield forced Jones to take an eleven-mile detour to Petersburg to cross the Potomac. From there he dispatched his dismounted men, artillery, wagon trains and a three-hundred-man cavalry escort back to the Valley via Franklin, dangerously reducing his force by nearly a thousand men.

With his remaining twenty-five hundred troops, Jones continued toward Oakton. A stubborn detachment of the 23rd Illinois met them at Greenland Gap, and Jones's men killed seven and wounded twenty-two before pushing them aside.[8] Eighty-three men delayed them for more than four hours while federal reinforcements rushed westward over the railroad to intercept Imboden.[9]

Low morale plagued the mud-splattered Confederates of Imboden's command after they completed the most wretched march they had ever endured. Imboden knew nothing of Jones's failure to sever the B&O.

Rumors of Union couriers carrying news of his advance to the garrison at Beverly caused Imboden great concern and prompted him to send twenty partisan rangers in an unsuccessful attempt to capture them. As his troops marched toward Beverly, the rumors proved false. The small garrison, about fifteen hundred infantry and cavalry, drew up in a line of battle two and a half miles south of the town. Recognizing that the Federals maintained a strong position, Imboden split his force, planning to envelop the enemy from two sides rather than suffer needless casualties with a frontal assault.[10]

He sent his cavalry west of town to sever the Union line of retreat on the Buckhannon Road. Col. George Lathan, the Union commander, noticed the Confederates on his right flank but across the Tygart River. Imboden sent his remaining regiments into the woods to turn the Federals' left flank. With the garrison thus surrounded, he raked them with skirmish fire and pounded them with his artillery. They held out for two hours before being forced to withdraw toward Phillippi.[11]

Imboden pursued the fleeing enemy for a few miles, but the thick woods, deep mud and approaching darkness caused him to abandon the pursuit. At Beverly, Imboden had captured $100,000 worth of supplies including a vast amount of badly needed ammunition, rations and forage, which was welcomed by the overjoyed Confederates. His command had suffered only three men wounded yet had inflicted sixteen casualties, including one killed, two wounded and thirteen captured, and a number of wagons and mules had been seized.[12]

The effect of the capture of Beverly on the federal authorities in western Virginia was immediate and powerful. Brig. Gen. Benjamin Roberts was upset and numbed by the news at his headquarters in Buckhannon. Roberts, fresh from the western frontier, wired General- in-Chief Henry W. Halleck in Washington to complain that the roads were impassable and that he was therefore unable to protect the B&O. Halleck immediately sent a scorching reply ordering him to collect his troops and defend the railroad. He questioned Robert's telegram by retorting, "I do not understand how the roads there are impassable to you, when, by your own account, they are passable enough to the enemy."[13]

On April 26 Imboden led his force out of Beverly, advancing toward Buckhannon. Reaching a position midway between Buckhannon and Phillippi, he was informed by his brother George that a fresh Union brigade had arrived at Phillippi by rail from New Creek.[14] It was the force at Phillippi that had gone west while Jones was fighting at Greenland Gap. Concerned, Imboden dispatched couriers to find Jones, knowing that if the latter had succeeded on schedule, the railroad would be out of working order.

Imboden met with his regimental commanders who all agreed that "the safety of the command requires that we should fall back to a position where escape would be possible if we were overpowered." Accordingly, Imboden returned with his column to Beverly, where he further studied the situation.[15] A Union force thirty miles west at Buckhannon and another thirty-two miles northwest at Phillippi caused him to stay where he was, especially since he had had no word from Jones.

Roberts grew apprehensive and drew all of his forces to Buckhannon, but soon began to worry about the safety of that position as well. Recognizing that Clarksburg, with its military stores and railroad, was the more vital position, he abandoned Buckhannon on April 28 and concentrated his force of twenty-eight hundred men there.[16]

That same day, when scouts brought Imboden word of the evacuation of Phillippi and Buckhannon, he immediately put his force on the road toward Buckhannon. As his weary troopers entered the town early the next morning, they found the warehouses still smoldering. Roberts had ordered them burned before his departure. The Confederates salvaged what supplies they could, and units were dispatched to the countryside to round up cattle and horses, which were sent to the rear. As Imboden awaited news of Jones, pickets took their places along all of the roads, and the remaining Confederates settled down to a well-deserved rest, feeding their horses with forage gathered from area farms.[17] In eight days many of them had marched more than a hundred miles and fought a battle in the most miserable weather imaginable.[18]

Imboden was not the only one who had not heard from Gen. Jones. On April 29, Lee wrote President Davis: "I have received a dispatch from Gen. Imboden dated April 28th. On the 26th he had penetrated the country midway between Phillippi and Buckhannon. . . . I have had no report from Gen. W. E. Jones."[19]

Imboden feared that his comrade was in great difficulty. Just as he began an advance toward Phillippi the next morning to assist Jones, the general and a small portion of his command arrived. His force had burned nine railroad bridges and had captured two trains, one artillery piece, five hundred prisoners, twelve to fifteen thousand horses and a thousand head of cattle.[20]

After considering the present situation, the two generals agreed to assault Clarksburg. On May 3 they shifted their forces to Weston, sixteen miles west of Buckhannon and twenty-three miles south of Clarksburg. Two days later the two commands joined in a parade through the town of Weston and were presented with a flag by the ladies of the town.

At this time, a very personal matter required the attention of the Imboden brothers. With the knowledge that this area of Virginia was to be abandoned for the time being, arrangements had to be made for their aged parents, who lived in Weston, to be moved to a more secure location. As Frank Imboden noted in his diary, "They have suffered martyrdom from the accursed abolitionists." The brothers "fitted up a five-horse team and loaded it up with the clothes and some bed clothes and other things in the house," then carried their sick father to the wagon "and started it through the mud, leaving the furniture and other things to share the fate of war treatment."[21]

While their troops enjoyed a leisurely time of playing baseball, writing letters and sleeping, generals Imboden and Jones took the next two days to decide what their next course of action would be.[22] Despite the addition of Jones's brigade, the Confederates were still too weak to attack the reinforced federal position. Imboden had detailed several detachments to guard the herds of cattle already shipped east and had left behind a large number of sick and exhausted men at Beverly and Buckhannon. After much discussion they decided to cancel the plan to attack Clarksburg and employ a different strategy.

The two commands were to separate again, with Imboden going south and Jones heading northwest. Imboden was to move toward Summersville with all of the captured livestock and the supply train, while Jones was to turn westward and attack the B&O.

Jones captured the railroad guard at West Union and Cairo, burned five more bridges and damaged a tunnel so that it was no longer usable. He then swooped down upon Oiltown, where he demolished the oil fields and equipment and burned a hundred fifty thousand barrels of oil, creating the largest fire ever in western Virginia. This accomplished, Jones headed southwest at a leisurely pace to join Imboden.[23]

Imboden, meanwhile, had moved southward through abominable weather. The march was slow and cumbersome, taking three days to cover the last fourteen miles. At Summersville he captured a twenty-eight-wagon federal provision train pulled by a hundred seventy mules, gathered a huge herd of livestock along the way and seriously damaged the Union supply depot and garrison.[24] When Jones linked up with Imboden at Summersville on May 14 both generals agreed that their mission had been accomplished, then separated for the last time.

Imboden began a slow march toward Lewisburg, but the Federals were not finished with him yet. A Union cavalry force attempted one last attack, but Confederate general John McCausland, with a force of three regiments and one battalion of cavalry, fell upon them at Fayetteville, thirty miles southwest of Summersville. They effectively prevented the Federals from raiding the miles of Imboden's vulnerable wagons.[25]

Imboden reached the Shenandoah Valley during the last week of May. Lee thanked him profusely for the more than five thousand head of cattle and twelve hundred horses that he brought with him and praised the men for the accomplishments of the raid. Two trains had been captured, twenty-four bridges destroyed, one tunnel damaged, countless buildings demolished, telegraph lines cut and the B&O left to rely on wagons and pontoon bridges for days. Other results included the burning of the oil field, the capture of a thousand small arms, the destruction or capture of several cannons and the seizure and sacking of many supply bases. Enemy casualties had amounted to eight hundred killed, wounded or captured.[26]

As for the Confederates, Imboden's forces had marched more than four hundred miles through enemy territory in thirty-seven days, had captured a vast amount of goods and had avoided battle except on their own terms. Losses had been slight, with only one lieutenant and one private killed, three men captured and two seriously wounded. Although eight sick men had fallen into enemy hands, approximately five hundred volunteers had been added to the Confederate ranks.

The greatest disappointment throughout the whole expedition was the mass desertion of Dunn's Battalion at Beverly in light of orders forbidding the looting of civilians.[27] Imboden had tried to respect the rights of civilians by issuing specific orders against raiding or seizing their property.

The effects of the raid were profound from a political viewpoint. The Unionist convention at Wheeling had been forced to break up and flee, and, as a result, thousands of federal troops had been dispatched to western Virginia. Upon the reassembly of the Wheeling convention, the representatives voted to secede from Virginia, later creating the new state of West Virginia illegally and without Virginia's consent.

Most of Imboden's troops were suddenly natives of an enemy state.

The High Tide

Imboden's force settled into camp at Buffalo Gap on June 1, where they enjoyed meals of corn, molasses, bacon and fresh beef from captured stores. This was a great respite for men who had been existing on salt beef and a half pound of meal per day while on the raid. Weary horses were replaced and fine new wagons took the place of those that were old and dilapidated.[1]

The stay in Augusta County was a short one, but for nearly a week the men rested and were given new issues of uniform items. Imboden then shifted his force west, to Monterey in Highland County. When Imboden's status was questioned by Maj. Gen. Samuel Jones, Lee responded by stating: "General Imboden's command was organized for service in Northwestern Virginia and the Valley, and he reports directly to me."[2]

Few were the days of inactivity, for on June 7 Imboden received orders from Lee at Fredericksburg to move the Northwestern Brigade toward Romney by way of the south branch of the Potomac through Franklin and Moorefield. His men were to cover the left flank of the Army of Northern Virginia as Lee began the opening maneuvers of the Gettysburg Campaign.[3] Imboden's mission was four-fold: he was to prevent Union troops guarding the B&O from reinforcing those at Winchester; detain federal troops at New Creek, Cumberland and Cacapon; and destroy bridges to prevent the transfer of troops to Martinsburg—all the while gathering supplies for the army.[4]

The brigade marched northwest into Hampshire County on June 8. En route they rounded up cattle and horses and toppled all of the important bridges on the B&O. By June 15th they had taken Romney.

Following these successes, Lee directed Imboden to support Gen. Ewell, who had defeated Milroy at Winchester and was poised with his II Corps for an invasion of Maryland. On Ewell's left flank, Imboden crossed into Maryland at Hancock and launched a series of attacks on the B&O.[5] He divided his command into two sections, one of which attacked the Chesapeake and Ohio canal. By cutting the embankments at vital places and damaging the dams, Imboden hoped spot destruction would prevent rapid repairs.[6]

For the next twelve days Imboden's troops burnt bridges, attacked isolated outposts and wrecked rolling stock, thoroughly disrupting the federal army's primary transportation link to the West. Lee acknowledged the effectiveness of Imboden's efforts in his report:

> He drove off the forces guarding the Baltimore and Ohio Railroad, and destroyed all the important bridges on that route from Martinsburg to Cumberland, besides inflicting serious damage upon the Chesapeake and Ohio Canal.[7]

Despite the destruction they carried out, Imboden's men kept a sense of humor. When the troops passed through a Northern town, the ladies would cheer and ask of them, "Whose men?" The soldiers told them almost anything, some answering "First Texas," others "2nd South Carolina," and so forth. By the time they had passed through, the townspeople would be telling one another that they had talked with soldiers from nearly all of the Southern states.[8]

From Hancock, Imboden flanked Lee's invading forces and occupied McConnellsburg, Pennsylvania, where his brigade suffered a setback. Capt. William Dickinson Ervin and twenty-two men from Company G of the 18th Virginia Cavalry fell into enemy hands through their own carelessness.[9]

Thanks to their many captures from the Union army, Imboden's brigade was one of the best mounted and equipped units to invade Pennsylvania. From McConnellsburg they marched to Mercersburg on June 30. While camped at Mercersburg on July 1 Imboden was handed a message from Gen. Lee. He was to march his brigade to Greenwood and relieve Gen. George E. Pickett's Division.[10]

On the morning of July 2 the Northwestern Brigade reached Chambersburg and took over as rear guard of Gen. Lee's army. Guarding the trains and rear of the army would normally have fallen to Stuart, but the latter had yet to arrive. Pickett's three Virginia brigades had been filling in for Stuart, but Lee had summoned them to the small crossroads town of Gettysburg where a great battle was raging. Imboden hastened to Gettysburg to meet with Lee, who ordered him to guard the reserve train parked between Greenwood and Cashtown, ten miles to the west, and instructed him to "pay strict attention to the safety of the trains, which are for present placed under your charge, and upon the safety of which the operations of this army depend."[11]

Imboden, with his twenty-one hundred men and six guns, passed the battle of Gettysburg without incident; from their position at the left of Lee's army a portion of the brigade could see the fierce fighting of July 3.[12] Though they took no active part in the battle, Imboden and his brigade were destined to play a vital role in the sad aftermath.

The Retreat

With the coming of night on July 3, 1863, the battle of Gettysburg came to a close. Lee's Army of Northern Virginia had been repulsed in the climax of the great battle on Cemetery Ridge. All of the Confederates knew that the day had gone against them, although the extent of the disaster was known only to those in command. Although the carnage had been great, the Southern army was not in retreat, and it was generally thought that with the coming of dawn the battle would commence again.

It was a warm summer's night. The weary soldiers were lying about, speculating on the coming day, when at about 11:00 P.M. a horseman brought to Imboden a summons from Gen. Lee. Imboden promptly mounted up and, accompanied by an aide, Lt. George W. McPhail, followed the courier about two miles toward Gettysburg. In a small meadow to the left of the roadside stood a half dozen small tents, Gen. Lee's headquarters for the night. When Imboden inquired after the general, he was told that Lee had gone to Gen. A.P. Hill's headquarters about a half mile closer to Gettysburg. Arriving at Hill's tent, he saw Lee and Hill sitting on camp stools and studying a map by the light of a flickering candle. Imboden dismounted and approached the two generals, but after a brief greeting was directed back to Lee's headquarters to await the general's return.[1]

When Lee finally rode up alone to his tent around 1:00 A.M., Imboden noticed that he was evidently wrapped in profound thought. He later wrote,

> When he arrived there was not even a sentinel on duty at this tent, and no one of his staff was awake. The moon was high in the clear sky and the silent scene was unusually vivid. As he approached and saw us lying on the grass under a tree, he spoke, reined in his jaded horse, and essayed to dismount. The effort to do so betrayed so much physical exhaustion that I hurriedly rose and stepped forward to assist him, but before I reached his

side he had succeeded in alighting, and threw his arm across the saddle to rest, and fixing his eyes upon the ground leaned in silence and almost motionless upon his equally weary horse, the two forming a striking and never-to-be-forgotten group. The moon shone full upon his massive features and revealed an expression of sadness that I had never before seen upon his face. Awed by his appearance I waited for him to speak until the silence became embarrassing.[2]

When Imboden ventured to remark in a sympathetic tone, "General, this has been a hard day on you," Lee looked up and mournfully replied, "Yes, it has been a sad, sad day to us." Then, relapsing into a thoughtful mood, Lee grew quiet. After a few minutes he turned to Imboden and in a voice filled with emotion, said,

I never saw troops behave more magnificently than Pickett's division of Virginians did today in that grand charge upon the enemy. And if they had been supported as they were to have been, but, for some reason not yet fully explained to me, were not, we would have held the position and the day would have been ours.[3]

After a moment's pause he added in tone filled with agony, "Too bad! *Too bad!* OH! TOO BAD!"[4]

Lee invited Imboden into his tent, where, speaking with feeling of all the fallen men and officers, he remarked:

We must now return to Virginia. As many of our poor wounded as possible must be taken home. I have sent for you, because your men and horses are fresh and in good condition, to guard and conduct our train back to Virginia. The duty will be arduous, responsible, and dangerous, for I am afraid you will be harassed by the enemy's cavalry. How many men have you?[5]

When Imboden replied that he had "about two hundred effective present, and all well mounted, including McClanahan's six-gun battery of horse artillery," Lee promised Imboden as much artillery as needed but could offer no additional troops. He laid out the route the brigade was to take, across the mountain over the Chambersburg road, then without halting to Williamsport. After giving Imboden directions and advice as to roads and best disposition of his troops, Lee gave him orders to collect all wagons and ambulances the next day and ready them for the trip south.[6]

As Imboden was leaving his tent about 2:00 A.M., Lee came out and in a low voice confided,

> I will place in your hands by a staff officer, tomorrow morning, a sealed package for President Davis, which you will retain in your possession till you are across the Potomac, when you will detail a reliable commissioned officer to take it to Richmond with all possible dispatch and deliver it into the President's own hands. And I impress it on you that, whatever happens, this package must not fall into the hands of the enemy. If unfortunately you should be captured, destroy it at the first opportunity.[7]

Early the next morning written instructions and the envelope addressed to President Davis arrived, but the wagons, ambulances, and wounded could not be collected and made ready to move until late afternoon. The day after the battle was dreadful for the entire army. Burial details were overwhelmed with caring for the dead, and the sickening stench of decaying bodies intensified in the July heat. Doctors and ambulance crews worked furiously to prepare the enormous number of wounded for transport.[8]

True to his word, Gen. Lee ordered eight Napoleon guns of the famed Washington Artillery of New Orleans, a four-gun battery under Capt. Tanner and one Whitworth rifled gun under Lt. Pegram to be sent to Imboden. He also ordered Hampton's cavalry brigade under Col. P.M.B. Young and Capt. James F. Hart's four-gun battery of horse artillery to cover the rear of the trains under Imboden's command.[9]

Shortly after noon on July 4 rain began to fall, and the force of the storm soon grew to the point that the rain fell in blinding sheets. Fields and roads became flooded. Thousands of wagons, ambulances and artillery carriages tried to assemble in the fields and on the roads leading to Cashtown but became a confused mass. As the afternoon wore on and the storm continued, the canvas wagon covers offered little protection. The wounded men lying on the boards of the wagons were drenched. Horses and mules were blinded by the wind and the rain.[10]

At 4:00 P.M. Imboden finally started the long train in motion toward the Potomac and safety, with the head of the column slowly ascending

the mountain toward Chambersburg. Luther Hopkins of the 6th Virginia
Cavalry described the scene he saw that evening while grazing his horse:

> [I suddenly heard] a low rumbling sound . . . resembling
> distant thunder, except that it was continuous . . . a
> number of us rose to our feet and saw a long line of wagons
> with their white covers moving . . . along the
> Chambersburg Road. . . . The wagons going back over
> the same road that had brought us to Gettysburg told the
> story, and soon the whole army knew the fact. This was
> the first time Lee's army had ever met defeat.[11]

The train was a procession of agony seventeen miles long. It took
thirty-four hours to pass any given point. The 18th Virginia Cavalry and
a section of McClanahan's battery served as advance guard, followed by
an ambulance carrying badly wounded generals William Dorsey Pender
and Alfred Moore Scales, with whom Imboden shared a little bread and
meat at noon. To resume the train's movement once stopped took hours.

Yet Harry Gilmor noted the overall orderliness of the retreat when he
declared, "There was not a rout . . . and all the silly stuff we read in the
Northern accounts of 'flying rebels' and 'shattered army' are pure fiction
prepared for the Northern market."[12] Randolph Shotwell of the 8th
Virginia described the retreat in this way:

> Beside the prisoners, a large portion of the wounded, such
> as were able to bear transportation in ambulances and
> wagons, took the road for Cashtown, Greencastle, and
> Williamsport.
>
> Soon the difficulty of the road which was narrow and
> rocky, added to the drenching rain, and the bottomless
> mud, caused the trains to become crowded, and
> embarrassed, filling the highways and rendering the
> movements of the footmen, i.e., the prisoners and their
> guards exceedingly wearisome.
>
> Wagons, ambulances, artillery, cavalry, stragglers,
> wounded soldiers, Yankees, and guards were irretrievably
> mixed, and the continued succession of momentary
> halts, to be followed by a rapid trot of a 100 yards, and
> then another halt, resulting from the breaking down of
> wagons, or difficulty in passing mud holes, were so
> inconceivably vexatious, and fatiguing that I have often

wondered why all the prisoners did not escape for the guards became almost indifferent; especially in the confusion after dark, when the crowded trains were painfully toiling up the winding pass at Cashtown. Doubtless more of the prisoners would have escaped had they not been too near physical and mental exhaustion to have the necessary energy.

We bivouacked at the top of Cashtown Pass in a wet swampy meadow where the water arose around our bodies as we lay in the dark grass. Fire was out of the question even if there had been fuel, for the rain fell increasingly, and of food we had none. During the day I had kept up with the moving mass through energy born of despair—a kind of reckless desperation of endurance. But this night threatened to be too much straw for the camel's back.[13]

Pvt. Norval Baker of Co. F, 18th Virginia Cavalry, agreed. He noted in his diary,

Twas an awful night, it rained all night, one thunder storm after another. The rain fell in sheets, and vivid flashes of lightning and so dark we could not see our hand an inch from our eyes when there was no lightning. The roar of the water and heavy bursting thunder, the cries of the wounded and dying soldiers made it awful.[14]

Imboden gave directions at Cashtown to place detachments of guns and troops at quarter mile intervals.[15] After dark he set out from the town to reach the head of the column, as it was important that there be no halt. He had to get things moving—if a wagon broke down or had an accident, it had to be gotten out of the road and abandoned. Despite the rough road and inclement weather, the column made respectably good time.

As Imboden hurried along he was never out of earshot of the groans and cries of the wounded, many of whom had now been without food for more than thirty-six hours. He described their agony:

Their torn and bloody clothing, matted and hardened, was rasping the tender, inflamed, and still oozing wounds. Very few of the wagons had even a layer of straw in them, and all were without springs. The road was rough and rocky from the heavy washing of the preceding day. The jolting was enough to have killed strong men, if long exposed to it. From nearly every wagon as the teams trotted on, urged by whips and shout, came such cries and shrieks as these:

"O God! why can't I die?"

"My God! will no one have mercy and kill me?"

"Stop! Oh! for God's sake, stop just one minute; take me out and leave me to die on the roadside."

"I am dying! I am dying!, My poor wife, my dear children, what will become of you?"

Some were simply moaning; some were praying, and others uttering the most fearful oaths and execrations that despair and agony could wring from them; while a majority, with a stoicism sustained by sublime devotion to the cause they fought for, endured without complaint unspeakable tortures, and even spoke words of cheer and comfort to their unhappy comrades of less will or more acute nerves. Occasionally a wagon would be passed from which only low, deep moans could be heard. No help could be rendered to any of the sufferers. No heed could be given to any of their appeals. Mercy and duty to the many forbade the loss of a moment in the vain effort then and there to comply with the prayers of the few. On! On! we *must* move on. The storm continued, and the darkness was appalling. There was no time even to fill a canteen with water for a dying man; for, except the drivers and the guards, all were wounded and utterly helpless in that vast procession of misery. During this one night I realized more of the horrors of war than I had in all the two preceding years.[16]

Darkness was the column's friend, since no distinction could be made between friend or foe. With the coming of day the Confederates knew there would be harassment by Union cavalry. Instead of traveling through Chambersburg, Imboden left the main road and took a shortcut on the Pine Stump Road. Daybreak on July 5 found the head of the column at Greencastle, having covered thirty miles. They were now only fifteen miles north of Williamsport and the Potomac, where they could cross into Virginia and safety.

Here Imboden's real troubles began. After the advance guard, the 18th Virginia Cavalry, had passed about a mile beyond the town, some forty citizens attacked the train with axes, cutting the spokes of about a dozen wheels and dropping the wagons in the street. Imboden sent a detachment of cavalry to capture the townsfolk and had them treated as prisoners of war. Then the Northern cavalry swarmed down upon them in small bodies, striking the column where there were few or no guards and creating great confusion. Imboden himself narrowly escaped capture by one of these parties when about fifty Yankees closed in on him. It caused him to turn two of McClanahan's guns, which were close at hand, and fire canister to drive the emeny off. His brother George heard the commotion and rode with his regiment at a gallop after the retreating Yankees, capturing the entire party.[17]

The head of the train reached Williamsport on the afternoon of July 5, and by early the next morning the rest of the wagons were on the banks of the Potomac. The route over which they had come was littered with broken wagons and men who had been left to die by the roadside. Since the great length of the train had made it difficult to guard effectively, more than a hundred wagons had been captured.[18]

Despite Imboden's relief that they had reached the Potomac safely, he was distraught to find the pontoon bridge washed away. The river was at flood stage and impossible to cross. They were low on ammunition and supplies. Although they were finally in sight of Virginia, the brigade was effectively cut off from Southern soil.

Williamsport

Imboden turned the town of Williamsport into one great hospital. A large number of surgeons had accompanied the train, and they wasted no time in tending to the suffering of the sick and wounded. The bodies of those who died were buried, while those wounded who could walk were ferried across the river on two small, flat-bottomed boats.[1] Imboden ordered every citizen of the town to cook provisions for the wounded. If they failed to cooperate, he threatened to send his soldiers into their kitchens to do the job.[2]

His troops went from house to house seeking supplies. They seized a large quantity of flour from a nearby mill, bought some bacon from a local merchant and secured wheat, straw and hay to feed their horses and mules. He met a fresh regiment from Staunton, the 54th North Carolina of

Robert F. Hoke's Brigade, and one just up from Winchester, the 58th Virginia of Smith's Brigade, who were detailed to hold the river crossing. The wagons parked along the river, under a bluff. Imboden had his back to the wall but was determined not to lose the wounded. The situation was desperate, but the river crossing must be held at all costs. The only factor in Imboden's favor was that his flanks rested on the banks of the Potomac and the Conococheague Creek, which permitted the use of two small ferryboats or flats that ran constantly, carrying wounded to safety and bringing back fresh ammunition.[3]

Early on the morning of July 6 Imboden was informed of the approach of a large body of enemy cavalry, a force of about seven thousand men with three full batteries of rifled field artillery from Frederick. He posted his guns on the hills that concealed the town, supported by the dismounted men from his command. To augment this force, Imboden armed about seven hundred wagoneers in companies of a hundred each, commanded by wounded line officers. Also armed and sent to defend the position were about a hundred walking wounded, the commissaries and quartermasters. About two hundred fifty of these men under Col. William R. Aylett were sent to the right flank near the river, the same number under Col. J. L. Black were sent to the left flank, and the remainder under Capt. J. F. Hart were used as skirmishers. Imboden's own command was placed in the center of the line.[4]

Imboden had the tremendous responsibility to protect not only the thousands of wounded, but about ten thousand horses and mules and nearly all of the wagons belonging to Lee's army, as well as several wagon loads of flour, a fine herd of fat cattle collected from Pennsylvania farms, and sugar and coffee procured at Mercersburg.[5]

The enemy appeared at Imboden's front around 1:30 P.M. from two directions. Every man in the ranks understood that if the enemy were not repulsed, Lee's army would be ruined. The fight began with the artillery of both sides. Firing from the Confederates was so rapid that the enemy was held off for some time. In about half an hour, however, J. D. Moore's battery ran out of ammunition. An ordnance train from Winchester and two wagonloads of ammunition saved the day when they were ferried across the Potomac. With this fresh supply, the guns opened up once more.

Leaving Black's wagoneers to support the guns, Imboden led his command forward. The 18th Virginia Cavalry and the 62nd Virginia Mounted Infantry were sent rapidly to the right to meet and repel five advancing regiments of dismounted enemy. McNeill's Rangers and Aylett's wagoneers also entered the severe fight. Hart, seeing how hard pressed things were, sent his troops forward against the enemy's right flank. As Eshelman's eight Napoleons and McClanahan's battery poured a furious fire into the enemy line, Imboden's troops bravely charged forward, driving the enemy back to their horses.[6] Pvt. Baker recorded in his diary:

> The fight commenced about 2 o'clock in the evening of the 6th, and continued till about an hour after dark, when Fitz Lee's division rolled up in the rear of the enemy's lines and cannon and all was saved. We slept on the field with our guns that night, the rain came down like cloud-bursts and drenched us.[7]

As night approached, Gen. Fitzhugh Lee arrived with his cavalry command, greeted by a wild yell from Imboden's ranks. Stuart's Horse Artillery arrived then and opened up on the enemy's rear. The Yankees broke and ran, but it was too dark to follow. About a hundred twenty-five of the enemy were captured, with Imboden's total loss amounting to about the same number. Imboden was extremely proud of the fighting ability displayed by the wagon masters, who fought so well that the fight became known as the "wagoneers' fight."

Imboden's total force numbered fewer than three thousand. By extraordinary good fortune, all of Lee's wagons were saved. One bold charge by the enemy cavalry could have broken the feeble lines.[8]

On the evening of July 7, some of Imboden's troops went northwest of Williamsport on a scouting mission. Encountering some Yankee troops, they had quite a fight, driving them to a mountain fort. A detachment from the Confederates was sent to keep them there until the wagons could cross the river.

Imboden's men would stay at Williamsport for several more days. Pvt. Baker recounted,

> It was an awful place, the dead horses and offal of the great number of beefs, etc., killed for the army packed around the little town made it very unpleasant for us when we returned to camp after night. The green flies were around us all the time and orders were not to unsaddle or unbridle our horses and be ready for duty all

The house where John Daniel Imboden was born stood on Christian's Creek, near Fishersville, Virginia. It was razed in 1993. *(Photo courtesy Joe Moyer)*

Old Tinkling Springs Church near Fishersville, Virginia, where Imboden regularly attended services. His first wife and two of his children rest in the graveyard. *(Photo by the author)*

George and Isabella
Imboden, parents of
John D. Imboden.
*(Previously unpublished
photograph courtesy
Nancy S. Garrett)*

This photograph of John D.
Imboden was taken shortly
after his promotion to
brigadier general in the spring
of 1863. *(Courtesy Tulane
University)*

Painting of John D. Imboden from photograph taken about the time of the invasion of Pennsylvania, summer 1863. *(Courtesy Michael H. Sullivan)*

This photo of General Imboden was taken during the winter of 1863-64. *(Courtesy U.S. Army)*

Hand-tinted photograph of John D. Imboden taken at the pinnacle of his career in the Confederate States Army. *(Previously unpublished photograph courtesy Nancy S. Garrett)*

Colonel George W. Imboden, brother of John D. Imboden. *(From author's collection)*

Captain Francis M. Imboden, brother of John D. Imboden. *(From author's collection)*

John D. Imboden during the 1870s, about the time he was commissioner to the U.S. Centennial celebration in Philadelphia. *(From author's collection)*

General Imboden in later life. Date unknown. *(From author's collection)*

General Imboden's gravesite in the Confederate Officers' section of Hollywood Cemetery in Richmond, Virginia. *(Photo by the author)*

the time. Our blankets were under our saddle and soaked with water and the green flies were working under the rawhide covering of our saddles and ulcerated the backs of our horses. . . .

This work was kept up for quite a while and quite a number of the soldiers fell with dysentery and were sent to the Virginia side of the river with the wounded. We fed our horses on sheaf wheat and the beards made the horses' tongues sore. Our regiment was about a mile or so south of the river with orders to unsaddle our horses. Our horses' backs were raw with ulcers, one and two inches deep and full of maggots. The green flies had put up a big job on us, our blankets were full of maggots in them and we had to wash them out with hot water and soap and it was months before the horses' backs were cured.[9]

More than four thousand prisoners taken at Gettysburg and the Confederate wounded were ferried across the Potomac. Imboden was chosen to escort the prisoners as far as Staunton, where they would be sent on to Richmond. After conferring with Gen. Lee, Imboden set out with the 62nd Virginia to guard the prisoners.

Pioneers from each division were sent to Williamsport to construct crude pontoon bridges to get the ambulances, medical wagons, ordnance wagons, and artillery across the river. Lumber was secured from a local yard, yet progress was slow. As a result, the cavalry was forced to swim the river and the infantry to wade.[10] Lee personally selected Maj. John Harman to oversee the work on the pontoon bridges.

When Imboden had gone no more than two miles toward Winchester, a courier overtook him with a message requesting him to return to Gen. Lee's headquarters in Hagerstown immediately. Lee had just learned that Imboden was very familiar with the fords of the Potomac from Williamsport to Cumberland and wanted him to describe them. While Imboden characterized ford after ford in minute detail, including the roads and surrounding countryside, a staff officer recorded the information verbatim. Afterward, Lee instructed Imboden to send the 18th Virginia Cavalry to act as guides for fording the river. As Imboden prepared to depart, Lee stopped him. "You know this country well enough to tell me whether it ever quits raining around here?" he asked. "If so, I should like to see a clear day soon."[11]

District Command

Imboden divided his four thousand prisoners into divisions and marched them in columns of four. The cavalry and artillery moved en masse between the divisions of prisoners while the infantry marched in two files, one on each side of the column. They averaged fifteen miles a day and, having encountered no major difficulty, the column reached Staunton on July 20.[1] During the march, Pvt. Baker had the opportunity to speak with many Yankee prisoners. In his diary he recorded what he learned regarding their reasons for fighting:

> The Yankee prisoners tell us it is to save the Union and
> if they thought it is to free the negroes they would lay
> down their arms and go home. . . . We meet thousands
> of men from Ireland, Russia, and Germany and they tell
> us they are paid so much money to fight and that is all
> they care for.[2]

Upon reaching the Shenandoah Valley, Lee's army rested and recuperated before crossing to the eastern side of the Blue Ridge.

Imboden had given the Confederacy valuable service in the last four months as he secured much needed livestock and supplies from western Virginia, screened the army's advance into Pennsylvania and, most importantly, guided the wagon trains safely south. In recognition of these accomplishments, Lee assigned him command of the Valley District—all of the country west of the Blue Ridge, north to the Potomac and south to the James River in Botetourt County. This district had been created in 1861 for Stonewall Jackson, and its boundaries remained the same throughout the war.

A native of the Valley who was active in business and politics, Imboden was acquainted with nearly all of its prominent citizens, and he knew the natural features and resources of the entire district. It was natural that he be chosen for the position, and he took command of the Valley District on July 21, 1863, a position he would hold almost to the end of the war.

Imboden commanded his own brigade of cavalry and mounted infantry (now made up of George Smith's 62nd Virginia Mounted Infantry), Maj. Robert H. White's 41st Battalion of Virginia Cavalry, George Imboden's 18th Virginia Cavalry and Hanse McNeill's Partisan Rangers. Also under his command were Gen. Gabriel C. Wharton's infantry brigade, John McClanahan's Battery of Horse Artillery, Harry Gilmor's Battalion of

Maryland Cavalry, Maj. Sturgis Davis's Battalion of Maryland Cavalry and
Capt. J. H. Bartlett's Valley District Signal Corps. His effective troops
numbered about three thousand, and he could also call upon the reserves
of the Valley counties and the Corps of Cadets at V.M.I.[3]

Since the command was largely mounted, there was great competition
for assignments to the Valley. Pvt. Baker recorded in his diary the feelings
between the mounted and foot soldiers: "The infantry never liked the
cavalry branch of the service because they had to foot it while the cavalry
could ride while on long marches." Many deserters from the infantry tried
to join the cavalry, often using such ruses as claiming that they were from
Maryland, but were usually found out and sent back to the ranks.[4] The
problem of deserters wanting to join his outfit plagued Imboden for the
rest of his stay in the Valley.

When Lee left the Valley in late July, the only federal troops left in
Imboden's district were a few guards posted along the B&O. As Lee was
facing Gen. George Meade's advancing Union army, he needed every
available man; therefore, since the Valley was in a state of quietude, he
ordered Wharton's brigade to rejoin the Army of Northern Virginia along
the Rappahannock.[5]

Lee and Imboden corresponded frequently. In July and early August
Lee often prodded Imboden to raid Grafton, New Creek and Piedmont,
wanting him to "[direct] small raids with the dual purpose of distracting
the enemy and gathering supplies."[6]

On September 7, 1863, Imboden sent a foray through Winchester to
Bath. Three officers and twenty-six men from Maj. Gilmor's battalion
surprised two companies of Col. John Wynkoop's Pennsylvania Cavalry
at Bath. They killed eight to ten soldiers and captured twenty-three
prisoners and fifty horses while suffering only two wounded.[7]

Following the success of this little brush, Imboden increased his raiding
activity. The Confederacy needed cattle, cloth, leather, iron and other
resources that raiding parties could collect; and Gen. Lee wanted him to
threaten the B&O. He especially approved of using locally raised troops
to campaign in the Union-held western counties, hoping they would bring
recruits into the army. When he learned that on their raid Gilmor's troops
had run into bands of deserters, Lee ordered Imboden to use every means
at his disposal to capture and destroy these dishonorable hoodlums. He was
to take them where he could, dead or alive.[8]

In his next raid, Imboden sent his brother Frank with Hanse McNeill
and Capt. Hobson and a force of a hundred fifty men toward Moorefield,

their objective being six companies of the 1st West Virginia Infantry camped near the town. At dawn on September 11 the raiders left their camp about four miles from Moorefield, posting a few men to guard Brock's Gap. They slipped behind the enemy pickets and a few minutes later charged through the sleeping camp, firing point blank into the enemy tents. The Federals were taken entirely by surprise; the Confederates had even captured a small patrol that came upon their rear without alerting the unsuspecting Northerners.[9]

The victorious cavalrymen paraded their prisoners through Staunton on the way to Richmond. J. Marshall McCue recorded:

> Captains McNeill, Imboden and Hobson made their appearance in our midst Tuesday last with 147 prisoners captured by their companies near Moorefield, Hardy County, a few days since. . . . Captain McNeill received a slight scratch and Captain Hobson had his hat shot off his head.[10]

Along with the prisoners, the raiders had captured all of the property of the camp and killed or wounded thirty men. The Confederate losses were three men wounded.[11]

Imboden now faced the Union Army of the Department of West Virginia under Benjamin Kelley. The Union troop strength in the area had increased from eighteen thousand to nearly thirty thousand. The garrison at Grafton alone numbered three thousand Yankees, double the total force under Imboden's command.[12]

Despite his active military involvement, Imboden did not lose his interest in political matters. In the fall of 1863, he emerged as a candidate for lieutenant governor, the running mate of Thomas S. Flournoy, the Whig candidate for governor. He won the majority of the military vote but lost the election. Democrats William "Extra Billy" Smith and Samuel Price were the victors,[13] although Imboden and the Whig party retained some prominence in Virginia politics.

The Dash on Charles Town

Imboden spent the remainder of the late summer and early fall of 1863 conducting many small raids, for which he needed more men. A number of his regular troops were dismounted, detailed or on sick leave, and many units in his district, such as Gilmor's and McNeill's, operated in semi-independent status and were not always available when needed. His frequent appeals to Lee for reinforcements were of no avail as Lee's army regrouped and recuperated after the loss at Gettysburg. With no troops to spare as he faced Meade, the only help Lee could offer to the Valley District was one small company of dismounted Missouri cavalrymen, recently exchanged prisoners of war.[1]

In mid-September Maj. David B. Lang of the 62nd Mounted Infantry led an eighty-man force into Randolph County, an attack typical of the many small actions in which Imboden's men engaged. At one o'clock in the morning of September 25 the Confederates quietly surrounded a Union cavalry patrol that had camped for the night near the crossing of the Cheat River about nine miles northeast of Beverly. Overwhelming the sleeping Yankees before they could offer any resistance, the Southerners captured thirty-six prisoners, including all of their weapons and equipment, without suffering a single casualty. The Harrisonburg newspaper commented on this incident the following week as the federal prisoners passed through town. "General Imboden, it will be seen, is affording the abolitionists of the Northwest the best facilities he can command to enable them to get quickly and safely on to Richmond."[2]

On October 2 Imboden embarked on yet another raid on the B&O railroad, but advanced only as far west as Wardensville. Heavy rains, unfordable streams and treacherous roads that had turned into seemingly bottomless quagmires forced the command to abandon its mission. Slowly the drenched troopers limped back into camp, where they enjoyed but a few brief days of rest before once again taking the offensive.[3]

Five days later, on October 7, Imboden received orders from Lee to move into the northern Shenandoah Valley. Once again the Northwestern Brigade was to act as guard for the Army of Northern Virginia's left flank as it advanced northward on the east side of the Blue Ridge Mountains to begin the ill-fated Bristoe Campaign.[4]

Following the Valley Turnpike as far as Strasburg, they marched through Front Royal and on to Berryville before encountering any difficulty. On October 17 they discovered a Union scouting party and chased them for more than four miles. Pvt. Baker recorded in his diary:

> They made a general run for it and the 18th regiment after them. We rode down quite a number of them and got more guns than we got prisoners. The road was dotted with hats, guns, canteens, etc. Indeed, they cut loose everything to lighten their horses.[5]

At 2:00 A.M. on October 18 Imboden was closing on Charles Town, his objective. He had expected the federal garrison stationed there to withdraw in light of the Confederate advance, but the Unionists held the town. Imboden divided his command, sending the 18th and Gilmor's Battalion to cover the Harpers Ferry Road, while he led the 62nd and McClanahan's battery on an attack against the town from the front in an attempt to surround and capture them.[6]

Conducted under cover of darkness, the movement caught the Union commander completely off guard. Col. Benjamin L. Simpson, a wealthy Baltimore businessman with little military experience,[7] had been confident that he could resist a Confederate attack and refused to abandon the town, but at dawn he realized that he had woefully underestimated his opponents. Less than two hundred yards in front of the fortified municipal buildings stood the 62nd Virginia Mounted Infantry and McClanahan's Battery drawn up in the line of battle.[8]

Aware that he must act quickly before Northern reinforcements could arrive from Harpers Ferry, Imboden sent McNeill into the Union lines under a flag of truce with a written surrender demand, allowing the Yankees five minutes to relinquish the garrison. The overconfident federal commander, still determined to resist a Confederate attack, tersely replied, "Take us if you can." Upon hearing the reply, Imboden declared, "Boys, unlimber that piece of artillery, and I'll take them out."[9]

One of the Confederate artillerymen recalled later:

> While we unlimbered [Imboden] dismounted and, sighting in the piece himself, fired straight into the door striking the adjutant and cutting off both his legs. The next shots went first through the wall to the left of the door and the next to the right. Then they came out like a swarm of bees, and Captain McNeill was ordered to take charge of them.[10]

Reported Imboden:

> I immediately opened on the buildings with artillery at less than 200 yards, and with half a dozen shells drove out the enemy into the streets, when he formed and fled toward Harpers Ferry. At the edge of town he was met by the Eighteenth Cavalry, Colonel Imboden, and Gilmor's battalion. One volley was exchanged, when the enemy threw down his arms and surrendered unconditionally.[11]

One Yankee major praised Imboden's tactics by saying:

> The Johnnies had some pretty damned smart officers during the war, and some of them that did the most effective work were the least heard of. Imboden was one of them. Imboden with a half dozen shells and a volley or two of carbine and pistol shots and considerable dash has scooped in pretty nearly as many as his own force.[12]

The jubilant Confederates captured four hundred thirty-four prisoners and numerous wagons, horses, mules, arms and other supplies, along with thirteen drums of various sizes. Soon the 62nd had one of the finest drum corps in the entire Confederate army.[13]

The prisoners and captured property were secured quickly. Knowing that the large Union force, a mere eight miles away at Harpers Ferry, would soon be breathing down their necks, the troops scurried about loading the Union wagons. As expected, within two hours,

> ...the Federals came up from Harpers Ferry and attacked our rear guard. When we heard the firing of shots, we pulled stakes and moved on, taking position and beating the enemy back from every hilltop for a distance of twelve miles; but we came out safely with prisoners and provisions which we had captured in little old Charles Town. When night came on, we were well-nigh spent, and our prisoners, in the language of the today, were simply "all in!"[14]

Another of Imboden's men recalled that they fought them to dark. Lt. Carter Berkley later recorded:

> We fired our guns *en echelon*, some firing and some
> retreating. Several times they came near capturing them.
> At one place I remember especially, they got on our right
> flank and within a few feet of us before we could turn our
> guns about, when Major Gilmor charged them and saved
> us. In the charge he recaptured two of our men that the
> enemy had taken.[15]

The Union major recorded how Imboden's force had fallen back in
good order:

> The whole day was a stern chase, but occasionally when
> Imboden was pressed too closely and in need of time to
> keep the prisoners and plunder ahead out of the way, he
> stopped long enough to give us a sharp taste of fighting
> that showed the mettle that was in him.[16]

When all was said and done, Imboden's brigade had suffered five killed,
thirty wounded and "ten or fifteen broken down men, struggling
behind."[17] Lee praised Imboden highly when he remarked, "This duty was
well performed by that officer on the 18th instant he marched upon
Charles Town and succeeded, by a well concerted plan, in surrounding
the place and capturing nearly the whole force stationed there."[18]

Imboden had set a new record in his operations against Charles Town.
Having marched his troops forty-eight miles in one day to attack the town,
the general had bettered Napoleon's record of thirty-six miles marched in
one day to fight a battle.[19]

Averell's Raids

Imboden's troopers were allowed little time to savor their victory, as
federal reinforcements were soon sighted galloping in their direction from
Harpers Ferry. The Confederates quickly gathered up the captured
equipment and withdrew southward with their prisoners. Enemy cavalry
pursued the Southerners for more than twelve miles but were held in
check with a series of hard fought, spirited rearguard actions. Imboden
pushed his men nonstop for twenty-eight miles before finally stopping to
rest near Front Royal.[1] Since high waters made the Shenandoah River
unfordable, they camped there until October 25.[2]

They then resumed the march southward at a leisurely pace, without
threat of Union attack. In addition to the large number of prisoners, the

Southerners had also captured huge amounts of provisions and military equipment at Charles Town. The captured provisions were sorely needed, especially clothing and shoes.[3] Supplies—including a few tents,[4] curry combs, horse brushes, halters, bridles and hams[5]—were received from the Confederate authorities in Richmond and distributed to the men. Despite an outbreak of chickenpox, the brigade's medical facilities remained adequate, and the men were well armed with .54 and .58 calibre Enfield and Austrian muskets.[6]

The unremitting duty of defending the Valley from Winchester in the north to Botetourt County in the south in especially inclement weather made the next several weeks a very unpleasant period. A typical day of service consisted of constant patrolling in the rain and sleet. Lt. Julian Pratt of the 18th Virginia Cavalry echoed the sentiments of the whole command when he wrote, "I hope we shall have no more very active duty this winter."[7]

In early November Lee urged Imboden to renew his attacks on the B&O Railroad. Imboden asked for reinforcements since his force was too weak to accomplish any significant mission, but nothing came of his request.[8] He ordered McNeill's command into western Virginia to observe the enemy and report any movements.

On November 1, 1863, Union general William Averell departed his camp at Beverly to raid southwestern Virginia with more than five thousand veteran troopers. He pushed southward, virtually unopposed, for five days. Notified by McNeill about this advance, Imboden set about organizing an adequate defense.[9] He assembled all available troops, including the Lexington Home Guards, a company of students from Washington College, and the Corps of Cadets from V.M.I.[10]

A small Confederate force under Brig. Gen. John Echols made a desperate attempt to block the Union raiders just north of Lewisburg. In the ensuing battle of Droop Mountain, the heavily outnumbered Southerners were driven from the field, clearing the way for the federal advance to Lewisburg.[11]

For the next nine days Imboden's men skirmished with Averell's raiding party, containing the Union force at Lewisburg until the enemy broke contact on November 14, retreated into Hardy County and established a camp near Petersburg. After the last skirmish and exchange of long-range artillery fire, Imboden ordered the home guards and cadets back to Lexington. Before dismissing the citizen soldiers, however, he assembled them for a word of commendation:

If the Valley counties will but act the part that Old
Rockbridge has done on this occasion, there will be no
need for reinforcements from General Lee to repel raids
against the Valley.[12]

His words were met with enthusiastic applause from the old men and
boys. In his official report Imboden praised the reserve forces as well:

I beg leave to call my testimony to the admirable spirit
displayed by the people of Rockbridge in coming to my
assistance. At 7 p.m., on Thursday, the 6th, the news
reached Lexington of this raid. By 7 p.m., the next day
800 men were 12 miles on their march to support me. My
thanks are especially due Colonel J. W. Massie,
commanding the Home Guards, and General F. H.
Smith, commanding cadets for their energy and zeal they
manifested and the skill which they moved their
commands so rapidly through the mountains.[13]

During this campaign Imboden earned the nickname "General Pizzen,"
because he was considered to be as deadly as poison to his enemy.[14] His
command remained in the area, ever ready to strike at any federal
movement.

Averell made the costly mistake of relaxing his vigilance. Late on the
morning of November 15 an eighty-five wagon supply train loaded with
commissary and quartermaster goods rolled out of New Creek enroute to
Averell's camp near Petersburg. Feeling that there was no threat, the
overly confident federal commander had detailed only a hundred men to
guard the mile-long train. The lumbering train made only thirteen miles
before stopping for the night near Burlington. Early the following morning
the Yankee wagonmaster resumed the journey, unaware that their
progress was being closely monitored by McNeill's Rangers and the 62nd
Virginia Mounted Infantry.

As the Federals rolled steadily southward, completely oblivious to the
impending danger, the wagon train passed an abandoned house midway
between Burlington and Williamsport. Confederate soldiers hidden in the
house fired upon the unsuspecting advance guard, which signaled a
full-scale assault on the train. The first volley emptied the saddle of a
federal lieutenant, who fell dead into the roadway. As the squad rushed
from the abandoned house, the 62nd attacked the front of the train and
McNeill attacked the rear. Confusion reined as the Northern troops found

their rifled muskets no match for the Confederates' shotguns, pistols and carbines, and they dispersed into the neighboring forest.

The destruction of the train was halted by the approach of an entire federal cavalry regiment, which sent the Confederates scurrying into the countryside where they eluded the pursuers on the intricate mountain trails.[15] The attack had netted, in addition to the destroyed wagons, two hundred forty-five horses and forty-three disgruntled teamsters. The Confederates suffered only four men slightly wounded.[16]

The Southern troops returned to camp ready to relax in winter quarters after the vigorous campaigns of the last eight months. Some of the more realistic troopers were not so optimistic, however. One soldier with the 62nd wrote home: "I doubt very much whether we shall see any winter quarters this winter as we have a very extensive country to protect. In fact it is more than Gen. Imboden can do. We ought to have more troops."[17] Less than a week later the trooper's words proved to be prophetic, for in the second week of December Averell went on yet another raid. Imboden's brigade once again took to the saddle to repulse this latest federal assault into southwestern Virginia.

Averell's troops raided southward into Craig County. Christmastime was near, and tables overflowed with hams, turkeys, chickens, venison and wine. Laughter, dancing and fiddle and banjo music echoed in the hollows. Then the opportunistic Yankees appeared, devouring the food, drinking the wine and taking hostage all of the unfortunate residents who got in their way.[18]

Once again Imboden called out the home guards and cadets. As his command reached Lexington on December 18, Margaret Preston recorded their arrival:

> At 11 o'clock, Imboden's cavalry and artillery passed through. It is the first time I have ever seen an army. Poor fellows! With their broken down horses muddy up to the eyes, and their muddy wallets and blankets, they looked like an army of tatterdemalions; the horses looked starved.[19]

The people of Rockbridge County gladly shared what they had with the soldiers from their skimpy supplies of foods and other goods. Imboden sent a letter to James D. Davidson, commissariat in Lexington, thanking him for the provisions, gloves and other articles of clothing:

We shall never forget the hospitality of good old
Rockbridge, every day I hear some misty looking veteran
say, "Well boys, I wonder when we will be marched
toward Rockbridge again?" And often you will hear in
camp, "Hurrah for the Rockbridge Home Guards."[20]

Lee ordered Gen. Jubal Early to the Valley. Averell pushed on as far as
Salem, wrecking railroad property and destroying large quantities of
supplies intended for Gen. James Longstreet's forces in Tennessee along
the way. Early arrived in time to come between the enemy and his base of
operations.

The Confederates then possessed numerical superiority. Along with
Early's infantry there were two brigades of cavalry under Fitzhugh Lee to
add to Imboden's small command. Also available from Gen. Samuel
Jones's Southwest Virginia Department was a brigade of infantry under
Gen. Echols and a detachment of unmounted cavalry under Col. William
L. Jackson.

Jackson's troops on the Virginia Central Railroad at Jackson River
Depot were in a good position to block Averell if he were to return by the
same route. Averell felt Covington to be lightly guarded and decided to
retreat via Covington and New Castle to his base at Petersburg.
Unbeknownst to Averell, Early had sent Imboden to Covington to cover
the bridges and attack the enemy should he proceed that way.[21]

Torrential rains pounded the Southern troopers, and high waters forced
them to take a roundabout route. Early sent Fitz Lee with a brigade of
cavalry to join Imboden at Covington. Lee felt that Averell would attempt
escape via Buckhannon, so he and Imboden moved their troops in that
direction. Averell, however, slipped by them and crossed the Jackson
River at Covington, gaining a two-day march on the Confederates.
Imboden and Lee had come close to stopping him, yet Averell got away.
His escape was opposed only by Jackson's five hundred men, who put up
a good fight but did not prevail.[22]

To counter further raids by federal cavalry, Imboden's engineers erected
fortifications seven miles from Goshen on the Cowpasture River and at
Buffalo and Jennings gaps. The V.M.I. cadets and Jackson's small force
fortified other sites leading across the mountains from the west.[23]

On Christmas Day 1863, Frank Imboden wrote in his diary, "XMAS.
Tonight, George, Jim, Jake, Ma, Pa, and myself are all at home, only the
General absent. Will we meet another XMAS?"[24]

As 1863 drew to a close, Imboden could look back on nine months of constant operations. The coming year would be no different.

The Start of a New Year

On the last day of 1863 the Northwestern Brigade was split for a two-pronged thrust into enemy occupied territory; McNeill's and Gilmor's units were sent with Fitz Lee, who led a foraging expedition into the South Branch Valley, while Imboden with the remainder of the brigade accompanied Early, who led a second Confederate column down the Shenandoah Valley toward Strasburg in a diversionary tactic.

The hardships of winter campaigning were very evident in this expedition. Snow and ice-covered roads forced Lee's wagons and artillery back to the Shenandoah Valley. The only significant capture by the greatly reduced Southern command was late in the afternoon of January 3, when a forty-wagon federal supply train was overtaken just north of Moorefield. The Confederates' hopes of obtaining sorely need supplies were dashed when it was discovered that the wagons contained only artillery ammunition and raw beef hides. Lee detached a detail to accompany the wagons back to the Shenandoah Valley while continuing northward with the remainder of his command, which defeated small Union detachments at Burlington, Williamsport and McLemar's Church. A major hailstorm cut short the raid on January 6th.[1]

While Lee was raiding with little success in Hardy County, Early's prong of the expedition had spent the week skirmishing constantly with the enemy in the vicinity of Middletown and Strasburg. Fitz Lee returned to Shenandoah County on January 7, and once again the Northwestern Brigade was united.

Finally having been relieved from duty in the northern Shenandoah Valley, the jaded troopers of Imboden's command went into winter camp. The 18th Virginia Cavalry set up their quarters at Bridgewater, McClanahan's Battery camped at Mount Jackson and the rest went into winter quarters at Mount Crawford. The entire brigade spent the next three weeks recuperating and refurbishing.[2]

During this brief period of inactivity Imboden was absent from his command, tending to political matters in Staunton. In his absence the brigade was under the command of Col. Smith of the 62nd Virginia Mounted Infantry. Although Smith did his best, there were some petty infractions of discipline that prompted Early to complain that Smith was unreliable. Early's disdain for and prejudice against Imboden's entire command was well known; he felt the men couldn't be depended upon and suspected that most of them were probably deserters from the regular army. He asserted that the brigade was inefficient, disorganized and undisciplined.

When one of Imboden's lieutenants killed a sergeant on the streets of Staunton, Early exploded in protest to Col. Smith and Fitz Lee. Imboden, who learned of Early's comments when he returned to the brigade, was outraged. He wrote to Robert E. Lee of the matter, describing Early's accusations as "sneers unofficially and publicly made which are calculated if true to bring me and my command into disrepute and contempt." He accused Early of "gross injustice by yielding to the disrepute of prejudice rather than reason."[3]

Imboden confronted Early on the matter and asked for a court of inquiry. Early concurred with convening such a court, noting that the brigade was in a "very bad state of discipline." Lee, who knew that much might be lost and little gained by such proceedings, promptly notified Imboden that a court of inquiry would not be "advantageous."[4] Lee evaluated Imboden as a department commander and found mostly minor defects, most of which were simply mere irritants; foremost among these shortcomings was discipline. On the other hand, Lee knew, Early had acquired a dislike of the cavalry and made no effort to acquaint himself with that branch or study its place in an army.

The brigade's period of rest came to an abrupt end on January 26 when Early once again summoned Imboden and his command northward. Unhappy with the results of Fitz Lee's earlier excursion, Early decided to personally lead yet another expedition into the South Branch Valley. Once again Imboden's command was divided as Gilmor's Marylanders, McNeill's Rangers and McClanahan's mountain howitzers accompanied Early into Hardy County. Imboden was directed to create a diversion to provide cover for the Confederate raiders.[5]

This second raid proved to be quite a bit more successful than the first. McClanahan's battery, accompanying Gen. Thomas Rosser's Confederate calvary, captured a sizeable federal wagon train. Rosser also destroyed several railroad bridges across Patterson's Creek and the Potomac River.[6] Imboden's command harassed Federals in the northern Shenandoah Valley for ten straight days. On February 5 Early returned to his camp near New Market, having appropriated seventeen hundred head of cattle and sheep, fifty wagons and a large amount of desperately needed commissary supplies.

Imboden then led his brigade south to Rockbridge County, where the command was broken up into detachments of company and squadron size and dispatched for scouting, picketing, collecting deserters, recruiting and gathering supplies.[7] While on these raids a heated disagreement arose between McNeill and Rosser over the latter's treatment of horses. Rosser was incensed that a mere partisan captain would question the actions of a West Point-trained general officer and wrote to Lee and Stuart condemning the Partisan Ranger Corps. Both Lee and Stuart agreed with Rosser and endorsed a plan to disband all partisan bands.

While Confederate authorities debated the importance of the partisans and their future, business went on as usual with McNeill and those semi-independent commanders within Imboden's district. Eventually the Partisan Ranger Act was repealed with certain provisions, one of which allowed the secretary of war to exempt companies serving within the enemy's lines. Thus McNeill's command was permitted to continue its operations, but under closer scrutiny.[8]

At the end of February Early returned to the eastern side of the Blue Ridge, leaving Imboden's command as the only Confederate force in the Valley. The brigade moved into Rockingham County and camped for the next two months at Bridgewater.[9] They had only slight encounters with the enemy during this period.

An incident that involved thirteen men of Co. A, 18th Virginia Cavalry exemplifies the type of warfare being waged at this time. On March 20, these troopers went into Barbour County to waylay enemy wagon trains. They found the trains to be too heavily guarded, so they rode into Tucker County, where they raided Wheeler's Store for supplies. There they encountered a vastly superior group of Lambert's Independent Scout Company of Tucker County and suffered two wounded and one captured.[10]

The brigade spent the months of March and April operating as scouts and pickets in Page, Warren and Rappahannock counties. The emergence of the Swamp Dragons, a pro-Union independent band who regularly committed acts of unspeakable violence on the civilian populations of western Virginia under the protection of the United States Army, caused some excitement for the troopers. A well-planned and well-executed raid by McNeill's Rangers in April completely destroyed the Swamp Dragons' camp and inflicted serious casualties, while the Rangers emerged completely unscathed.[11]

This period gave Imboden time to catch up on his administrative duties, among which was a series of courts-martial for infractions of military justice committed during the preceding year. At least one civilian had also been arrested. Robert E. Lee wrote to Imboden concerning the case of Michael Yoakum:

> I have been informed that you have in arrest a citizen of Hardy County named Michael Yoakum, who is charged with outrages committed upon the person and property of some of our citizens of that county, and that you proposed trying him before a court-martial. I am also informed that a writ of *habeas corpus* has been sued out by Yoakum, to which you have made return claiming jurisdiction over the case. You have the power to afford immediate protection to our citizens against threatened or attempted violence, but where an offense has been committed by one not in the military service of the United States or our own you have no jurisdiction to try the offenders by a court-martial. You can arrest and deliver him to the civil authorities, who alone are competent to try him. If the facts of this case be such as I have represented then above, I desire that you will surrender the accused to the civil authorities, in obedience to the writ to be dispersed of by the court of jurisdiction.[12]

The most common offenses prosecuted were absences without leave (AWOL) and desertion. A fine line existed between AWOL and the much more serious charge of desertion; most men charged with the latter had the charges lowered to AWOL. The usual sentence for convicted offenders was confinement to the guardhouse with a ball and chain attached to the left leg and extra duty. One exception to this was Pvt. John Mick of Co. C, 62nd Virginia Mounted Infantry. While away from camp, Pvt. Mick had joined the notorious Swamp Dragons and so was charged with desertion. The court found him guilty and sentenced him to death by a firing squad. Pvt. Mick was executed before the assembled Northwestern Brigade on March 18, 1863, near Imboden's camp in Rockingham County.[13]

Another court-martial involved Hanse McNeill. McNeill was called up to answer to charges of violation of the Partisan Ranger Act relating to dispersal of public property and for "knowingly receiving and entertaining a deserter from other than his own company and refusing to deliver him up." McNeill was completely exonerated by the court on both charges.[14]

Against Sigel in the Valley

In March of 1864 President Lincoln appointed a general from the western theater to the supreme command of all Union armies. Ulysses S. Grant inherited mass confusion from his predecessor, who had done little to bring cohesion to the several armies scattered throughout the various military districts and departments.

Grant launched an all-out offensive against the Confederacy that included a five-pronged assault against a thousand-mile arc that reached from Virginia to Alabama. The Army of the Potomac under Gen. George Meade was to move against Robert E. Lee's Army of Northern Virginia in front of Richmond. Gen. William T. Sherman was to lead a force through the heart of Georgia, Gen. Nathaniel Banks was to attack Mobile, Alabama, and Benjamin Butler was to strike Richmond from the James River.

The fifth prong of the attack was to be a thrust through the Shenandoah Valley by an army led by German-born Maj. Gen. Franz Sigel. The Valley was a vital economic and strategic region of the Confederacy, a prime source of produce and livestock essential for the sustenance of Lee's powerful army defending Richmond against the expected federal onslaught. Railroads traversing the Valley linked the eastern and western theaters of the embattled Confederacy. The far southwestern sector of Virginia's great valley contained the valuable lead and salt mines of Wythe County.[1] Conquering it was vital to Grant's plan.

The only Confederate defense against Sigel's seven thousand-man force was Imboden's command: the 62nd Virginia Mounted Infantry, 18th Virginia Cavalry and McClanahan's Battery—less than two thousand men. Company A, 1st Missouri Cavalry under Capt. Charles H. Woodson was attached to the 62nd Virginia. The few other resources available included Bartlett's Valley District Signal Corps, Capt. William T. Hart's Engineer Company, the Augusta and Rockingham County Reserves, Davis's Maryland Battalion, Gilmor's Maryland Battalion, McNeill's

Partisan Rangers, Col. John S. Mosby's Partisan Rangers and the cadets from V.M.I.[2]

Lee anticipated that the Shenandoah Valley would play a major role in the spring offensive. Unable to send reinforcements to Imboden, he wrote to the new commander of the Department of Southwest Virginia, Maj. Gen. John C. Breckinridge, instructing him to "act in concert" with Imboden.[3] The tall, handsome Kentuckian was a Mexican War veteran, politician, former vice president, presidential candidate and veteran of the Army of Tennessee.[4] His department was a vast area that included all of southwest Virginia, eastern Tennessee and parts of Kentucky as well as what had become West Virginia.

By the end of April Imboden knew that Sigel was in command, with headquarters at Winchester. On the 2nd of May the Confederates broke camp at Mount Crawford, about seventy miles from Winchester, and moved forward to determine Sigel's strength and report it to Lee.

About a hundred of Imboden's scouts were positioned on either side of Sigel. Imboden, with 1,492 effective troops, had notified the reserve commander at Staunton, Gen. William Harman, to be ready to march at a moment's notice. The reserves consisted of men over age forty-five and boys between the ages of sixteen and eighteen as well as men detailed to work in shops, at furnaces and other critical duties. Gen. Francis Smith at V.M.I. had been notified to ready his three hundred cadets. The Confederate troopers were well mounted and equipped for hard service. The reserves, undisciplined and armed only with hunting rifles and shotguns, were less than a thousand strong.[5]

On May 3 Imboden reported enemy troops from Romney to Wardensville. Kernstown and Winchester were occupied with a good deal of enemy artillery and at least three thousand cavalry. On May 4 Imboden arrived at Rude's Hill between New Market and Mount Jackson. The enemy cavalry was at Maurertown, and Sigel had moved his force to Front Royal.[6]

When Imboden reached Woodstock on May 5, Sigel was at Strasburg, only twelve miles away. With intelligence from his scouts and the citizens of the area, Imboden was able to estimate the strength of the enemy accurately. When it was determined that he faced nearly ten thousand men, appeals were sent to Gen. Lee for reinforcements. Then the signal corps operating in the mountains to the west reported an additional force of seven thousand at Lewisburg, a hundred miles west of Staunton, that were apparently waiting to link up with Sigel. Lee's reply to Imboden's earnest request was that he was hard pressed by Grant and could spare no troops. He ordered Imboden to do all that he could to block Sigel's advance without being surrounded.[7]

Outnumbered by more than four to one, Imboden could not risk a full-scale engagement with the enemy. Too weak to stop his opponent, he could only slow the Federals' advance with diversions and sharp, quick guerilla attacks. The efficacy of this plan would be well proven by the fact that it would take Sigel two weeks to move his troops a mere fifty miles.

Imboden's first attempt to relieve pressure on his understrength force was to order McNeill deep into enemy territory to draw federal attention from the Valley with yet another attack on the B&O Railroad. Shortly after sunset on May 3 McNeill set off with sixty rangers. On the second night they crossed into Maryland at a ford on the south branch of the Potomac. A short ride eastward brought them to the little hamlet of Bloomington on the main line of the B&O. By dawn they had captured the small town and seized an eastbound freight train. From Bloomington they rode in high fashion on the captured train the two miles to Piedmont Station, the site of vast stores of railroad supplies and numerous machine shops.

The locomotive was detached and two rangers mounted the cab. With a flag of truce flying, they entered Piedmont without incident, followed by the remainder of the command on horseback. The little Union force stationed there surrendered without a fight.

Within a half hour of leaving Bloomington, they had begun the destruction of Piedmont. Seven machine shops, nine locomotives and more than a hundred fully loaded rail cars were detroyed in place. Six other locomotives were put under a full head of steam and sent streaking into New Creek. In less than an hour the Confederate partisans had destroyed more than a million dollars in federal property.

While McNeill was busy at Piedmont, a smaller ranger force under Capt. John T. Peerce was creating further havoc along the B&O. His men wrecked two heavily laden freight trains and destroyed valuable federal stores. Peerce rode up to a third train that arrived with two passenger cars loaded with Union troops and demanded surrender. Intimidated by the Confederate's audacity, the Union commander surrendered his hundred-man detachment to the eleven partisans without firing a shot.[8] The Southerners then rode south to the safety of Virginia with their prisoners, where they joined McNeill. Knowing that federal troops would soon be on their trail, McNeill withdrew deep into the mountains.

Enraged by the success of the Confederate raiders, the Federals quickly organized a force to pursue and capture them. Alerted early on the morning of May 8 to the departure of two bodies of Union cavalry from Sigel's camp, Imboden saw an opportunity to fight a fragment of the enemy with the odds in his favor. He planned to attack these detached units before they could reunite with the main enemy force.[9]

Imboden was well aware that his movements would be reported to Sigel by Union sympathizers in the area. As a cover, he let it be known that he was moving his command toward North Mountain to obtain better grazing for the horses. Leaving Col. Smith with the 62nd at Woodstock, he rode with the 18th and two guns of McClanahan's battery to join McNeill and overtake the enemy party that had gone west toward Moorefield.

Just before dawn on May 10 Imboden joined McNeill north of Wardensville. With a numerical superiority of more than two to one, the Confederate commanders devised a plan to punish the unsuspecting Federals. Crossing North Mountain at a pass known as the Devil's Hole and travelling all night, the command reached Lost River in Hardy County before dawn. Learning that the enemy had spent the night at Moorefield, Imboden prepared to ambush them as they left town.[10]

To decoy the unsuspecting Yankees, McNeill's Rangers skirmished briefly at the entrance to Lost River Gap before slowly falling back. The Union cavalry, five hundred well-equipped troopers of the 22nd Pennsylvania and the 15th New York, rushed headlong into the gap hot on the heels of the retreating Rangers, unaware of Imboden's presence. A half mile into the gap they galloped straight into the waiting Confederates. In just a few seconds the tables were turned, and the heavily outnumbered Northerners reversed their course and fled frantically northward, closely pursued by the jubilant Southerners.

A member of the 18th Virginia Cavalry wrote, "We got them on a stampede and run them all day."[11] The Confederates pursued them for more than sixty miles, driving them across the Potomac to Oldtown, Maryland. The day-long retreat cost the Federals their train of eight fully loaded wagons, an ambulance and fifty men, all captured. More importantly, Sigel's force had been reduced by five hundred men.[12] Triumphantly, Imboden's men returned to Lost River.

The following day, May 11, the rangers reached Mathias, where they rested for a day before crossing the mountains back into the Shenandoah Valley. From New Market Imboden called for the reserves, the cadets, and help from Breckinridge. If he could hold off Sigel until all of the reinforcements arrived, he could fight the coming battle with nearly equal numbers on each side.

The same day an incident occurred that significantly improved the Confederate chances in this campaign. Davis's Maryland Battalion, having delayed the Union advance all day, fell back, allowing the Union army to enter Woodstock late in the afternoon. The telegraph office was captured before its records could be destroyed, and from the captured dispatches Sigel learned that Breckinridge was advancing to reinforce Imboden. Rather than continue his advance, the Union commander hesitated long enough to give the Confederate forces time to consolidate.

On May 12 Imboden received welcome news from Breckinridge, who reported in a dispatch that his force was now at Staunton and moving north. If the enemy could be delayed another two days, the two commanders could be united. The Confederates would then have an effective force of five thousand men and eighteen guns.[13]

On May 13, while in the area of Rude's Hill, Imboden's command became aware of a second Union cavalry column that had ridden from Sigel's camp five days before. Young Davey Crabill, who had left home at the age of sixteen to join the 18th Virginia Cavalry, was with a small detachment on picket duty on the Luray Road east of New Market. Lying by a rail fence in the late afternoon sun, he spotted the blue column coming through the gap. Jumping up, he shouted, "Lieutenant, lieutenant, come out here. Sir, I see men riding through the Gap."[14]

Imboden called out the 18th and 23rd Virginia Cavalry regiments. The 23rd was sent to the bridge over Smith's Creek to meet the enemy column head on, while the 18th and two of McClanahan's guns were sent around to the rear to cut off a Yankee retreat. The Union force rode into the position held by the 23rd and was repulsed; in an attempt to retreat, they ran into the 18th, and a rout ensued. Part of the enemy force managed to forge through the line of the 18th Cavalry but only after losing seventy-five men as prisoners and many killed and wounded. Young Elon Henkel of New Market recorded the Southern pursuit of the fleeing Yankees as "neck and neck, the horses hoofs hammering the pike, the scabbards of the sabres rattling, and the cavalrymen giving the rebel yell."[15]

The remainder of the Yankee force scattered into the mountains. Lt. James M. Potts of Co. G, 18th Virginia Cavalry, wrote:

> [We] drove them into Massanutten Mountains, capturing nearly the entire detachment. We sent the

prisoners up the Valley, but kept their splendid horses to
take the place of our badly jaded stock.[16]

Capt. James H. Stevenson of the 1st New York wrote, "Our men were
seen running in all directions on foot, . . . their horses having given out or
got fast among the rocks; while some of the horses rushed along wildly
without riders, the saddles under their bellies."[17]

In three days the hard-riding Imboden had smashed two enemy forces
more than thirty mountainous miles apart, caused a hundred and fifty or
more casualties and rendered eight hundred federal troops ineffective.
The odds were now narrowing for the impending battle.

The Battle of New Market

Imboden had crippled the entire Union cavalry corps in the Valley. When
Sigel discovered that the only force facing him was Imboden's tiny
command, he pushed southward, driving amid Imboden's pickets on the
Valley Pike. As the blue-clad soldiers from the North dashed into Mount
Jackson they met Maj. Harry Gilmor and his Marylanders. In a heated
engagement, Gilmor was badly wounded, along with several of his men
and horses.[1]

The next day, May 14, Imboden threw his brigade across the pike at
Rude's Hill, four miles north of New Market. Leaving Col. Smith in charge
of the brigade, he rode to meet Breckinridge at Lacy Springs, ten miles
south of New Market. Breckinridge had sent word that he would be there
by noon.

While conferring with Breckinridge over dinner, Imboden received
word of desperate fighting at Rude's Hill. The courier's message was
underscored by the sound of engaging artillery. Without hesitation,
Imboden rose from the table and rode to his men with orders to hold New
Market at all cost.[2]

Arriving at New Market while an artillery duel was in full swing,
Imboden discovered that Smith had deployed the brigade across the front
of the opposing force in single ranks to give the impression of a much larger
force. The Confederate line ran from the hills west of the town, across the
pike and Smith's Creek, into the woods on the right. McClanahan's
artillery was on the extreme left, at the top of the hill, providing a
commanding position from which to fire across the town and down upon
the enemy guns nearly two hundred feet below. From the position of the
battery, Imboden had full view of the enemy's placement. With the

exception of the artillery, which was engaged, and a few advanced cavalry, the enemy troops were not yet formed into a line. The fighting lasted past 11:30 P.M. The Confederates had fought against overwhelming odds, yet had delayed the Union forces for more than nine hours. Lt. Potts of the 18th Virginia Cavalry observed that the enemy "gave us a very hard afternoon's work."[3]

New Market, a beautiful old town with a population of a thousand, lay between natural protective barriers to the west and east. Just beyond the cultivated, sloping hills to the west of town meandered the formidable North Fork of the Shenandoah River. To the east of the Valley Turnpike, the main thoroughfare, was Smith's Creek, a millstream at the foot of the steep slopes of Massanutten Mountain.

The night became intensely dark as it began to rain. Sigel used the cover to move his infantry to a plateau northwest of the town, yet their campfires revealed their exact position.[4]

Imboden fell asleep well after midnight by the roadside near the center of his line but was aroused about two hours before daybreak by the light of a tin lantern shining in his face. It was Gen. Breckinridge, reporting that his troops would be in position by sunrise. As daylight broke, his weary, ragged, muddy troops moved into position on the Confederate line.

The two generals studied the terrain and decided to await Sigel's advance. Breckinridge had brought with him two small infantry brigades, veteran troops seasoned on many battlefields, commanded by brigadier generals John Echols and Gabriel C. Wharton; plus Maj. William McLaughlin's six-gun artillery battery; a section of the cadet battery from V.M.I.; and the entire corps of cadets, two hundred twenty-five present under the command of Col. Scott Shipp.

Imboden's largest regiment, the 62nd Virginia Mounted Infantry with five hundred fifty men, was ordered to dismount and placed with the cadets in the center of the infantry line. His remaining units were to form the extreme right wing of the Confederate line along Smith's Creek.[5] With the cadets was Imboden's youngest brother, Jake, a boy of seventeen.[6]

The Confederates expected the Yankees to attack at dawn, but an hour after daybreak only an occasional shot fired by skirmishers deployed in and around the town broke the stillness. Where was Sigel? Imboden led his cavalry in a feigned attack and then retreated, hoping to draw the enemy, but Sigel refused to respond.[7] Finally Breckinridge decided, "We can attack and whip them here. I'll do it." All of the troops were ordered to advance as rapidly as possible. Imboden was sent with his cavalry and

McClanahan's battery to take a position on the extreme right flank. In little more than an hour the "ball was opened" by McLaughlin's guns.

Imboden's troopers were concealed from the enemy at their front by woods, which he filled with mounted skirmishers several hundred yards ahead of the main line. The battle began in earnest when the Confederates came under tremendous artillery fire from the other side. The town lay between the contending forces, who were too far apart to use small arms.

Breckinridge advanced his infantry steadily. At times a gap was made in the line by an exploding shell, but it was quickly filled as the troops marched on in parade ground formation. While Echols, Wharton, the 62nd Virginia and the cadets were coming under a galling fire, the troops on the extreme right were only occasionally bothered by a stray shell thrown their way.[8] Jessie Rupert, a resident of New Market, described the action: "Cannon balls and shells rolled and exploded in every direction. The air was filled with dust and smoke, and curses and shrieks."[9]

As the infantry reached the edge of the town, Imboden rode into the woods in his front to ascertain what force, if any, the enemy had on the other side. When he discovered Sigel's entire cavalry force massed in a field just beyond the woods, he moved his command forward at a trot and swept down Smith's Creek to the bridge on the Luray Road. Gaining the top of a small hill, McClanahan's battery unlimbered and got off a shot before being discovered by the enemy. Their position was less than a thousand yards from the Yankee cavalry and gave a commanding view of the troops massed in their front. The first discharge from the Southern cannons threw the Northern cavalry into total confusion. While McClanahan kept the enemy troopers at bay, Imboden led his cavalry down the creek undetected, heading for his enemy's rear.[10]

Unaware that the woods were held only by a skirmish line, the Union cavalry turned to the right and rapidly retired out of range. In doing so they left exposed one of their batteries, which began to exchange fire with McClanahan. Breckinridge noticed the activity on his flank and pushed his infantry forward, covered by McLaughlin's and McClanahan's guns. The shells from the Confederate guns began to fall upon the flank of Sigel's infantry. Pressed from the front and harassed on his flank, Sigel pulled back a half mile.

Along with the cadets, Echols's, Wharton's and Smith's troops passed through the town followed by McLaughlin's guns, which occupied the ground formerly used by the federal batteries. With each passing moment the conflict became more intense. One six-gun battery, with some elevated guns west of the turnpike, was especially destructive in its fire upon Breckinridge's infantry. Smith's 62nd Virginia Mounted Infantry and the Corps of Cadets were instructed to silence the battery, which was positioned directly in front of them, either by dislodging or capturing it.[11]

The rain that had been falling all day turned into a heavy downpour. Breckinridge gave the order to advance, and the first line of federal infantry crumbled with ease. Continuing at a steady pace, the Confederates came under the concentrated firepower of the Union infantry and artillery just beyond the Bushong farmhouse. The 62nd pushed ahead, but the 51st, on their left, was stopped cold. Far in advance of the other Confederate units, the unsupported 62nd was forced to fall back to the cover of a small ravine to reform. During the advance they had suffered substantial casualties, including the wounding of their entire color guard.

Desperate to silence the Union artillery, Capt. Woodson led his company of Missourians from the cover of the ravine. The expert Missouri marksmen shot down so many federal gunners in just a matter of minutes that the Yankee cannons were temporarily silenced. During the same period the Missourians lost forty of their sixty men, either killed or wounded.

At this critical point in the battle, Breckinridge ordered the cadets forward. The cadets, who would have advanced in rear of the 62nd, were now called upon to fill the gap that had opened to the left when the 51st gave way.

Just as the Confederate line was reestablished, around 3:00 P.M., the federal infantry launched a counterattack. The partially protected Confederates laid down a withering fire, easily repulsing the ill-fated federal attack.[12]

As the Federals began their withdrawal, the entire Confederate line surged forward. The Unionists made a brief stand, then fell away before the onrushing Southern tide.[13] The boys from V.M.I., out in front, suffered severely. Young Jake Imboden was knocked down and temporarily disabled by a canister shot as he advanced from the gulch. The order was given to charge "at the double-quick," and the day's work was soon done when most of the the Yankee gunners were captured, along with most of their guns. A rebel yell went up as the battery was taken.[14]

Simultaneous with the charge on the Union battery, Echols and Wharton charged the whole enemy infantry line, which gave away. A long-range pursuit of the fleeing Yankees lasted until midnight.

Imboden rode to find Breckinridge, since the two had not seen one another since the fight began and found the officer about three miles north of town, in sight of Rude's Hill, where an artillery duel had developed. As his infantry filled their cartridge boxes in preparation for a charge, Breckinridge ordered Imboden to take cavalry around to the left with McClanahan's battery and head straight down the pike toward the enemy. When Sigel realized what was in store, he led his troops down the hill and across Meem's Bottom, north of Rude's Hill.

When McClanahan's battery reached the top of the hill, the enemy troops had already crossed the bridge over the Shenandoah River. A few rounds were fired after them before the Confederate cavalry reached the top of the hill, their advance being delayed by knee-deep mud. As they watched helplessly, the bridge was completely destroyed, rendering further pursuit impossible that night.[15]

Although a complete Southern victory, the price of the battle had been high. The ground was strewn with dead and wounded. Col. Smith's 62nd Virginia Mounted Infantry suffered the highest casualties—of five hundred fifty men led into action, two hundred forty-one were killed or wounded. The cadets had begun the fight with two hundred twenty-five men, of whom eight were killed and forty-six wounded. The company of Missourians lost forty-seven of their seventy troops. In all, the Confederate losses totaled forty-two men killed, five hundred twenty-two wounded, and thirteen missing of about forty-five hundred engaged. The Union force of sixty-five hundred incurred losses of ninety-three killed, five hundred fifty-two wounded, and a hundred eighty-six captured.[16]

Mrs. Eliza Clinedist wrote of the aftermath of the battle:

> They commenced carrying the dead from the field. . . .
> They carried some of them by our door, and the red blood
> dripped and dripped on the pavement. . . . Oh, what a
> sickening sight after the battle. . . . A cold rain was falling
> and so many shivered with such severe chills, and we
> helped carry the wounded into the Old Rice home. We
> made a fire and gave them warm drinks but many died
> that night. Our poor soldiers, how they suffered and died
> that day. Even now it brings a tear to my eyes. . . . Old
> Dr. S.P.C. Henkel, our old worn doctor, went to work,
> and stayed all night with the wounded. I saw a pile of
> arms and legs that were cut off and buried in the field.
> The sixty-second Virginia Regiment suffered and lost so

many men in the battle. The long rows of graves in our cemetery tell the tale of how these brave men fought that day.[17]

As word spread out of the Confederate victory at New Market, Lee issued General Order Number 41, which read, "A part of the enemy's force threatening the Valley of Virginia has been routed by Gen. Imboden, and driven back to the Potomac, with the loss of their train and a number of prisoners." Lee's message to his troops about the victory raised their morale and increased their devotion to the cause.[18]

The battle of New Market was recorded as a complete Confederate victory, despite its fearful cost. The most important little battle of the war left the Confederates in control of the vital Valley—at least for a while.

Guarding the Valley

On May 17, despite strident objections from Imboden, Breckinridge left the Valley with the 62nd Virginia to join Lee's hard-pressed army, which needed reinforcements for its battle with Grant at the Wilderness. In the mistaken belief that the Confederate victory of New Market would discourage further federal invasion of the Shenandoah Valley, Breckinridge left Imboden with barely a thousand men to guard the Valley.[1]

Imboden detached a hundred men to rebuild the bridge at Meem's Bottom. The lumber was secured nearby and, with the services of a professional bridge builder, they completed the bridge in three or four days.[2] With the bridge intact, Imboden sent a party to scout after Sigel.

After the battle the Unionists had marched seventeen miles without stopping, abandoning eight or ten wagons and burning many more along the way. On May 19, during a tremendous rain, the enemy sent hospital supplies to New Market under a flag of truce. That day the cadets returned to Staunton.[3]

Sigel, a former lieutenant in the Prussian Army, was relieved of his command four days after the battle of New Market and replaced by Maj. Gen. David "Black Dave" Hunter, a sixty-two-year-old West Pointer. The dark-complected, broad-shouldered Hunter, who dyed his mustache black and wore a dark wig, was given to fits of violence. The son of a Presbyterian minister, Hunter was resentful of his upbringing and of his family's rich Southern heritage in the Valley of Virginia. His checkered army career was marked by courts-martial and fights. He had been brought from the frontier as a captain of dragoons to serve as an escort on the train carrying Lincoln from Illinois to Washington for his inauguration, after which he led the White House guard before taking field command. He had served in Missouri and Kansas and had headed the Department of the South when he led the force that captured Fort Pulaski, Georgia. While in Georgia he ordered freedom for all of the slaves in Florida, Georgia and South Carolina, an order that Lincoln forced him to rescind. Hunter had organized the first colored regiment in the Union army, also illegally. Throughout the South, Black Dave Hunter had been branded a felon and carried a price on his head.[4]

Grant's orders to Hunter were to move on Staunton, Gordonsville, Charlottesville and Lynchburg. Only Imboden's small force lay in his path, as the Confederate cavalry bands of generals John McCausland and William L. "Mudwall" Jackson were in the mountains keeping an eye on a Union cavalry force under Gen. George Crook. Imboden had for support the partisan rangers of McNeill, Gilmor and Mosby, who wove in and out of the mountain passes, raiding the enemy's flanks. They continued to attack supply trains and the railroad and snatch prisoners from isolated posts.[5]

On May 22, Hunter gave his troops their marching orders. The Yankee soldiers were issued an extra pair of shoes and socks, a hundred rounds of ammunition, four pounds of bread, ten rations of coffee, sugar and salt. They were ordered to live off the land and expected to subsist on the hogs, cattle and horses of the Valley residents. Because of the partisan raids harassing his flanks, Hunter did not begin his march southward until May 26. From the start, foraging parties were sent out.[6]

Imboden had established his headquarters at New Market with an outpost at Woodstock. He appealed to Richmond for reinforcements, but there was not a man to spare in Lee's whole army. Lee even retained the 62nd Virginia, advising Imboden to call up the reserves. Once again the old men, boys, and detailed men were all pressed into service.[7]

Imboden was in a serious predicament. Facing ten thousand enemy troops at his front, with at least ten thousand more somewhere in the mountains to the west, he had but a thousand men to guard the precious breadbasket of the Confederacy.

Facing Hunter in the Valley

Hunter had with him infantry, cavalry and artillery—ten thousand men and twenty-two cannon. His infantry commander was Brig. Gen. Jeremiah Sullivan of Indiana, thirty-four years old and a strict disciplinarian. Brig. Gen. Julius Stahel, an exiled Hungarian nobleman and well-educated journalist, commanded the cavalry. Stahel had seen considerable service in the Valley as a cavalryman. Capt. Henry A. du Pont of Delaware was Hunter's artillery chief.[1]

By the time Sullivan's advance reached Woodstock, Imboden had sent pickets and scouts to harass him. Hunter had already begun his odious and unprecedented war against civilians. Before leaving Strasburg his troops had set fire to the Boyden house, as he suspected it was "a rendezvous for bushwackers."[2]

At Newtown (now Stephens City), Gilmor's partisan rangers struck a train of sixteen wagons coming from Martinsburg with an eighty-three-man escort from the 15th and 21st New York Cavalry. Catching the Yankees completely off guard, Gilmor burned the wagons, inflicted several casualties and took a few prisoners.[3] In retaliation, Hunter sent Maj. Timothy Quinn with a detail of two hundred men to burn all of the homes, storehouses and outbuildings in Newtown, sparing only churches and the home of an old doctor who had acted kindly toward the Yankees. As they rode to carry out Hunter's evil order, Gilmor heard about it and sent word that he would hang four Union prisoners if the town were burned.[4] Although faced with the impending deaths of his own men, Hunter insisted that the torch be put to Newtown. Only the disobedience of Hunter's own officers spared the little town.

Hunter halted his army at Woodstock for the night, where he sent out foragers to gather beef, sheep, grain and flour. He ordered his scouts to burn houses in the area that might have been used to harbor Southern guerillas. The citizens of Woodstock proved to be less than cordial to Union inquiries regarding such activity, and the troops returned without burning any homes. Hunter's violent temper was then directed toward his own men for not carrying out his orders. Not only did he believe that burning should be used as a reprisal for guerilla attacks, he also felt it was good policy to burn something daily as general punishment for being a slaveholding state on the wrong side of the war.[5]

Confederate attacks against Hunter's flanks persisted, necessitating special vigilance. As Hunter continued to march and burn, Imboden's scouts kept him informed of every move. The information was passed directly on to Gen. Lee.

On May 29, Hunter's army pressed on to Edinburg, where they destroyed a large quantity of salt. They continued onward, through Mount Jackson, and established headquarters at Rude's Hill. Early the next morning Hunter sent out pickets and scouts to ascertain Imboden's position and wreak havoc on the surrounding countryside.[6]

On June 1 Hunter drove Imboden's small force from New Market. Fighting all the way and contesting every foot of ground, Imboden fell back to Lacey Spring, where a serious skirmish occurred. While the Northern troops reconnoitered the Confederate position and awaited more troops to be brought forward, they were attacked in the rear by some of McNeill's men, which caused great excitement in the Union ranks. Imboden had planted a considerable amount of misinformation, and the Unionists had no idea of what they were facing.

Imboden's force was too small to resist the Union troopers effectively, and the next day they fell back to Harrisonburg with the federal column close behind. As the Northwestern Brigade passed through, cannonballs from the Yankee artillery fell on the town, and Imboden hurriedly threw up a skirmish line just outside of the town limits. When the Yankees saw the Southern troops lined up for battle, they broke off their advance.[7] The Confederate troopers maintained their thin skirmish line, manned by approximately a hundred sixty home guards and a small group of cavalrymen, and the town was quickly secured.

The Union cavalry challenged the Confederates' far right, and before long, the opposing forces were hotly engaged all along the line. The Union troops forced the Confederates back, then a Southern counterattack drove the Yankees back. A Confederate cannon opened up on the Union line from a position about one mile south.

Despite their stubborn resistance, the Confederate line could not be held, and the Southerners retired toward Mount Crawford, where Imboden fortified the North River. By throwing up defensive works on the hilltops overlooking the bridge and felling trees across the fords for several miles above and below the town, he hoped to slow the Yankee advance long enough to allow reinforcements to reach him. His line was stretched paper thin. His right was at Rockland Mills and his left at Bridgewater, a distance of seven miles.[8]

The Yankee invaders appreciated the beauty of Harrisonburg, and the citizens of the town had offered Christian charity to wounded Union troops all during the war. Yet the beauty of the town and the charity of its residents were not enough to protect it against the ravenous hordes descending upon it. The enemy soldiers made it hard on the citizenry by ransacking their fine homes and taking food and other valuables. Horses were stolen, and pillaging by individual soldiers was widespread. Several Yankee officers tried to stop the looting, but Hunter himself did nothing to stop the destructiveness of the invaders.[9] When offices of the Harrisonburg *Register* were sacked and the burned ruins of its broken machinery were scattered in the street, freedom of the press ended in this Southern town.[10]

When Hunter learned from his scouts of Imboden's fortifications on the North River, he decided to detour eastward to Port Republic and then south to Waynesboro rather than risk a frontal assault. His objective was the railroad at Staunton. On Saturday, June 4, he issued orders to advance. The march began at 5:00 A.M., with the infantry, formed in three columns, preceded by the cavalry.[11]

Imboden prepared to meet him, all the time fully aware of Crook's and Averell's forces somewhere west of him in the mountains. His plan was to fight Hunter at the earliest moment, defeating him if possible, then turn on Crook and Averell and do the best he could. He had one great advantage—he knew every road and every farm over which Hunter would pass.[12]

Preparing for Battle

As Hunter carried out his program of looting and burning, Imboden worked diligently to build up his tiny force. In twos and threes, the reserve forces of Augusta and Rockingham counties trickled into camp. They had been called upon in August and December of 1863 and in January 1864. Now they again answered the call to duty. Armed with their own hunting guns and mounted upon farm horses, they were ready for action.

Reserves from Augusta, Rockingham, Rockbridge and Page counties answered Imboden's call, bringing the total of reserve troops at his disposal to somewhere between a thousand and fifteen hundred. Four companies of reserve cavalry arrived under the command of captains J. F. Hottle, Robert W. Stevenson, James C. Cochran, and John Nunan; and the boys' artillery battery under Capt. J. C. Marquis of Staunton was available.[1]

Col. Edwin G. Lee, who had been given command of the reserve forces of the Valley, was appointed enrollment officer while convalescing from wounds at Staunton in late May. On May 27 he issued an order requiring the enlistment of all males seventeen to fifty years of age in the Valley. The Staunton *Vindicator* ran the following announcement:

> It is deemed unnecessary to make an appeal to Virginians to step forward, without coercion, and lend their aid to the noble armies that are now winning, at such costly sacrifice, our independence; our bleeding Country points to her wounds in an appeal stronger than words.[2]

Imboden continued to complain about the removal of the 62nd Virginia Mounted Infantry from the Valley and beseeched Breckinridge for their return. "That regiment is small now, and will be of little value to you," he wrote, "but inestimable to me as a nucleus to form the reserves upon."[3] To make matters worse, he could no longer depend on the cadets from V.M.I. since they, too, had been summoned to Richmond.

With Hunter's menacing force in his front, Imboden continued to worry about the enemy west of the mountains. Scouts had informed him on May 25 of Union troops massing at Beverly, obviously intent upon descending on Staunton. Imboden relayed this intelligence to Gen. Lee, who alerted McCausland at Christiansburg and suggested that he move his little cavalry force to Millboro and the Cowpasture River to keep an eye on this threat.[4]

As the situation grew more desperate, Imboden complained to Adjt. Gen. Samuel Cooper that the reserve battery at Staunton was ready for the field but for a lack of horses. The quartermaster at Staunton, Capt. Randolph Luck, refused to release any horses to Imboden although they were available in Staunton stables. Imboden wrote to Cooper, "Can I have them a few days? Am preparing for the best fight my means can afford."[5] His request was granted, and the sixteen- and seventeen-year-old reserves joined him at North River under Capt. Marquis, a veteran of Jackson's Valley Campaign.

At Imboden's request, Col. Lee issued orders calling for quartermaster and commissary troops, shopmen, telegraphers and all furloughed soldiers.

Imboden then called in the various squads from guarding the mountain passes, but left William Jackson's force on the Jackson River near Covington to keep an eye on the large enemy force in Greenbrier County.[6]

Again calling upon Robert E. Lee for reinforcements, Imboden wrote, "There is no point this side of Mount Crawford where I can successfully resist him, and there is very doubtful, though I will do my best."[7] Though

Lee still could spare no troops, he replied that he would direct Grumble
Jones to come to Imboden's aid.[8] On May 29 Imboden telegraphed Maj.
Charles S. Stringfellow, Jones's adjutant: "Is it possible for you to aid me?"[9]

Reserves continued to arrive. Two complete units—Capt. Henry
Harnsberger's company of men over fifty-five years of age and Capt.
George Chrisman's company of young boys—were mustered in and
assigned to Capt. Thomas Sturgis Davis's command of about fifty
Baltimoreans.

On Monday, May 30, at Glade Springs near Bristol, Jones received word
from Lee to proceed to Staunton with all troops available. The next
morning the 36th, 45th and 60th Virginia regiments and the 45th Virginia
Battalion with Thomas A. Bryan's artillery battery of six guns started north
by train. Along the way they stopped at every hospital and shop to impress
men. On Wednesday Imboden telegraphed Capt. James F. Jones of the
Niter and Mining Corps in southwest Virginia to bring his men to
Staunton by Friday.[10] The general also travelled to Staunton to enlist
postal workers, telegraphers, clerks, tax collectors, and other men who
were not yet in the army. Throughout the county he issued a broadside
calling for recruits:

> Headquarters, Staunton
>
> May 31st, 1864
>
> The Genl. Commanding this District has this moment
> notified me, that "every man who can fire a Gun is
> urgently required at Mt. Crawford" — He says: "I see no
> reason why Magistrates and Constables should not *fight
> for their homes* in a pinch like this." "A man should be
> ashamed to claim such a *pitiful* exemption." "If it becomes
> necessary to *make them fight,* I will DECLARE MARTIAL
> LAW in this District until the danger is over and MAKE
> every man shoulder his musket." "A man who will
> deliberately refuse to defend his home, wife and children
> for a few days ought to be forced into the ranks. IF KILLED,
> THE LOSS IS TRIFLING."
>
> > Beverly Randolph
> > Major Commanding.[11]

Beverly Randolph was an ordnance officer in Staunton who had
assumed the post of town commandant to replace John Q. Nadenbousch.

The reserve companies continued to file in, often led by veterans. Company B was under the command of Robert Doyle, a veteran of the Stonewall Brigade and Imboden's Partisan Rangers, who had retired because of age. Company K was led by Monroe Blue, who had been wounded two months earlier. Capt. Blue had previously served as a non-commissioned officer in the 33rd Virginia and as second lieutenant in the 18th Virginia Cavalry. Worn from capture and confinement at Johnson's Island for ten months, Blue had retired to the reserves. The hundred men of Company D were led by Henry H. Peck, while John Newton Opie, who had fought with the 5th Virginia early in the war and was with J.E.B. Stuart at Brandy Station and Gettysburg, commanded Company E. He had been at home, recuperating from wounds, when called for reserve duty.

These companies were all in Harper's brigade, and another brigade of reserves was improvised under the command of Gen. William H. Harman. Both men were combat veterans of the Mexican War and had been generals in the Virginia militia. Harman had also seen action at Manassas as colonel of the 5th Virginia.[12]

Imboden continued to appeal to Lee for help. He telegraphed, "Is it possible for you to give additional aid to the Valley?" On June 3, Lee replied, "Gen. W. E. Jones is, I hope, by this time with his troops in Staunton."[13] Indeed, Jones arrived late Friday afternoon and hurried to the North River.

Capt. James F. Jones had organized the hundred thirty miners in his Niter and Mining Corps into two companies, one under Capt. W. L. Clark and the other under Quartermaster Capt. F. P. Clark. Upon their arrival in Staunton the men drew old smoothbore muskets without bayonets or cartridge belts from the old depot in Staunton and marched that night to join Imboden. Meanwhile, Imboden also received word that Brig. Gen. John Crawford Vaughan was on his way with a brigade of Tennessee mounted infantry.

Bryan's artillery detrained at Staunton, but their horses had not yet arrived over the macadamized pike from Bristol. Horses were impressed, harness fitted and singletrees devised. Soon they, too, were on their way.

While Imboden was busy patching together his force, McNeill kept him informed of the enemy's strength with fair accuracy.[14]

As squads of laborers erected breastworks along the rain-swollen stream and trees were strewn across all possible crossings, Imboden posted his artillery at defensive positions. At the centerpiece of Imboden's line was

Marquis's Boys Battery, sixteen to eighteen year olds equipped with enormous field guns, including a twenty-four-pound howitzer and a twenty-pound Parrott rifle planted at the bridge in Mount Crawford.

On Friday night, with the expert help of his adjutant, Capt. Frank B. Berkley, Imboden began organizing his troops into two brigades. Jones's troops, who had not been organized above company level as they rushed to the front,[15] formed the nucleus of the first brigade under the command of Col. Beuhring H. Jones of the 60th Virginia. It also included the 60th and 36th Virginia Volunteer Infantry regiments and a regiment of convalescents, guards and detailed men. The second brigade, commanded by Col. W. H. Browne of the 45th Virginia, consisted of the 45th Virginia Volunteer Infantry Regiment and Lt. Col. H. M. Berkley's 45th Battalion Virginia Volunteer Infantry, plus two regiments of reserves. A reserve division of seven hundred men from miscellaneous groups was placed under the command of Lt. Col. Charles Robertson.

In addition to McClanahan's six guns and Marquis's two, Bryan had four long-range guns—a twelve-pound howitzer and a three-inch bronze rifle. The artillery was further supplemented by thirty Maryland cannoneers released from the defenses of Charleston, South Carolina.[16]

Coming from Staunton, Grumble Jones arrived at Imboden's headquarters, the home of Mrs. Robert Grattan, before sunrise and, as the ranking general, at once approved the organization set up by Imboden. Although Jones was in command, Imboden held considerable influence because of his knowledge of the terrain. By mid-morning the miners had arrived and were assigned to the infantry command of Maj. Richard Brewer. Vaughan's Brigade of mixed cavalry and mounted infantry, numbering between five and seven hundred men, appeared about noon, the first meeting between Imboden and Vaughan since the start of the war. Vaughan, who had received his commission a little earlier than Imboden, became second in command. The Tennesseans were placed on the heights overlooking the North River.[17]

The Confederates expected an attack the next morning. The little army, filled with what Imboden described as "a spirit of defiant optimism,"[18] awaited battle.

The Battle of Piedmont

The forty-five hundred Confederates under Jones, Vaughan and Imboden faced Hunter's Union force of more than eleven thousand five hundred. The Southerners had fourteen pieces of artillery, and the Yankees had between twenty-two and thirty-one guns.[1] The Confederates were nonetheless determined to hold out at all costs.

Fully expecting an attack early in the morning of June 4, the Southerners were perplexed at the absence of the enemy on their front. Imboden sent his brother George with the 18th Virginia Cavalry and Peck's and Opie's reserve cavalry companies across the North River to find out what Hunter was doing. As the 18th rode along, they ran into increasing numbers of enemy scouts offering serious opposition. Before noon, as the cavalry skirmished north of the river, pickets brought news of Hunter's army moving in three columns toward Port Republic by way of Cross Keys. It was clear now that Hunter was attempting to outflank the little Confederate army.[2]

Jones and Imboden consulted regarding the change of events. Since Imboden knew the area, Jones consented to allow him to select the site where they would battle Hunter. Imboden chose an eminence known as Mowry's Hill, three miles south of New Hope and eight miles northeast of Staunton.[3]

The 18th continued to scout north of the river while the remaining cavalry rode eastward, leaving the artillery, Vaughan, the reserves and the two infantry brigades with Jones to occupy Mowry's Hill. Imboden led his cavalry to picket the fords and harry the enemy flanks, thereby delaying the federal advance by forcing early deployment. That afternoon, Imboden and Jones rode together for a few miles along the Valley Pike, then Imboden left for Mount Meridan to find the enemy. Jones halted near Mount Sidney and dispatched Opie's and Peck's companies across Middle River toward the village of Piedmont, which was just north of New Hope.

That evening, Jones's men rested in their camp along the Valley Pike. The horses for Bryan's Artillery arrived, but it was too late to change the harness and gear of the caissons. The impressed horses were kept with the guns, and the veteran horses held in reserve. During the night a courier arrived at Jones's camp with a telegram from Gen. Lee, which Jones read and then thrust into his pocket without divulging its contents. Pickets were posted as the camp slept. They were to be on the march an hour before dawn.

Meanwhile, Imboden had shifted his cavalry east of Middle River. The 18th had been recalled to the south bank of North River, and all of the fords picketed. That night, Imboden's scouts reported that Hunter was in

Port Republic and that his engineers were laying a pontoon bridge across North River. The 18th camped the night of June 4 at Bonnie Doon, the Crawford farm, a mile south of Mount Meridan. The remainder of the cavalry bivouacked near New Hope, a few miles out. Imboden set up pickets just north of Mount Meridan at a crossroad on the Alex Givens farm. He had orders to avoid a risky encounter but to do everything possible to delay the enemy advance.[4]

Before dawn, while the 18th was eating breakfast, Jones's infantry forded Middle River. The 18th mounted up and galloped toward the sound of firing north of them. They met the pickets fleeing from a horde of Union horsemen. They drove the enemy back and took up a position along the high ground to the right. Dismounting behind a rail fence, they prepared to receive an attack from the seasoned 1st New York Cavalry, which was covering Hunter's advance.

The New Yorkers had marched out of Harrisonburg on Saturday morning and brushed aside pickets at Mount Crawford. At Port Republic they had captured thirteen wagons and burned a large woolen mill.[5]

Stirred by the success of their initial attack, the 18th plunged northward. The 1st New York, now reinforced by the 21st New York Calvary, combined to push the 18th back. Frank Imboden and his company were cut off from all support, overpowered, and the whole company captured.[6]

The encounter of the 18th Virginia with the 1st New York Cavalry was the prelude to battle. The enemy's advance had been slowed by inexperienced engineers building a pontoon bridge across the river, but du Pont's artillery and some cavalry had found a ford a mile west of Port Republic and crossed there. The remainder of Hunter's army awaited completion of the bridge before crossing the swollen stream.

Reinforcements continued to swell the federal ranks. The 1st New York (Veteran), 1st Maryland, 14th Pennsylvania and 15th New York cavalries, plus the 20th and 22nd Pennsylvania, joined in the assault on Imboden's cavalry. Together they drove the 18th back through Mount Meridan for almost a mile before the Confederates were reinforced.[7]

Imboden personally led his troops and ordered their withdrawal. He barely escaped capture by leaping his horse over a fence and dashing down a side lane toward the river. The enemy could not pursue him, and he soon rejoined his men at Bonnie Doon, where they made a stand along the road. Davis's Battalion of Marylanders, with Capt. Harnsberger's old men and Capt. Chrisman's young boys, rode up from the south and joined the 18th. A few miles to the south the 23rd Virginia Cavalry heard musketry and sped northward.

Captains Opie and Peck were near Piedmont when they heard the roar of cannons. The reserve officers ordered their men to eat a hasty breakfast and saddle up. A courier from Imboden caught up with them, and they joined the 23rd. Approaching the sound of combat, Opie took command of Peck's company and dismounted them, leaving one in every four to hold the horses, before marching them into battle.[8]

The Confederates deployed behind a rail fence parallel to and on the edge of a thicket. The rapid fire of Opie's men and the reckless charge of Harnsberger and Chrisman, followed by a surge of the 23rd, drove the enemy back. Several charges by the Union troops were repulsed until the Federals moved on the right flank. The Confederates fell back to a new position on a thinly wooded height, as the federal assaults continued, each one increasing in strength.

Imboden could now see long lines of infantry and several pieces of artillery moving toward his position. He quickly sent word to Jones, requesting that an artillery section and five hundred infantrymen be brought to his assistance, as soon as possible.

The reinforcements arrived in less than an hour, including Carter Berkley's section of two guns from McClanahan's Battery, sent on Jones's orders. As they rumbled northward through the little village of Piedmont, shouting and singing, they were cheered on by women who stood on their porches and waved to them.

Increasing pressure pushed Imboden back to a new stand above Crawford Run, barely a mile from Jones's line. Berkley planted his two guns overlooking his front, supported by Opie's cavalry on a rocky bluff beside the road. His first shot knocked out a gun in Capt. Chatham L. Ewing's Union battery. Another shell ripped through the Yankee cavalry. For a half hour Berkley's guns blasted away, until a ten-gun barrage from du Pont's artillery forced them back.[9]

During the artillery duel, Imboden was puzzled at the celerity with which the reinforcements had come. It was physically impossible to ride from Mowry's Hill to his position south of Mount Meridan in such a short time. Riding to the rear in an effort to find Jones and confer with him about the developments, he found Jones not at Mowry's Hill, where they had agreed to make their stand, but much closer, at Piedmont. This position offered the Confederates very little advantage, and Imboden told Jones so. "We have no advantage of ground, and he outnumbers us nearly three to one and will best us."[10] When Jones replied that he did not want any advantage of ground because he could whip Hunter anywhere, Imboden countered,

> General, I will not say you cannot whip him here, but I
> will say, with the knowledge I have of his strength, that
> if you do, it will be at the expense of a fearful loss of life
> on our side, and believing we have no right to sacrifice
> the lives of our men where it is possible to avoid it as it is
> now, if you will even yet fall back to Mowry's Hill, I enter
> my solemn protest against fighting here today.[11]

At Jones's retort of "Sir! I believe I am in command here today," Imboden returned, "You are, Sir, and I now ask your orders and will carry them out as best I can; but if I live, I will see that the responsibility for this day's work is fixed where I think it belongs."[12]

The Confederate line was set by this time, for in less than an hour the two armies would be locked in combat. While the cavalry fell back once more, Jones and Imboden rode in front of their troops in the Confederate position along the road that led to the Finley house. Before leaving for their tour, Jones ordered his staff to remain under cover, saying in a jocular tone, "Gentlemen, I don't want any of you killed, and I don't want to be killed myself."[13]

From their barricades of rail fences, the Confederate infantry cheered their commanders who rode parallel with their lines. When they emerged from a clump of trees five hundred yards from the road and were fired upon by the federal batteries, the two generals rode rapidly back to their lines. Jones stopped in front of the troops and directed them to "aim low, boys, and hit 'em below the belt."[14]

Berkley had retired; the forward section of Bryan's Battery was on the left, near the river, firing upon any target in range. The two companies of miners, moving forward almost a mile ahead of the main line in support of the battery, held the line for an hour before being assailed by the federal cavalry. The Yankees drove back Bryan's guns and forced the miners to retire behind the rail fence to the left of the 36th Virginia.

All of Jones's troops were in position on the heights by now, with the rail fence sheltering the infantry. The reserves were spread out along the crossroads leading from Piedmont to the Valley Pike. Vaughan moved to the right of the east road, which connected Port Republic to Staunton, leaving a gap of several hundred yards between his left flank and the infantry's right flank. Jones ordered Imboden to move to the right of Vaughan and keep watch on any movement that might threaten the right flank or rear.[15]

Imboden's impassioned warnings against this weak position had had no effect on Jones, and this was where the battle must be fought. In Imboden's words, "his over-confidence had led him into a grave error."[16] The stage was set for one of the worst disasters ever to befall the Confederate army in the Shenandoah Valley.

Confederate Defeat

A light drizzle began to fall as the 18th Connecticut moved across Crawford Run in an effort to flank the Confederate left. They bunched up against the bend in the run just before reaching the Confederate works, and Southern snipers began to pick them off, one by one. This little action was the first of many minor battles to erupt on this day.

By 11:30 A.M. the Confederate line was ready for battle behind the rail fence, with skirmishers out in front, feeling out the enemy. The cavalry remained in position on the right while the artillery unlimbered and took up a firing position. A Yankee shell demolished a house beside McClanahan's Battery, forcing them to abandon their position and retire to the heights south of the village. Bryan's Battery withdrew to a position south of the junction.

Hunter's infantry brigades were lined up below the heights, far to the north. In the distance heavy smoke could be seen from a burning mill at Mount Meridan. Noon was approaching. It was time for the federal assault.[1]

Piedmont was a little village of only nine or ten houses, although several prosperous farms, owned mostly by conscientious objectors who remained neutral during the war, were nearby. Grain and cattle were their principle products. The gently rolling terrain was heavily timbered and drained by numerous rills that emptied into Middle River. The river meandered northwest of the village, bounded by cliff-like banks that protected the Confederate left flank.

Whereas land to the south of Piedmont was timbered, the area to the north contained open clover fields extending for nearly a mile. Vaughan was posted on the north edge of the woods with his horses tethered in the woods behind him, his line extending for half a mile to where it joined Imboden's. The latter's line curved to the right of Vaughan's along the northern fringe of the woods. He had orders to post his flank pickets on

Round Top Hill, east of New Hope. Imboden and Vaughan were to remain on this line until they received further orders.[2]

The reserves and the irregulars were stationed behind the main line of Confederate infantry. Opie's, Peck's and Davis's units served as scouts, snipers, and river guards. Throughout the coming battle, Imboden and Vaughan remained on the right with a gap of several hundred yards between them and the infantry. The Confederate artillery maintained a commanding position with Marquis's Boys Battery, behind the 60th Virginia, covering the gap between the infantry and cavalry. To its right and rear, near the road junction, were Bryan's two short-range guns, with McClanahan's six guns farther to the right. Near Imboden's right wing were Bryan's four long-range guns.[3]

The Confederates faced nine thousand Union infantry, twenty-five hundred cavalry, and five hundred twenty artillerymen stretched across their front. Before noon the rain stopped, and the air was thick and balmy. Enemy troops began to drive in the Confederate skirmishers and assail the rail fence. The Confederate infantry clambered over the rails, taunting their enemy with cries of "New Market."

As the gray line surged down the hill, the Union troops gave way. Capt. du Pont's gunners countered by pouring a withering fire into the Southern ranks, and an attack by the Union infantry was followed by a cavalry demonstration against the Confederate left. The Union artillery blasted great holes in the rail defenses, scattering rails and driving the Southerners back. Marquis's Boys Battery was riddled until forced to retire.[4]

Capt. Bryan detected an enemy flanking movement off to the southeast under the cover of woods. He turned his guns on the ravine through which they moved but was ordered by Jones to direct them back toward the front. A third federal assault was repulsed, and Jones was confident of victory. He sent word to Vaughan to prepare a cavalry pursuit of the fleeing Yankees. The artillery of both sides were particularly effective, inflicting a number of casualties.

The Confederate infantry emerged through the gaps in the rail fence, pursuing the Yankees, and a hand-to-hand fight ensued. Jones sent a courier to Imboden with orders to send Bryan's long-range guns to the front, but the messenger never reached the cavalryman. Jones saw the need to close the gap and brought up the reserves. Hunter interpreted the move as readying for attack and advanced his fresh brigades.

This new assault caught the Confederates by surprise. Du Pont's guns were all in action, shelling the rail fence. Desperately, Jones sent orders for Imboden and Vaughan to charge, but it was too late. The federal line swept on through the knee-high clover, a sudden onslaught that forced Jones to throw all of his troops into action. The reserves fought bravely, yet in the furious, desperate hand-to-hand combat that followed, it took merely a half hour for the Confederate defenses to collapse.[5]

Jones had by no means conceded defeat, however, and rode from unit to unit, toward each new burst of fire, shouting encouragement. In an attempt to stem the Confederate retreat, he rushed his troops impetuously to the front: Carter Berkley's section of artillery and Harper's and Harman's home guard units. There they encountered the 34th Massachusetts, which turned and poured a deadly volley into them. Jones fell, shot through the head, near the spot where Capt. Bryan had observed the flanking movement in the ravine. Grumble Jones was dead before he hit the ground.[6]

Federal cavalry charged over the rails and the Confederates fled in panic. They raced toward the river, pursued by the blue horsemen. The Confederate line was in shambles. Wounded soldiers were strewn over the battlefield, many bayoneted to death by the Northern victors. Great hordes of prisoners were taken. Jones's body was discovered and identified by Yankee soldiers, who found that morning's message from Lee. It had been orders to fight Hunter before he could join forces with Crook.

Confederate casualties amounted to a thousand captured, sixty wounded, six hundred killed and a thousand small arms captured. No artillery was lost, thanks to the fresh horses held in reserve. Federal losses were estimated at a hundred fifty killed, six hundred fifty wounded and seventy-five missing.[7]

The battlefield itself showed the ravages of the battle. Limbs were torn from large trees. The clover and wheat had been trampled to the ground. The green corn in the bottom along the river had been cut down as if by a scythe.[8] The devastating battle was over.

The Fall of Staunton

Imboden and Vaughan watched the Confederate army dissolve into a mass of fallen, fleeing, and surrendering men. The two generals conferred, unsure as to what should be done next. Imboden suggested falling back to Mowry's Hill, but Vaughan felt that it was futile to attempt further resistance. He outranked Imboden, so it was decided to attempt an orderly retreat. Since Imboden was familiar with the area and the terrain, Vaughan deferred to him on the details of the withdrawal.

Vaughan was to lead the retreat south to New Hope, with Imboden following and covering any federal attempt to attack. The men were mounted and moving in less than ten minutes, and all of the wagons and artillery were moved safely from the field. One section of Bryan's artillery, completely cut off from the remainder of the army, moved unprotected along the Valley Pike but soon caught up with the Confederate ambulances full of wounded. The artillerymen helped to fix a broken wheel on one of the ambulances, then proceeded to Staunton. The miners were the last to leave the field, joining Vaughan on the withdrawal.[1]

Imboden posted Davis and Opie at the church in New Hope to halt the refugees from the battle and group them for the retreat to Fishersville. Vaughan sent a courier with a telegram to Gen. Lee with news of the defeat, stating, "I will try to protect Staunton, but unless reinforcements come at once, I cannot do it." Farmers serving with the reserves hurried home at once to drive off their livestock for protection before the federal invasion.[2]

Well into Sunday night, the Confederate troops plodded into the town of Fishersville, the head of the column arriving at 9:00 P.M. While the army bivouacked along the Staunton-Waynesboro Road southwest of the village, Vaughan set up his headquarters at the Schmucker house and sent news of the disaster at Piedmont to Col. Lee at Staunton. Vaughan's official report of the battle, sent to Secretary of War James A. Seddon, read, "Artillery and wagon trains safe. . . .The enemy is pursuing. . . .Staunton cannot be held."[3]

Imboden arrived at Fishersville around 11:00 P.M. The two generals telegraphed Richmond, requesting a copy of the telegram Lee had sent to Jones earlier that morning. When the duplicate telegram arrived in a half hour and revealed that Lee had no reinforcements available, Vaughan was convinced that Staunton must fall and decided to have his forces fall back through Waynesboro to Rockfish Gap, west of Charlottesville. Before long most of Jones's surviving infantry units had reached Fishersville. The strength of Vaughan's force now numbered less than three thousand.

Lt. Col. Charles O'Ferrall arrived at midnight, and Vaughan entrusted him with a note to Hunter requesting the bodies of Jones and the other Confederate officers. O'Ferrall set off for Piedmont with an ambulance and three soldiers.[4] When his small party reached Mowry's Hill and saw a squad of Union cavalry, O'Ferrall ran up a white flag and rode down to meet the Yankee cavalry leader, Maj. Charles G. Otis. O'Ferrall's request to deliver the note personally to Hunter was denied, but Otis sent a courier with the message. An hour and a half later, Hunter returned a curt note refusing to deliver the corpse.

Again O'Ferrall insisted, and again a courier rode off. While O'Ferrall and Otis sat under a tree awaiting Hunter's reply, an old man, George W. Mowry, rode up and demanded that the Yankee prisoners be hanged. When he was told of the result of the battle and the circumstances under which the meeting on his land was taking place, he rode off in terror. Another hour and a half passed before a preemptory reply from Hunter arrived, stating that all "Rebel" dead were buried and all wounded were being cared for. O'Ferrall bade Otis farewell and returned to Rockfish Gap empty-handed before sunset. Originally buried where he fell, Jones's body was moved after the war to Old Glade Springs Church in Washington County, Virginia, and laid to rest beside his wife.[5]

Imboden had established an intricate signal system in the Valley, to be used to alert Staunton by midday of the battle's progress. As Col. Lee had no troops with which to defend Staunton, other than a few quartermaster troops, he had all available wagons and freight cars loaded with all that could be salvaged. Nine hundred sacks of salt, leather, office papers, ammunition, bank valuables, official records, and other valuables were hurriedly shipped off. On Sunday night, word of the rout and Jones's death reached Staunton. The wagon trains from Staunton started down the Greenville Road toward Lexington, and the rail cars were sent to Lynchburg. Col. Lee remained in control, but few slept at Staunton that night.

Just after midnight on Monday, June 6, Secretary Seddon telegraphed Gen. Braxton Bragg for confirmation or denial of the rumor of defeat at Piedmont. The Confederate authorities in Richmond expressed surprise at the fact that Imboden—who most considered to be the most able—was not in command in the Valley. Seddon wanted to know what could be done to stop the advancing enemy, to which Bragg replied that no force was available to assist the Valley.[6]

On the afternoon of June 6 Hunter entered the town of Staunton, a prize that had eluded the Federals for three years. The arrogant Union victor seemed oblivious to the beautiful town's gentle rolling hills and hundred-year-old homes. He ignored the stately Augusta Female Seminary and was blind to the simple majesty of Staunton's churches.

Instead, Hunter saw a hotbed of Confederate activity—the railroad, arsenals, factories, supply depots and prisoner of war camps must all be destroyed, and the foul secessionists and slaveholders who built and supported them must be made to suffer.

As more than ten thousand Yankee soldiers surged into the narrow, dusty streets, shots rang out. The streets echoed with the shouts and cheers of federal soldiers. Somewhere in the distance a military band played "Hail Columbia." Hunter and his staff met with Maj. Nicholas Trout and a number of prominent citizens at the Virginia Hotel, where Stonewall Jackson had his headquarters in 1862. Hunter told them that he would confiscate or destroy all military supplies and would torch all factories, shops and storehouses. He then warned the residents, with a smile, that "some disorder" could be expected.[7]

On June 7 the destruction began bright and early, and by mid-morning a pall of black smoke hung over the town. Troops wielding torches and explosives set fire to the woolen factory of Crawford and Young, the Staunton Steam Mill, the distillery, all government workshops, stables, forage sheds, the railroad depot, twenty-six rail cars, the arsenals, the stage depot, the flour mill and the shoe factory.[8] On Hunter's specific orders, troops destroyed all of the town's firefighting equipment.

A frenzy of destruction and looting followed as a mob of federal soldiers, former slaves and camp followers broke into the stores. Blankets, shoes, clothes, saddles, tobacco and food were stolen. Soldiers under orders of the provost marshal rolled confiscated barrels of apple brandy into the street and broke them open. The liquor cascaded over the cobblestones and rushed into the gutters, picking up papers, horse dung and dead rats. Nevertheless, dozens of Union soldiers fell to their knees and drank greedily as the concoction flowed along.[9]

Hunter burned private homes, private stores and shops—whatever he felt needed to be destroyed. He sought out Imboden's home but spared it when he found that it had been recently purchased by a Union sympathizer. His cavalry visited every home in town, cleaned out every pantry and ran off or killed all of the livestock. From June 8–10, the destruction continued. The Federals confiscated twenty barrels of flour, ten barrels of meal, six hundred sacks of salt, a hogshead of sugar, five bales of cloth, eight bales of yarn, a thousand wooden buckets and fifty wagons, plus miscellaneous saddles, spurs, horseshoes, clothing, harness, spikes and shovels.

The three-story building housing the Staunton *Spectator* was gutted, and, as in Harrisonburg, the press and type were thrown into the street. Stolen furniture and more than a thousand confiscated private firearms were dumped into a pile and burned.[10] Railroad tracks were torn up as far as Goshen, and the bridges at Swoopes, Craigsville and Goshen were burned. Many culverts and smaller bridges were destroyed. East of Staunton the tracks were torn up as far as Christian's Creek, and the rails were bent around trees. The bridges at Christian's Creek and Fishersville were burned.[11]

The mayor and all leading citizens were arrested, while all of the wounded Confederate soldiers were forced out of their beds and thrown into the streets. The jails were opened, and military and civilian criminals of every sort joined the mob, free to destroy, pillage and even murder under the relaxed gaze of the Union soldiers.[12] Two of the Union officers who oversaw the shameful destruction of Staunton were future presidents of the United States—Col. Rutherford B. Hayes and Lt. William McKinley.

"Many women look sad and do much weeping over the destruction," wrote one Yankee soldier. "We feel that the South brought on the war and the State of Virginia is paying dear for her part."[13]

At noon on June 8 Crook and Averell joined Hunter at Staunton. They agreed to march upon Lynchburg by way of Lexington. On June 7 Grant had dispatched Maj. Gen. Phillip Sheridan to meet Hunter at Lynchburg, but Sheridan took a circuitous route and would be defeated on June 12 at Trevillian Station, Virginia.[14]

Hunter left Staunton on June 10 to march toward Lexington, leaving the residents without arms with which to protect themselves. With no law enforcement, marauders roamed unchallenged and gangs of freed slaves plundered openly. Women and children huddled behind locked doors in fear.

Two days later Confederate forces reoccupied Staunton,[15] but the crown jewel of the Shenandoah Valley would never regain its former importance to the Confederacy.

Slowing Hunter's Advance

Imboden and his associates had held Hunter's force in Augusta County while Lee repulsed Grant at Cold Harbor, and the battle of Piedmont had bought precious time for the Confederates, permitting reinforcements from Lee's army to reach Lynchburg, where they hoped to head him off.

The battle had cost the Yankees dearly in arms and supplies, but even more damaging was the loss of many lightly guarded wagons to Mosby's Partisan Rangers.

Breckinridge, who had been badly injured in a fall from a horse shot from under him on June 3 at Cold Harbor, arrived at Rockfish Gap on June 8 with a small force. Upon his arrival, Breckinridge assumed command and immediately began preparing for the defense of Lynchburg. John McCausland and his brigade of cavalry were ordered to keep in front of Hunter and delay and harass him as much as possible.[1] Generals Wharton and Vaughan were assigned to work out the details of the army's march to Lynchburg. On June 9, before leaving Rockfish Gap, Breckinridge delivered a powerful oration before his assembled troops.[2]

Hunter's army left Staunton on June 10, with Crook, Averell and Sullivan taking different routes along the western base of the Blue Ridge. General Alfred Duffié took his brigade east of the mountains into Nelson County, where he was to destroy the Orange and Alexandria Railroad and damage the military stores at Amherst Court House before advancing to the James River. Duffié's raiders took the Waynesboro Pike toward the Tye River Gap, leaving Staunton at 3:00 A.M. and demonstrating against Imboden and Vaughan's infantry defending Waynesboro. Part of Duffié's force pinned down the Confederates, which allowed the main force to proceed unmolested. They reached the gap by nightfall and crossed the mountains the next day.[3]

Because of the arduous service they had seen lately, only four hundred troops were available to Imboden[4]—badly mounted and armed—yet he hurried to stop Duffié. The citizens of Nelson and Amherst counties had never had the enemy in their midst, and his arrival caused a great deal of concern.

Duffié sent his force to Arrington to destroy the O&A depot. A Confederate artillery unit at Amherst Court House was warned by the citizenry, and Capt. Henry C. Douthat led his hundred-man Botetourt Artillery on a commandeered train to within six miles of Arrington. The Confederates hoped to reach the bridge over Tye River before the Federals could burn it. The Union cavalry encountered Douthat and withdrew after a brief skirmish, mistakenly thinking that they had encountered a large infantry force, and the bridge was saved.[5] Imboden continued to harass and slow Duffié's advance all the way to Lynchburg, engaging them in small skirmishes along the way.[6]

Alone in the Valley and lacking the men for a frontal assault, McCausland had little success as he tried to slow Hunter's advance. By nightfall on June 10 Hunter was within ten miles of Lexington. As Hunter skirmished with McCausland the next day, the Confederates fell back on Lexington and burned the bridge over the North River to slow the Yankee advance. Confederate artillery positioned along the river shelled Hunter as he approached, and Confederate sharpshooters fired upon the advancing Union troops from the roof of V.M.I. By mid-afternoon, facing overwhelming odds, McCausland and the V.M.I. cadets abandoned Lexington.

With the fall of Lexington, Duffié returned to Arrington and destroyed the depot there. Duffié was now in front of Lynchburg, whose defenses were under the command of Gen. Francis T. Nicholls. Nicholls mobilized his small defense force of home militia and recruits from the hospitals, and citizens from eighteen to eighty years of age flocked to defend their city. Douthat rushed to join Nicholls, and together they awaited the attack.

However, having been called to Lexington by Hunter, Duffié altered his course. At Piney River Imboden blocked the way, but after a brief encounter, the Federals sidestepped him and moved through White's Gap, reaching Lexington the next morning. Duffie had captured a hundred men and three hundred horses on his raid and had destroyed five miles of railroad and the depot at Arrington. The reconstruction did not take long, though, for the Confederates had the railroad rebuilt in two days.[7]

One of the worst acts against a civilian committed by Hunter happened before he reached Lexington. At Brownsville he hanged old David S. Creigh without benefit of trial, witnesses or council for the "crime" of defending his family from a drunken Yankee soldier in November 1863. Upon returning to his home, Creigh, a highly respectable member of the community, had found the drunken soldier using insulting language to his wife and daughters while rifling through the family's belongings. When he asked the Yankee soldier to leave, the soldier drew a pistol and threatened him. Creigh attempted to defend himself, and the Yankee fired, grazing the elderly man in the face. A struggle ensued, and both men tumbled down the stairs and out onto the portico. A Negro woman who had seen the entire episode handed Creigh an axe with which to defend himself. After dispatching the robber, Creigh buried the body, and nothing was said of the matter until Hunter arrived.[8]

At Lexington Hunter continued the burnings he had begun at Staunton, igniting mills, furnaces, storehouses, granaries and all the farm tools and machinery that he could find in the town and surrounding countryside. He burned the Virginia Military Institute and all of the professors' houses save the superintendent's, where he established his headquarters. He originally intended to burn Washington College, but yielded to the pleas of the trustees to respect the honor of the father of his country. He opted instead to destroy the philosophical and chemical apparatus, the libraries and all of the furniture. He reneged on a promise made to Mrs. Letcher to save the home of Governor John Letcher, and many other private stores and homes were ravaged by his fires. Capt. Matthew White, formerly of the Rockbridge Cavalry, was arrested at his home and shot without a trial. In all, the destruction to private property alone amounted to more than $2,000,000.[9]

Hunter's destruction of private property with no military value elicited the disgust of some of his own men. Union soldier William Stark described the ransacking of an occupied Southern mansion:

> From top to bottom they took clothing, plates, and money and destroyed much that was of no use to them. They played upon the piano and then pocketed the keys. I was disgusted with the whole affair. Hunter burned country court house records, and set fire to V.M.I. He rubbed his hands together and chuckled with obvious delight: "Doesn't that burn beautifully?"[10]

From Lexington, Hunter proceeded to Buchanan in Botetourt County, where he destroyed the plantation of Col. John L. Anderson, burning the magnificent mansion for no apparent reason. From Buchanan he marched to Lynchburg by way of the Peaks of Otter.[11] When he arrived in Lynchburg, he found Imboden waiting for him.

The Battle of Lynchburg

On the day that Hunter left Lexington, June 14, Lee sent Jubal Early from Richmond with the entire II Corps, some eight thousand men, to repulse the Yankee invaders. Early reached Charlottesville on June 16, where he received word from Breckinridge that Hunter was in Bedford County, only twenty miles from Lynchburg.[1]

Breckinridge had reached Lynchburg on June 15, and the citizens of the city had rushed to cheer him and his troops. One resident recorded that "it was a reassuring sight, and never were a lot of bronzed and dirty looking veterans, many of them bare-footed, more heartily welcomed."[2] Breckinridge himself was in poor physical condition. Still crippled by his injury at Cold Harbor, he was running a high temperature.

Early wanted all available trains on the O&A Railroad routed to Charlottesville to transport his troops to Lynchburg. He sent word to Breckinridge, saying, "If you can hold out until morning and the railroad does not fail, all will be well."[3] Confined to his bed, Breckinridge transferred command of his troops to Vaughan.

It was a hot, dusty day as Hunter advanced upon Lynchburg. After passing through Liberty, he divided his army into three parts. Duffié, with the cavalry, took the Forest Road, while Crook took most of the infantry over the Virginia and Tennessee Railroad, tearing up track all along the way. The remaining troops followed Averell along the Salem Turnpike.

Averell easily pushed McCausland aside in his advance, but the latter resolved to make a stand at New London. Earlier that day Imboden had arrived in Lynchburg and reported to Breckinridge, who sent him to McCausland's relief. He joined McCausland at New London with two thousand additional troops, and their combined forces stopped Averell in his tracks. At nightfall Sullivan's division arrived to Averell's relief, and they advanced to attack. In the face of the superior Union force, the Confederates fell back to a better position and pitched camp. That night Hunter arrived at New London, determined to take Lynchburg before Early could reinforce it.[4]

In Lynchburg, Breckinridge had found Confederate generals Daniel Harvey Hill and Harry Thompson Hays convalescing in one of the city's hospitals. Since he was still incapacitated, Breckinridge asked the two to plan for defense of the city. The generals set about at once, preparing redoubts and trenches along its the western edge. Soldiers and civilians alike rimmed the hilltops. The city was as ready as possible for a Yankee attack.

As the morning dawned and the anxiously awaited trains arrived in Charlottesville, Early loaded Stephen Dodson Ramseur's Division and one brigade of John Brown Gordon's Division on the first train. The remainder of Gordon's Division and Robert Rodes's Division were ordered to march along the tracks to meet the train on the return trip. Early telegraphed

Breckinridge from Charlottesville at 7:30 A.M., advising that his corps would be in Lynchburg after noon.[5]

Meanwhile, Imboden and McCausland battled Hunter's advancing troops along the Salem Turnpike. They retreated before the federal advance for several miles before making a stand only eight miles from Lynchburg. At 10:00 A.M., Averell struck at the Confederates on the Samuel Miller farm. As the Southerners withdrew, federal troops ransacked the home. Now only a few hours from Lynchburg and believing the city to be poorly defended, Hunter slowed his advance.

At 1:00 P.M., the remainder of Early's troops arrived in Lynchburg. Hanging to the sides and tops of the rail cars, the Confederate soldiers were greeted by citizens of the city who were wild with joy. Two hours later, when McCausland left Imboden to check Duffié's advance along the Forest Road,[6] Imboden decided to make a stand at an old stone Quaker meetinghouse only four miles west of College Hill.[7] Averell was the first to come in contact with Imboden's small force. After bitter fighting, Averell withdrew. Crook then came up with two brigades of infantry, but Imboden gave stubborn resistance until du Pont's artillery was brought into action.

Early and D.H. Hill rode out to the meetinghouse where they found Imboden about to give way in the face of the Yankee onslaught. Early described the action:

> Two brigades of Ramseur's division arrived just in time
> to be thrown across the road at a redoubt about two miles
> from the city, as Imboden's command was driven back by
> vastly superior numbers. These two brigades, with two
> pieces of artillery in the redoubt, arrested the progress of
> the enemy, and Ramseur's other brigade and the part of
> Gordon's Division which had arrived, took position on
> the same line. The enemy opened a heavy fire of artillery
> on us, but, as night soon came on he went into camp on
> our front.[8]

Shells could be seen exploding in the air at College Hill while the Federals fought Imboden from the beginning of the engagement until late twilight.[9]

When Early arrived at the meetinghouse, he had personally led Ramseur's troops into battle. Riding at the head of the advancing troops, he was heard to cry out to the Yankees: "No buttermilk rangers after you now, damn you!"[10] His reference was to a popular song of the period that described a disconsolate soldier who wanted to go home as a buttermilk ranger. Early's slur was an unfair slap in the face to Imboden's hapless troopers who had delayed Hunter's advance and held against Averell's more numerous and better-armed troops. It typified his unwarranted disdain of the cavalry.

While Imboden thus battled with Hunter, McCausland had his hands full with Duffié, whose Yankee troops pushed into the city limits and burned the Forest Depot. McCausland fell back in the face of superior numbers as night fell.

That night Hunter set up his headquarters at Sandusky, the home of Maj. George C. Hutter, a retired U.S. Army paymaster, while his main force bivouacked near the stone meetinghouse. Hunter had known Hutter before the war and treated him courteously. That night, when Hunter learned that Lynchburg had been reinforced, he reconnoitered the lines himself. The Confederate soldiers likewise stayed busy all through the night, strengthening their earthworks.[11]

The next morning, the Union pickets pushed forward, and their artillery opened up on the Confederate lines. The twenty-eight federal guns were answered by Early's ten cannons, whose gunners were extremely accurate and caused extensive damage. Union advances failed to force their way through Early's strong defenses.

McCausland, meanwhile, had occupied fortified works just beyond Blackwater Creek. He had an enviable position, in which the enemy must cross four hundred yards of open ground before attacking. Federal charges were repulsed, and occasional artillery fire continued until 5:00 P.M. During the night Hunter planned his retreat at Sandusky.[12]

The Confederates sought revenge on Hunter for the atrocities he had committed. Pursuit of the fleeing Yankees resulted in a sizeable fight at Liberty, twenty-five miles from Lynchburg, where Ramseur's Division drove the Federals through the town, leaving their dead in the streets. Yet the pursuit was abandoned, since the Confederate artillery failed to arrive until after dark. Because Imboden's orders had not reached him in time and McCausland took the wrong road, no cavalry took part in the fight.[13]

On the 18th of June, Maj. Gen. Arnold Elzey arrived from Richmond to take command of Breckinridge's infantry and dismounted cavalry, superseding Vaughan. Early restructured the cavalry by organizing Imboden's, McCausland's, Jackson's and Bradley L. Johnson's brigades into a single division under Maj. Gen. Robert C. Ransom.[14]

With Early in the Valley

On the morning of June 19, 1864, the Confederate cavalry again took off after Hunter's retreating army, spending the next three days in vigorous pursuit. A series of spirited rearguard actions took place, yet Hunter's cavalry succeeded in screening the retreat of the Union army.[1]

Believing Hunter's retreat would follow the route over which he had advanced, Early sent Ransom across the Peaks of Otter to intercept him at Buchanan or Fincastle. When they arrived in Bedford they learned that the Yankees were retiring westward, through Salem, toward Buford's Gap, so Ransom led his troops via the Peaks of Otter to Hanging Rock, where they circled to the front of Hunter's force. It took all night.

For more than two hours they stood still, watching the enemy's rapid movements through the gap. Lt. Berkley of McClanahan's Battery, McCausland and Imboden urged the cautious Ransom to attack. Finally he conceded, and Berkley's guns ran forward to fire on the Union column. Eleven Yankee cannons were captured, some fully equipped, while many wagons were destroyed and several horses and men killed.[2]

The cavalry's pursuit of the fleeing Federals continued through the mountains as the Confederates tried to cut them off before they could reach the safety of the western side of the Allegheny Mountains. Imboden followed the retreating enemy as far as Covington before discontinuing the pursuit at Early's orders.[3]

With all Union troops now completely out of the Valley, Early decided to move northward, to threaten the federal capital itself. Imboden led his troopers through Fincastle, Lexington and Brownsburg and met Early at Staunton, where they rested for several days.

During this pause at Staunton, Col. Smith and the 62nd Virginia Mounted Infantry received welcome orders to rejoin Gen. Imboden's command and be remounted. While serving under Breckinridge's command they had seen hard duty, and Breckinridge had been so impressed by their fighting ability that he sought to retain the unit in his command, stating that he "had not served with as gallant a regiment during the war."[4]

When the Northwestern Brigade was reunited, Early gave them an independent assignment: to destroy the B&O bridge that spanned the south branch of the Potomac River. Imboden led his men northward from Valley Mills through Bridgewater on June 28 and on through Dayton to the head of Lost River on the 29th, crossing the mountains by way of

Brock's Gap. On July 3 they reached their objective and found it to be heavily guarded.[5] Nevertheless, the next morning they engaged the Yankee defenses. An unknown diarist with Imboden's cavalry penned, "Morning of the 4 Reached the RR and commenst scrimishing the Yanks got in their Block [house] we cannonaded them with out affect and marched by the X Rd. & go on to B[ath]."[6]

The blockhouse, built following the bridge's destruction the previous summer, prevented the Confederates from getting their artillery into effective range for shelling the bridge. An armored railroad car further protected the strategic bridge. Unable to destroy the bridge itself, they concentrated their fire on the armored car. A well-aimed shot entered one of the portholes, ignited its magazine and caused it to explode.[7] Still unable to ravage the bridge, Imboden led his command eastward along the south bank of the Potomac River, tearing up railroad tracks and wrecking lesser bridges along the way.

On July 5, Imboden fell seriously ill with typhoid fever. As the command continued along in search of Early, his health worsened, and he was unable to continue. On July 7 he turned over command of the brigade to Col. Smith and returned to Winchester to recuperate.[8] The nearly fatal attack of typhoid and its lingering effects would seriously impair his continued effectiveness as a cavalry officer.[9]

While Imboden had been busy with the bridge, Early had crossed the Potomac into Maryland, still heading toward Washington. Bradley Johnson took his cavalry brigade south of Baltimore to burn railroad bridges and cut telegraph wires in an attempt to free Confederate prisoners at Point Lookout, Maryland.[10] Meanwhile, McCausland had entered Hagerstown and Frederick, levying ransoms of $20,000 and $200,000 respectively.[11]

By the time the Northwestern Brigade caught up with Early, his hardened veterans had already won the battle of Monocacy, south of Frederick, against the combined forces of major generals James Ricketts and Lew Wallace. After sharp fighting along the Monocacy River, Early's infantry put Ricketts' infantry into full flight toward Baltimore. The Confederates then poured across an unburnable iron railroad bridge and by 4:00 P.M. had Wallace's army in retreat as well. The Union casualties had been thirteen hundred, the Confederate seven hundred.[12]

The Northwestern Brigade led the advance as the Confederate army moved toward Washington on July 10. They passed through Rockville on July 11, then turned left and advanced through Silver Spring toward Fort

Stevens, the northernmost of the sixty-eight forts and fortified gun batteries ringing Washington.

The scores of huge siege guns outranged the Confederate horse artillery. As skirmishers moved forward, battling with the fort's defenders, a distinguished observer watched the action. President Abraham Lincoln was present among the pensioners, hundred-day volunteers, government clerks and convalescents from the city's hospitals who were manning the fort's guns.[13] As bullets from the Confederates' muskets whistled past his head, the president was persuaded to take cover.

Unbeknownst to the Confederates, the Federals were prepared for the worst. At the Washington Navy Yard ships were waiting under a full head of team to carry Lincoln, the cabinet and federal gold away to safety should the city fall.[14]

When Early arrived on the scene, he observed reinforcements arriving at Fort Stevens and decided to wait until the next day to order a full-scale attack. Weary Confederates hurriedly searched for shade and water. More Union reinforcements arrived during the night, greatly outnumbering the Confederates. With the overnight delay, the Confederate window of opportunity had closed.[15]

Early prepared to withdraw to Virginia. The two forces skirmished throughout the afternoon, but no large-scale Union attack was launched. Soon after dark the Southerners started back up the Seventh Street Pike. They reached Rockville early on July 13, then moved west to Poolesville and south to the Potomac, where the infantry crossed at White's Ford on the morning of July 14. While guarding the ford as the infantry waded across to Virginia, the Northwestern Brigade fought one last skirmish on Maryland soil.

After resting for a day on the Virginia side of the river, Early started his army toward Leesburg. From there they marched through Hamilton and Purcellville, guarded by Bradley Johnson's cavalry. The Northwestern Brigade served as rear guard. On July 16 the wagon train was attacked by some Union cavalry, who broke through Johnson's cavalry. More than sixty wagons were captured, including all twelve belonging to Imboden's brigade. In a letter to his wife, George Imboden pointed out that it was Johnson's troops who gave way, not those of his brother's brigade.[16]

Late that same day Early's army crossed Snickers' Gap and moved to the Shenandoah River. On July 18 a portion of Crook's command attacked the Confederate infantry at Castleman's Ferry and was repulsed with great loss. Part of the 18th and 62nd regiments were attacked the next day at Berry's Ferry by two full brigades of Yankee infantry and six pieces of artillery. Imboden's men were outnumbered at least ten to one yet were able to drive their attackers back to Ashby's Gap after a day-long fight. The Confederates' loss was about fifteen, yet they inflicted a hundred fifty-eight casualties on their enemy.

The Northwestern Brigade marched through Front Royal on July 20 and reached Strasburg the following day. While they were there, Gen. Imboden took back his command. Still very much weakened, he nevertheless was glad to be back with his troops. For two days the brigade remained in camp, recuperating from the vigorous campaign of the past month.

It would prove to be the last break they would enjoy for some time to come.

Against Sheridan in the Shenandoah

The battle-hardened veterans of the Northwestern Brigade had a do-or-die resolve about them. Still partisan rangers at heart, they fought best when on familiar ground. However, the war had taken its toll on these Southern patriots, who were tired, underfed and ill-clothed.

Their commander also showed strains of the long, seemingly endless days of continuous combat, and his recent bout with typhoid fever had left the general pale, weakened and seriously ill. Typhoid fever, an infectious and often fatal intestinal inflammation caused by a bacterium ingested with food or drink,[1] frequently reached epidemic proportions among Confederate troops in Virginia. The disease made its first appearance in the Confederate army in August 1861, and by the summer of 1864 was responsible for a fourth of all the deaths from disease.[2] Given the high fatality rate, it is surprising that Imboden survived to return to his brigade.

On July 24 Imboden's troops were once again thrown into battle, this time at the second battle of Kernstown. In this well conceived and executed assault, Jubal Early was able to drive the foe from Virginia soil. Imboden's troopers pursued the Yankees as they fled through Winchester to Martinsburg. One of the men recounted, "[We] charged them 10 miles, caused them to burn all their train artillery abundance of Provision ammunition."[3] The next day the Yankees retreated into Maryland.

Early's army spent July 27 and 28 destroying the B&O Railroad in the vicinity of Martinsburg. On July 28 Early sent McCausland's and Johnson's cavalry along with all available horse artillery, including McClanahan's battery, on a raid to Chambersburg, Pennsylvania, to collect a ransom. If the ransom were not paid, they had orders to burn the town in response to Hunter's recent fiery raid of the Shenandoah Valley. The raid on Chambersburg was meant to show the Yankees that both sides could operate in this fashion. When the residents refused to pay the ransom, McCausland burned several blocks of the town.[4]

After the burning of Chambersburg, McCausland raided Cumberland, Maryland, before encamping in the mountains near Moorefield. While in camp the Confederates were routed by a surprise attack. Despite a heroic fight, several men of McClanahan's battery were captured. Pvt. Norval Baker of the 18th Virginia Cavalry commented, "Our General Imboden was never surprised. He was one of the best watchers I ever saw, always posted his men well and was always on the lookout."[5]

While McClanahan's battery accompanied McCausland, the rest of Imboden's brigade scouted for Gen. Early. During the first nine days of August they scouted in Berkeley and Jefferson counties and, from information gathered there, reported a massive enemy buildup in the Harpers Ferry area. Early also learned that he was facing a new federal commander—Phillip H. Sheridan.[6]

Grant had appointed Sheridan to command the Union Middle Military Division on August 5 with these orders:

> In pushing up the Shenandoah Valley, as it is expected you will have to go first or last, it is desirable that nothing should be left to invite the enemy to return. Take all provisions, forage, and stock wanted for the use of your command. Such as cannot be consumed, destroy.[7]

Early received reinforcements to counter this new threat, as Fitzhugh Lee's cavalry and Joseph B. Kershaw's infantry division were sent to the Valley.[8] From early August to mid-September there was constant maneuvering by both sides as well as frequent skirmishing and movements by the cavalry. The Confederate cavalrymen rode far, raiding and burning enemy installations. Pvt. Baker recorded:

> The weather was sultry and the dead animals were in all stages of decomposition and millions of buzzards gathered to the Valley. We could always tell when the Yankees

were coming by the birds raising high up and sailing around. It was fight every few days and sometimes every day all summer.[9]

Imboden's first major conflict with the enemy arose on August 11 at Double Tollgate, southeast of Winchester. Imboden and Vaughan ran into a superior enemy force and, after a hard-fought battle, drove them back toward Charles Town.[10] After this sharp fight, Imboden reported to Early considerable accession to the cavalry from Grant.[11] According to Pvt. Baker, "the enemy had about ten to fifteen men to one of us."[12]

Imboden's brigade was posted on the Confederates' extreme right flank at Front Royal, grouped with those of Johnson, McCausland, Jackson and Vaughan into a division under the command of Maj. Gen. Lunsford Lomax. With fewer than seventeen hundred men, Lomax's division continued to operate primarily as individual units under their brigade chiefs. The cavalry still lacked strong discipline and never truly acted as a unified force on the battlefield, but Early lacked the time and aptitude to do much to improve them.[13]

For the next several weeks, the Northwestern Brigade skirmished almost daily, fighting the Union advance as Sheridan moved slowly forward. After a meeting with Grant on September 17 Sheridan laid out his plans to lay "the Shenandoah Valley into a barren waste . . . so that crows flying over it for the balance of this season will have to carry their provender with them."[14]

At dawn on September 19 the Union cavalry splashed across Opequon Creek and pushed through Berryville to the outskirts of Winchester. Imboden's brigade was at Stephenson's Depot, just north of Winchester, when attacked by Averell's Division. For the next seven hours, they fought against overwhelming odds. They were driven back inexorably, yet they made their Yankee opponents pay dearly for every inch of ground. By 4:30 P.M. Sheridan had forced the Confederate defenders into the city of Winchester. He then launched an all-out offensive that broke the Confederate line. The Confederates retreated through Winchester and headed south on the Valley Pike.

Pvt. Baker recalled,

> After fighting all day, we joined up north of Malboro along the Cedar Creek Pike after dark, like many birds calling together. We could hear the boys calling for their companies and regiments, all along the line. They had

been jammed around all day, until companies were mixed
and a soldier would fight wherever he could get in line.[15]

The next morning Early's army continued their retreat southward,
passing through Strasburg before taking up a defensive position on Fisher's
Hill.

From Fisher's Hill to Cedar Creek

The Northwestern Brigade had suffered terribly at the third battle of
Winchester, as had all of Early's army. Many men were missing from the
ranks at dawn on September 20, 1864, leaving Early just ten thousand
men to face Sheridan's thirty-five thousand.

Once again the Northwestern Brigade comprised the extreme left flank
of the Confederate line, which was stretched thin along a four mile front.
The left flank was separated by a small valley from the base of Little North
Mountain.[1]

Sheridan sent Crook with the Federal VIII Corps on a flanking
maneuver against the Confederate left. Crook positioned his two infantry
divisions and three batteries on September 21, and the next day moved
his troops to Little North Mountain. At 4:00 P.M., General Lomax saw
more than five thousand Union soldiers advancing on his thousand-man
division from the woods at the base of the mountain. Outnumbered five
to one, there was little the Confederates could do. Despite their gallant
efforts, Lomax's little command was overrun.

Early's men fought with all they had, but they, too, soon gave way to
superior numbers. Here and there, small groups of Confederates tried to
make a stand but were soon enveloped by the blue mass. Early retreated
on the Valley Pike, stopping at Woodstock at nightfall. Imboden's brigade
spent the night rounding up the horses that had run off at the beginning
of the attack.[2]

For the second time in four days the Confederates had been forced to
abandon the field to the enemy, and again the Northwestern Brigade had
suffered heavily. In the pre-dawn hours of September 23 Early assigned to
them the duty of protecting the right flank of the army as it retreated
southward. Later that day they made a determined stand on Bowman's
Ridge between Forestville and Timberville, holding back a large force of
federal cavalry and allowing Early to get his wagon train safely across the
North Fork of the Shenandoah River.

On September 25, when the Northern cavalry did not press the

Confederate retreat south of the river, Early withdrew another thirty miles up the Valley to the village of Cross Keys. The next day they were forced to move eastward to Brown's Gap when the Union army moved into Harrisonburg. For the next ten days Sheridan used Harrisonburg as his base while his cavalry carried out daily raids in Augusta and Rockingham counties. The greatly outnumbered Confederates could only carry out an occasional cavalry attack on an isolated federal unit.[3]

The devastation of Augusta and Rockingham counties was only a prelude to the wholesale destruction of the Shenandoah Valley. On October 6 part of the Union army fanned out from Harrisonburg across the entire breadth of the Valley. A separate column was sent east of Massanutten Mountain to lay waste to the Page Valley. They moved slowly northward, wantonly destroying everything in their path. Between October 6 and 8 Sheridan's troops burned two thousand barns, seventy-three mills and thousands of acres of corn and wheat and destroyed or drove off thousands of heads of cattle and sheep. An Ohio trooper remarked, "A heavy cloud of smoke hung over the entire Valley like a pall."[4]

The Northwestern Brigade sought to delay the Yankee column in the Page Valley, but there was little the greatly outnumbered troopers could do to retard the federal advance. They could only follow in the wake of this devastation and occasionally strike a blow to the Union rear guard.[5]

On October 13 Imboden's brigade reached Milford, between Luray and Front Royal, and established a strong defensive position with rifle pits and trenches. They remained in these entrenchments until October 18, when Gen. Early instructed Imboden to move to a position near the Valley Pike in the vicinity of Newtown, now known as Stephen's City. This position was in the rear of Sheridan's army, which was now camped along Cedar Creek at Middletown.[6]

At dawn on October 19 Early launched a surprise attack against the federal encampment that drove the Yankees northward, beyond Middletown. There the Federals regrouped, and in the afternoon they launched a counterattack that drove Early from the field.[7]

The battle of Cedar Creek, which had begun as a Confederate success, ended in crushing defeat as the Southerners were driven across the creek and through the town of Strasburg.

Imboden, meanwhile, had led his troopers north from their position at Milford. They marched through Front Royal, driving in the Union forces stationed in their front, then advanced to cut off the federal retreat from

Cedar Creek. They waited throughout the afternoon, but it was not until late in the evening that a courier brought word of the Confederate defeat. Imboden regretfully ordered a withdrawal down the Page Valley.[8]

They rode down the Valley, past the entrenchments of Milford, before finally halting at Luray, where the brigade took up a defensive position guarding the gap leading to New Market. Since the Union army did not pursue them, Imboden led his brigade back to Milford on October 22. Three days later they took position in their previously constructed entrenchments, only to be attacked by a federal calvary force under Gen. William H. Powell, who was attempting to get at Early's flank at New Market. On October 25 and 26 Imboden battled Powell, finally forcing the Yankees to withdraw.[9]

For the next two weeks, they alternated duty with the rest of Lomax's division in guarding the gap, a short period of relative inactivity for the Northwestern Brigade. Yet as the brigade rested, their general's health grew worse. It would not be an easy winter for Imboden or his men.

Reassignment

With the lull in activity, the Northwestern Brigade resumed a routine of scouting and picketing duties in Page, Warren and Rappahannock counties. During this period they focused their attention on a long neglected but extremely vital subject—the desperate condition of their horses. The almost constant campaigning of the previous six months had taken an extreme toll on their mounts. A full seventy-five percent of the 23rd Virginia Cavalry's horses were unserviceable, and other regiments suffered likewise. Unlike his counterpart in the Union cavalry, who was issued a government mount and replacements as needed, the Confederate cavalryman was responsible for obtaining his own horse.

The shortage of serviceable horses had become so critical that the very existence of the Northwestern Brigade was in jeopardy. Gen. Imboden had no alternative but to send the majority of his brigade on a huge horse procurement mission. Capt. Hannibal Hill, a trustworthy veteran of the 62nd Virginia Mounted Infantry, was appointed the leader. Hill led his contingent of three hundred eighty men into Highland County.[1]

When an intensive search failed to locate the needed number of horses there, the bold Capt. Hill decided to get them in a hit-and-run raid against the Union garrison at Beverly in Randolph County. His command was badly outnumbered, so Hill knew that in order to succeed the element of surprise had to be on his side. Keeping to the woods to avoid discovery by Union sympathizers, Hill led his men to within a mile of their objective before sunset.

The Confederates spent a long, cold night without heat or shelter. Shortly before daybreak on October 29 the weary Southerners were awakened from a fitful sleep by the sound of reveille coming from the Union camp. In a matter of minutes the Confederates were on their feet and formed for an attack. A rebel yell resounded as they drove in the federal defenses and charged through the enemy camp, where the attack quickly erupted into hand-to-hand combat. When the Yankees realized how few Confederates had attacked them, the tide of the battle changed. Despite a valiant effort, the Confederates were overwhelmed. They found themselves in a race for survival as they tried to elude the encircling enemy.[2]

The survivors of the fight at Beverly rejoined the remainder of the brigade in time to support Early's advance north from New Market. Imboden's brigade formed a line of battle at Newtown, awaiting a federal attack that never came.

The brigade returned to the Page Valley on November 14 as bad weather set in, ending all campaigning for the winter. In December they suffered greatly from the inclement weather and the lack of forage for their horses. The situation was so desperate that there was talk of disbanding the brigade until spring. To compound their grief, Early, whose dislike for the cavalry was well known, treated them unfairly. When the rest of the army was paid, the cavalry was not. Even more distressing was an instance in which clothing intended for the cavalry was given to the infantry instead; Imboden's brigade receive not a single blanket nor overcoat. Yet despite their treatment, scarcely a murmur could be heard among the men.

In early December Imboden requested a transfer for medical reasons. It was generally believed that spending the winter in the warmer climate of the deep South would speed his recovery and give him a chance to regain his strength. On December 6 he received orders relieving him of command in the Shenandoah Valley and directing him to report to South Carolina for duty with federal prisoners of war.

Command of the Northwestern Brigade was given to the general's brother, Col. George Imboden. Upon learning of their general's departure, the men in the ranks were very upset, but they were convinced that he would return in the spring.[3]

Late in December Imboden left his beloved Shenandoah Valley[4] and travelled over the poor railroads of the Confederacy south of Richmond. On January 4, 1865, he wrote to Gen. Lee concerning the Piedmont Railroad, a subsidiary of the Richmond and Danville Railroad, which he described as "the worst managed railroad on earth."[5] It had taken fourteen hours to make the forty-eight mile trip from Danville to Greensboro, the biggest problem being the wet, green wood used to fuel the locomotive. At one point, he reported, they had to stop and tear down a rail fence to use as fuel.[6]

On January 6 Imboden reached Columbia, South Carolina, where he reported to his immediate superior, Brig. Gen. John H. Winder.[7] A former U.S. Army career officer, Winder had resigned his commission to become provost marshal of Richmond. In 1864 President Davis had given him command over all prisoners of war east of the Mississippi.[8] Winder ordered Imboden to assume command of all Confederate prisons west of the Savannah River with temporary headquarters at Aiken, South Carolina.[9] Although the brave cavalry officer had faced many tough assignments in Virginia, he was now about to embark on the worst duty of all.

The Confederate Prison System

By early 1865 the Confederate economy had nearly collapsed. The South's railroads were breaking down, and many government functions were bogged down as a result. Never very effective at its best, the Confederate commissary system and railroad network had now nearly ceased to function. The Confederate government could no longer feed, clothe or provide for their fighting men, and the situation for troops guarding prisoners and their charges was far worse.[1] Food, water, clothing, shelter and medical supplies were scarce, resulting in cruel suffering and even death.[2]

Prior to the spring of 1864, when the Lincoln government had ended the exchange of prisoners, a parole and exchange system had been established by both governments in the Dix-Hill Cartel of July 22, 1862.[3] This included soldiers captured on the battlefield who could be released upon signing a pledge not to take up arms or offer assistance to his allies. Men actually taken into custody could expect to be swapped in a prisoner exchange where the two governments would trade men rank for rank. Such practices came to a halt because Grant, in his efforts to crush Lee's army, wanted no reinforcements to reach Southern armies through exchange. Lincoln supported his decision. Before long, tens of thousands of federal captives poured into Confederate prisons ill-prepared to receive them.[4]

The Confederacy impressed laborers to improvise shelter for the prisoners. The lack of lumber and building materials drastically slowed construction of new facilities, and overcrowding was a constant problem. Sanitary conditions were less than adequate, leading to polluted streams that served as water supplies and resulting in disease. With no ready supply of doctors, medical attention often was lacking. Food, especially meat, was scarce. The guards were primarily old men, convalescents and young boys.

The worst of the prisons in Imboden's district was Camp Sumter at Andersonville in Sumter County, Georgia. This prison consisted of pine log walls and guard towers surrounding a yard absent of trees, but overflowing with shebangs, makeshift huts fashioned from scrounged shirts, blankets and sticks. Terrible heat compounded the general misery, as did a polluted stream that served both as water supply and latrine. To make matters worse, the prisoners were split into two groups—the Raiders, or bullies who preyed on fellow prisoners, and the Regulators, who tried to protect the weaker prisoners. One inmate observed that "our own men are worse to each other than the rebels are to us."[5]

The commandant at Andersonville was Maj. Henry Wirtz, a native of Switzerland and citizen of Louisiana who left his career as a physician to volunteer for service in 1861. He was wounded at the battle of Seven Pines and lost the use of his right arm. Following a furlough in Europe, he was assigned duty at Andersonville in February 1865.[6]

Other prisons in Imboden's region were at Eufaula, Georgia; Florence and Columbia, South Carolina; Salisbury, North Carolina; and Cahaba, Alabama. There were also temporary holding areas at Thomasville and Blackshear, both in Georgia. All of the facilities shared a lack of wood, water, food and shelter and were plagued by mud, stench and an insufficient number of guards.[7]

Imboden realized the immensity of the task at hand and set about to do the best he could to correct it.

Tackling the Abyss

After a few days with Winder in Columbia, Imboden went to Augusta, Georgia, where he set up an office and installed Lt. George W. McPhail as officer in charge of prompt and convenient communications with all of the prisons in his district. He then returned to Aiken to set up his headquarters. His first official action was to dispatch Lt. Col. Bondurant to inspect all of the prisons in the department with instructions to report on the conditions he encountered.

Imboden was soon forced to flee Aiken as Union general Judson Kilpatrick's cavalry, operating on the flanks of Sherman's army, reached the outskirts of town. Kilpatrick occupied the town less than four hours after Imboden's departure. Imboden established his headquarters at Augusta and found a place to live a few miles out of town at a little place called Berzelia on the Georgia Railroad.

Based on Bondurant's report, Imboden decided to close all but two of the prisons in his department, Andersonville and Eufaula. He believed that two larger prisons could operate more efficiently and economically than several scattered ones.[1]

On February 6 Gen. Winder fell dead from a massive heart attack at the prison in Florence.[2] With no superior officer, Imboden should have reported directly to the secretary of war, but communications were slow and difficult at best, as Sherman's army was moving through Georgia. Imboden tried to establish contact with Richmond, but to no avail. A newspaper that fell into his hands reported that Gen. Gideon Pillow had succeeded Winder, but no official word of this ever reached Imboden.

After receiving a communication from Maj. Wirtz, Imboden decided to visit Camp Sumter, a difficult task as the nearest railroad to Andersonville was more than seventy miles away.[3]

Before leaving Augusta, however, Imboden had to deal with a report from Capt. H.A.M. Henderson, the commanding officer at Cahaba, Alabama, that a mutiny had occurred there on January 20. After rushing the guards and disarming them, the prisoners had held them in the water closets. Two sentinels at the main gate had escaped and sounded the alarm. Other sentries, reserve troops and a piece of artillery had been brought forward to restore order, and when the field piece was brought to bear on the rioters, they had soon quieted down. Rations were being withheld until the ringleaders of the uprising were brought to justice. Imboden ordered a trial for the main conspirator—a Capt. Hanchett, alias George Schellan. He also issued an order declaring that any prisoner confined in Georgia, Alabama or Mississippi who engaged in mutiny or attempt to escape should be fired upon, and that any armed prisoner was to be shot instantly.[4]

Imboden arrived at Andersonville in late February, unannounced and unexpected, and personally made a thorough inspection of the entire camp. What he found was appalling. Clothing, shoes and hats were in short supply. The prisoners' rations consisted mostly of cornmeal and a little bacon. There were absolutely no suitable medicines. The Union government had declared medicine contraband of war, and the blockade of Southern ports had effectively shut off the importation of it to the Confederacy.[5] The mental condition of the prisoners was poor, and thousands crowded around Imboden eager for information regarding exchange.

The guard force consisted of one brigade of Georgia militia under the command of Brig. Gen. Gartrell. The post at Andersonville was commanded by Col. Gibbs, while Maj. Wirtz was in command of the prison. The guards were dressed in rags, most of them barefooted and without overcoats. Some huddled under blankets for warmth. No discrimination in food existed, as guards and prisoners alike received the same daily rations: a third to a half pound of meat (bacon), one to one and a half pints of cornmeal (with salt), and an occasional potato or some wheat flour.

While Imboden was at Andersonville, six Yankee prisoners were detained by the Regulators for taking advantage of other prisoners. Imboden allowed the prisoners to try the offenders, who were found guilty of stealing and cheating. They were sentenced and hanged by their fellow inmates.

During his inspection Imboden was approached by a federal captain who felt that he had some influence in Washington and could possibly effect an exchange if paroled. When the prisoner agreed to return in thirty days if his mission failed, Imboden accepted his offer. The captain managed to get through the lines, but after thirty days he returned without having achieved his goal.[6]

On Wirtz's recommendation, Imboden ordered more shelters to be constructed for the prisoners. A hundred or more prisoners were paroled daily to cut trees from the forest, and log houses with chimneys and floors were constructed. Soon fifteen hundred of the prisoners in the most feeble health occupied these new shelters.

Wirtz informed Imboden that there were many shoemakers among the prisoners, and Imboden ordered a tannery to be built and the shoemakers put to work. Thousands of cowhides were tanned , and in a few weeks many formerly barefooted prisoners were supplied with rough but serviceable shoes. Acting on a suggestion from the medical staff, Imboden allowed the brewing of corn beer, which eased the suffering of those with scorbutic taint.[7]

Despite his gallant efforts, Imboden was able to do only a little to improve the lot of the prisoners under his care. Since the prison was cotton country, no wheat, corn or vegetables were readily available. All of the cattle and hogs were gone, and the entire region was destitute of clothing and the material from which to make it. Imboden's only recourse was to find some way to get rid of the prisoners.

The Collapse of the Confederacy

Imboden went from Andersonville to Macon, where he conferred with generals Howell Cobb, the overall commander of Georgia state troops, and Gideon Pillow. Pillow still had not received orders from Richmond appointing him to replace Winder.

Although they had no official communication from Richmond, the three generals agreed to parole the prisoners under their command without exchange if the Federals would accept their offer. They arranged to send the prisoners to the nearest accessible federal post under parole.

Imboden sent fifteen hundred prisoners to Jackson, Mississippi, for Gen. Richard Taylor to deliver to federal authorities. Taylor, commander of the departments of Alabama, Mississippi and Eastern Louisiana in the field, did not want additional prisoners sent to him for fear that they would pick up valuable military secrets along the way that might be used against him in battle.[1]

There was no rail line to Savannah, Sherman having destroyed it on his march through Georgia. The only Union post then accessible from Andersonville was St. Augustine, Florida. The route was by rail from Andersonville to Chattahoochie, by river to Quincy, Florida, by rail to Jacksonville, then an overland march to St. Augustine. When they were within a day's march of the Federals they would open communications with the commander.

In mid-March an officer from Imboden's command was sent to Florida to reconnoiter. In a few days a telegram arrived that read, "Send on the prisoners." All who could bear such a journey were readied. Three days' worth of cooked rations were prepared for the more than six thousand federal prisoners who made the difficult trek. When they reached their destination, however, the commander of the federal post refused to accept the prisoners, stating that he could not take them under control without some sort of official communication from Grant. Since the only line of communication open from Florida to Virginia was by sea, it would take weeks to get such permission, assuming it were granted.

Still acting without authority from Richmond, Imboden had no recourse but to order the prisoners back to Andersonville. Provisions were sent, and in a few days they returned, indignant that their government would turn its back on them in their time of need.

On April 1, 1865, the Confederate Army of Northern Virginia under Robert E. Lee left the trenches at Petersburg, Virginia, where they had been under seige for nine months, and retreated westward through central Virginia, allowing the Confederate capital to fall. Grant's victorious troops entered Richmond close on Lee's heels. The Confederate government fled to Danville, Virginia, where they established a new capital. On Palm Sunday, April 9, with nowhere left to go, Lee surrendered his army to Grant at Appomattox Court House.

Seventeen days later Gen. Joseph E. Johnston surrendered the Army of Tennessee to Sherman in North Carolina. As Union general J. H. Wilson's federal cavalry approached Andersonville from the west, Imboden, not wanting his command to be captured, once again sent his prisoners off to Jacksonville. The post at Andersonville was broken up, and all of the Georgia state troops were sent off to Cobb at Macon.[2]

On May 3, 1865, Imboden was captured and paroled as a prisoner of war at Augusta, Georgia.[3] Two days later he issued his last order as a Confederate general, paroling all federal prisoners in his department.[4] A few days later he was sent to Hilton Head, South Carolina, with other parolees. There he met more than two thousand former Andersonville prisoners, all of whom were glad to see that Imboden was safe. Four days later he embarked on the steamer *Thetis* for Fort Monroe, Virginia, with several hundred of his former charges.[5]

Still weak and not fully recovered from his bout with typhoid, Imboden started his homeward journey unsure as to what the future would hold.

The Trial of Henry Wirtz

Imboden's first stop on his homeward journey was in Charlotte County, Virginia, where he was reunited with his wife and family. He spent the next several months there, recuperating from the recurring fever and trying to regain his health.

The South had been devastated by the war. All of the banking and financial institutions had collapsed. Industry was nearly at a standstill, as most of the mills and factories had been burned or destroyed. The agricultural base had been destroyed, with the fields overgrown or barren, fences torn down and burned. Livestock had been killed or driven off; the barns left standing were empty.

In addition to the physical effects of the war, the human cost had been enormous. More than ten percent of the adult male population had perished, with countless more left as physical wrecks from wounds, disease or imprisonment. The entire labor system of the South had been disrupted. Relationships between former slaveholders and the newly freed slaves were strained at best. As a result of their abrupt emancipation, the former slaves were forced into a lifestyle for which they were not at all prepared. The economic loss to the South as a result of the abolishment of slavery was tremendous. The South had endured four long years of harsh and relentless warfare; now its citizens were paying the price.

Imboden, a lawyer, fell on especially hard times. Federal troops occupied the South, and military courts replaced civilian ones. Unable to provide a living for his family and in ill health, Imboden's future looked very bleak.

In late August Imboden received a subpoena to testify at the trial of his former subordinate, Maj. Henry Wirtz, in Washington, D.C.[1] Wirtz had been captured on May 10, but instead of being paroled, as were most Confederate officers, he was sent to Old Capitol Prison. On August 23 a military commission was convened by President Andrew Johnson to try Wirtz for alleged war crimes relating to the treatment of federal prisoners at Andersonville.

Two day later a hundred sixty witnesses were called by the prosecution; far fewer, including Imboden, were called by the defense. Wirtz was brought up on thirteen charges that ranged from shooting a prisoner to stomping and kicking prisoners. He was also charged with placing a prisoner in the stocks on August 20, 1864, although he had not been present on that date. Additional charges included personally beating the inmates and ordering guards to shoot them. In nearly every count the name of the prisoner and the date of the alleged crime were missing.[2]

The main witness against Wirtz was a former prisoner by the name of Felix de la Baune, who had received an appointment at the Interior Department just before the trial began. Many former prisoners who asked to testify on Wirtz's behalf were barred from the proceedings.

When Imboden presented himself at the building where the trial was taking place he was treated coldly and ordered to sit in the hallway. After an hour he was dismissed without having a chance to testify on Wirtz's behalf.[3]

On November 11, 1865, Henry Wirtz was hanged. Eleven days after his death the government's chief witness was unmasked as a fraud. Felix de la Baune was discovered to be a federal deserter by the name of Felix Oeser.[4]

Getting on with His Life

Mary McPhail Imboden had never been very healthy, and on September 21, 1865, she died of consumption.[1] Heartbroken, Imboden had little time to grieve. With his children to care for and no visible means of support, he turned to the important task of finding gainful employment.

Near the end of September he received an invitation from an old friend, Michael Harmon, to join in a business venture that would meet the shipping and express delivery needs of the South. With the financial backing and support of Richmond bankers Charles W. Purcell and L. W. Glazebrook, Harmon summoned former Confederates, all of whom needed employment, to Staunton for the organizational meeting.

The meeting continued in Richmond, where Joseph E. Johnston was elected president. The board of directors consisted of Harmon, Purcell, Glazebrook, John Echols of Staunton and Benjamin Hart, a New York businessman. James L. Kemper, an old friend of Imboden, was elected treasurer. Others involved in the company were Patrick Moore, Thomas L. Rosser and John Dooley, all former Confederates.[2]

On November 15 Imboden was elected general superintendent of the company,[3] and before the end of the month permanent corporate headquarters had been established in Richmond. On December 12 the National Express and Transportation Company was incorporated in Virginia to "do an express and general transportation business, by land and by water, for the conveyance of persons and property of every kind throughout or beyond the limits of Virginia."[4] The company's main service was the transportation of small parcels, money orders and letters.

Suddenly a business executive, Imboden was forced to travel to various cities across the nation on business, expanding the line from New York City to St. Louis via Cincinnati and south to Columbia and Charleston. Shares in the company sold well for $100 each. Despite stiff competition from established companies and the railroads, the company was off to a good start. With $9,000,000 in subscribed capital, their business was one of the major corporations headquartered in the South.[5]

On January 30, 1866, Imboden resigned as general superintendent to become the company's chief legal counsel. As such, he was instrumental to the continued success of the thriving business. He would remain with the company for two more years.[6]

During his stay in Richmond Imboden met twenty-five-year-old Edna Paulding Porter, the daughter of Commodore N. D. Porter and Elizabeth Beale and granddaughter of Commodore David D. Porter. On October 2, 1866, she and Imboden were married[7] and established their family home in Richmond. Imboden's children settled well with their new stepmother.

Before long, Imboden again became interested in politics and, on December 18, 1867, accompanied his long-time friend John Howard McCue to a convention to organize a new political party. Former Democrats, Whigs and Know-Nothings were joining together to bring control of Virginia back into the hands of Virginians. Virginia and the South had been ruled by the Radical Republicans since the war, a party of Negroes led by carpetbaggers and scalawags who had adopted a new state constitution and run the state further into debt. The state government under Radical rule had reached new lows of corruption, and leaders like Imboden saw the drastic need for Virginia to return to its prewar greatness, although three more years would have to pass before Virginia could rejoin the Union and bring Reconstruction rule to an end. Imboden was too busy making a living to take an active role in politics, but he did belong to Virginia's Conservative party and supported its candidate.[8]

Virginia established a State Board of Immigration for the purpose of attracting people to Virginia. In 1867 the board appointed Imboden the Domestic State Agent of Immigration, with an office in Richmond and a branch in New York City. In 1869 the name of the agency was changed to Virginia Land and Aid Immigration Company. Six months later, when the emphasis changed from increasing population to land development, the name again changed, this time to Virginia Lands and Southern Real Estate Generally.[9] Imboden's charge was to bring Northern and foreign capital to Virginia for investment in land development, especially the development of natural resources, an area of particular interest to him.

On May 6, 1870, Edna died suddenly and unexpectedly at their home in Richmond.[10] Once again, Imboden found himself a widower with several children to rear. In August 1870, while in Mecklenburg County in connection with a railroad promotion, he met Annie Harper Lockett, the daughter of Howard Lockett and Augusta Harper. Letters of courtship flowed from Imboden's pen, exclaiming how he had been attracted to her since their first encounter.[11] The courtship blossomed, and on March 15, 1871, they were married at her father's estate, Lombardy Grove, in Boydton. The only child of this union, Helen Maguire, was born on May 5, 1874. She brought years of joy to her father.

With his family once again intact, Imboden was about to embark on a new career that would span the next twenty-five years.

Natural Resources and Railroads

As Imboden became more involved in land development, his long-abiding interest in railroads increased. He recognized their value in Virginia's early history, had employed them creatively during the war, and foresaw their increasing importance to the Commonwealth.

The first railroad in Virginia, the Petersburg and Weldon Railroad, was chartered in 1830. By 1840 there were three hundred miles of track employed by various lines including the Winchester and Potomac, which connected the Valley with the B&O at Harpers Ferry; the Seaboard and Roanoke, which ran from Portsmouth to the Roanoke River; the Richmond-Fredericksburg and Potomac, which connected those two cities with the nation's capital; the Louisa Railroad; and the Richmond and Petersburg.

The first train crossed the Blue Ridge mountains in 1849 when the Woodhead Tunnel was completed. In 1858 Claudius Crozet finished his tunnel through the Blue Ridge on the Virginia Central line ,and regular traffic connected east and west. Other railroads were built throughout the state.

In 1860 Imboden had been the first to use a railroad for military purposes when he persuaded the Virginia Central to furnish cars to transport his troops to Richmond for a training exercise.[1] Military use of railroads escalated during the war until they were used extensively by both sides to transport troops and supplies.

As early as 1869, while attempting to market Virginia land, Imboden's interest in railroads came to the fore. He knew that businesses needed reliable transportation to carry people and goods and that the presence of railroads would boost land sales by inducing large companies to invest in Virginia.

As early as 1866, Imboden had shown an interest in mining. Motivated by a flourishing economy, he investigated his product so as to determine how its intrinsic value might be used to generate sales. He became a devoted student of mineralogy and used his knowledge to sell land. In an 1866 letter to James D. Davidson he wrote:

> We are going to wake up that part of Rockbridge in a short time by digging a mint of money out of its hills and mountains. I know of no such opening in Virginia just now for big returns on a comparatively small capital. Won't some of you Lexington gentlemen want to take a little stock in the Rockbridge Mining Company and help develop your county's wealth, and pocket good dividends?[3]

In 1872 he published a book, *The Coal and Iron Resources of Virginia*, that for many years was of great value in assessing the quality, quantity and worth of these two mineral deposits, both of which were critical to the railroad industry. Coal was rapidly replacing wood for boiler fuel, while iron was used for rails, rolling stock and most hardware. Coal also fueled the furnaces that converted ore into pig iron.[2]

In the fall of 1872, Imboden struck out on his own, establishing a land sales office at 902 Main Street in Richmond. He was at the same time involved in several other business enterprises, including the Leheigh Granite Quarry and the Goochland and Pittsylvania Asbestos Mines.[4] Imboden enjoyed working with land and the various rocks and minerals it provided.

Imboden was a good salesman, his native ability enhanced by his magnetic personality and an exhaustive knowledge of his product. He learned more about the resources of the various sections of the state as his knowledge of mineralogy increased, and his legal background was of great value to him in establishing business connections.

In the spring of 1873 Imboden sailed to London to solicit British capital for speculation in Virginia lands, being especially interested in obtaining investment for exploration and development of coal mining in southwest Virginia. He spent several months in London and succeeded in attracting several affluent financiers for his endeavors. Two of these, a Lord Hardy and geologist David Thomas Ansead, along with some monied Pennsylvanians, founded an investment group for coal mining operations called the Gauley Coal Company.

Following his return to the states, Imboden resumed his business ventures from offices he had established in New York City and Richmond.

By the end of 1873 the Gauley Coal Company had acquired the Hawk's Nest Coal Mines, at the time the largest mines to be situated on the Chesapeake and Ohio Railroad, and the Victoria Furnace at Goshen, an important railroad town thirty-six miles southwest of Staunton.[5]

These two operations occupied a great deal of Imboden's time during 1874 and 1875. On October 19, 1875, his old friend and the current governor, James Kemper, wrote that Imboden was better acquainted with the mineral lands of Virginia than any other known person.[6] Indeed, his reputation as a mineralogist was well established, and in 1875 he was elected an honorary member of the Mineralogical Society at Roanoke College in Salem.[7]

As the development of the railroads continued to interest him, Imboden devoted a considerable portion of his time to railroading and the design of useful improvements for the rail industry. On October 23, 1875, the *Scientific American* notified him by letter that his patent for a railway car lifter that was operated by compressed air, readily available from the locomotive, had been approved by the United States Patent Office.[8] He had exhibited his invention in 1874 at the annual fair of the Virginia State Horticulture Society. The lifter provided a way to adjust the wheels on the railway cars so they might be on tracks of different widths or gauges. There was little standardization of railroad track gauges in the early days, especially in the South, and Imboden's invention helped to overcome this stumbling block. This was the first of several ideas that Imboden applied to railroad improvement.

In November of 1875 Imboden delivered a speech to nine hundred delegates at the National Railroad Convention in St. Louis on the connection of coal mining to railroad operation.[9] In fact, coal would be used to fuel steam engines for the next sixty years and more. At the convention Imboden promoted his inventions and encouraged the sale of land.

Appointed by the United States Centennial Committee to serve on the board for Virginia,[10] Imboden looked forward to the International Exhibition of 1876 in Philadelphia. The state board was to present Virginia's products and industry at the exhibition, which would run from May 10 to November 10, 1876, in Philadelphia. He arrived in early April to establish himself in the city and make acquaintances who might aid his railroad and land promotion.[11]

Imboden's agreeable manner, personality and knowledge of Virginia attracted much interest. On April 22, 1876, the Executive Committee of the International Exhibition selected him to serve on the board of judges at the centennial celebration.[12] He was a judge of awards for the full six months of the exhibition, commuting from his home in Richmond to Philadelphia.

On May 22, 1876, Imboden's rail car lifter met with approval from the railroad industry. The C&O and the Clover Hill railroads began to build cars based on his model, and he expected the Philadelphia and Reading to soon follow suit. On July 26, 1876, his car lifter was put on display at the exposition. The B&O and Erie railroads became interested.

Railroads were expanding all over the country. A new development coming into rapid use was the steam-powered streetcar. The first commercially successful line had opened in Philadelphia. Always putting his keen mind to use to dream up innovative new ideas, Imboden conceived a design for a streetcar that used an engine powered by a more efficient steam system.[13]

On October 4, 1876, the Centennial Commission appointed Imboden as one of the marshals of the Centennial National Tournament to be held at the Centennial Grounds on Virginia Day, October 19, 1876.[14] On the closing day of the exposition, the Commission presented him with a special bronze medal for his valuable and efficient service.[15]

In 1877 Imboden became very well acquainted with the city of Pittsburgh, which, as a center of rail transportation, held special appeal for him. He easily made friends there, generally finding the Pennsylvanians willing to invest in land, mines and railroads. While in Pittsburgh he received word that he had been elected vice president for Virginia to the permanent free exhibition in Philadelphia. The exhibition, headquartered in the National Machinist Hall at Fairmont Park, was to continue indefinitely.[16]

Imboden travelled often, mostly by rail, to New York, Tennessee, Pennsylvania, North Carolina and England during 1877. His main purpose was the development of land, mining and railroads.

In 1880 Imboden moved from Richmond to Abingdon in southwest Virginia, a region that held great possibilities for mining and railroads. Abingdon, in Washington County, was situated in the heart of coal and iron country. The town's population had increased from seven hundred fifteen in 1870 to a thousand sixty-four in 1880.

Imboden was the first person to call attention to the vast coal and ore deposits in Dickinson, Russell, Washington and Wise counties, a region with phenomenal natural mineral wealth. To this day vast quantities of coal are mined from these counties. Rich timber and iron deposits also added to the area's attractiveness.

For the area to yield substantial benefit to the state's economy, Imboden knew that a reliable railroad must move its resources to market. He became involved with the Virginia and Tennessee Railroad, which later became the Norfolk and Western. The line was established in 1830, and though it was somewhat damaged during the war, it remained the finest in the region. During the 1880s the line expanded to 1,638 miles of track, and in 1881–1892 it extended three additional lines into the coal fields.[17]

Imboden, whose home was on the main line of the N&W in Abingdon, was primarily interested in the New River branch line. He travelled extensively for the Connellsville Coke and Iron Company, promoting the sale of their product, and did similar service for the Tinsalia Coal and Iron Company as their general agent. He also served as president of the Bristol and North Carolina Narrow Gauge Railway Company, with his main office in Elizabethton, Tennessee,[18] where on July 10, 1883, he was kicked by an ornery horse. Broken bones and a crushed foot incapacitated him for several weeks.[19]

On July 30, 1883, Governor William B. Bates of Tennessee selected Imboden to represent his state at the Louisville and Boston expositions.[20] As the official representative of Tennessee, he was to promote industrial progress for that state. The old general, who thrived on this kind of activity, attended both events.

In 1885 Imboden, still deeply involved in the promotion and expansion of railroads, moved from Abingdon to Bristol. At the request of the United States Bureau of Statistics he wrote an exhaustive study of the mineral potential of Virginia, providing a comprehensive statistical analysis of the state's mineral wealth in a three-hundred-page report. His work proved to be very popular and Congress had twenty-five thousand copies printed.[21] Imboden received widespread recognition as an expert in his field.

He continued to travel widely and almost constantly, visiting Richmond, Washington, Philadelphia and New York City in the spring of 1887. That summer he moved back to Abingdon.

Imboden became president of the Damascus Enterprise Company in March of 1888 and established the Mineral Bureau of Southwest Virginia, East Tennessee and West North Carolina. The purpose of this group was to promote the national resources of Appalachia, especially those of the planned town of Damascus. He had engineered the location and established and developed the entire town by himself. Although the town was still on the drawing boards, the bureau sponsored a railroad line to its proposed site, which was expected to be completed by 1893. He wanted desperately to build the town, wishing to see mills built and an industrial community thrive, and found investors in Pennsylvania who bought huge tracts of timberland.

By 1892 the streets of Damascus were laid out, but that was as far as the project went. Imboden's grand plans for a magnificent hotel, numerous businesses, a post office and other enterprises were thwarted by the economic panic of 1893.

Undaunted, Imboden built his retirement home there. Despite his age, he continued an active interest in business matters, his last venture being a spring water bottling plant.[22] He continued to eke out a living for himself and his family, and often wrote of his wartime experiences. In 1892 the sixty-nine-year-old general attended the Columbian Exposition in Chicago. The old general had finally begun to accept retirement.

The Imboden Family

Although John Imboden was busily engaged in various business affairs after the war, he remained in close contact with his brothers.

He and his eldest brother George were always close and managed to avoid their political differences. George entered Confederate service as first sergeant in his brother's artillery battery. In May of 1862 he was promoted to captain and in September to major in the partisan rangers. On December 15, 1862, he was promoted to colonel of the 18th Virginia Cavalry, remaining in command of that regiment until December 23, 1864, when he was badly wounded in the lower jaw at Gordonsville. George was a life-long Democrat and lawyer who married Mary Frances Tyree of Fayette County in 1859. They lived for a while in Crittenden County, Kentucky, after the war, then moved to Fayette County, West Virginia, where George served in the West Virginia legislature. When Mary Frances died in 1889, he married Anglina Mildred Dickenson. George died on January 8, 1922.

Brother Frank joined the militia in 1859 and was present with his brothers at Harpers Ferry. On July 19, 1860, he entered V.M.I. and was ordered to Richmond as a drillmaster at the outbreak of war. He resigned this position to serve under Gen. Henry A. Wise before being promoted to captain and assigned to McCullough's Rangers of New Orleans. He was captured at Roanoke Island, North Carolina, on February 8, 1862. After his release from federal prison, he rejoined his brothers as a captain in the 18th Virginia Cavalry. On June 5, 1864, he was captured at Piedmont and remained a prisoner of war at Johnson Island, Ohio, until late summer of 1865. In the postwar years he worked closely with brother John in timber and coal in Richmond and New York until 1872, when he was elected commander of the Richmond Light Infantry Blues. Frank married Nantie Palmer on October 20, 1881, in Saltville, Virginia. In 1885 he left for Honduras and upon his return lived in Colorado and Arizona, where he worked in land sales and mining. He died on June 7, 1929, leaving six children.

Brother James, called Jim, was not yet eighteen when the war broke out, yet he rose to the rank of sergeant major in the 18th Virginia Cavalry. After the war he married Elizabeth Shepherd Smith of Albemarle County, and together they had nine children. While living at Glade Springs near Saltville, Jim worked for his brother John at Damascus. He was also active in timbering, railroading and farming. Jim died on April 9, 1928, and is buried at Arlington National Cemetery.

The youngest brother, Jake, entered V.M.I. on March 31, 1864. He served in Co. D of the Corps of Cadets at New Market, where he was wounded. Later in the war he joined Mosby's Partisan Rangers. He graduated from V.M.I. in 1867 and married Johnnie Meems of Kentucky. She died suddenly, and he later married Anna Stuart Dickenson of West Virginia, the sister of his brother George's second wife. They had three children. Jake was involved in mining in West Virginia and Missouri and became superintendent of a mine in Georgia. He organized a Honduran expedition and married there for a third time, having four more children. He served as the U. S. Consul to Tuscaran until 1892. On December 5, 1899, he died from a gunshot wound received in a scuffle while trying to save a friend, Dr. W. W. Gold. Jake was buried in San Pedro Cemetery near Puerto Cortez, Honduras.

Imboden's sister Kate married John Thomas Gibson, who died of typhoid while serving in the Confederate army in 1862. They had two children.[1] The general's parents moved to Nelson County after the war, where his father died in 1875, his mother in 1887.[2]

The only grandchild Imboden ever knew was Hunter Imboden Snyder, the son of his daughter Jennie and Henry Wilkerson Snyder of Roanoke. Hunter spent many happy hours at Damascus with his grandfather in the 1890s and later earned a degree in civil engineering from the University of Knoxville. He was licensed in Florida, Illinois and Colorado. Hunter died in Denver on January 29, 1928.

After studying engineering at the Virginia Agricultural & Mechanics College in Blacksburg, Imboden's son Frank Howard went to Honduras with his uncles Frank and Jake and a cousin, George Gibson. He married Carmelata Randales and fathered three sons and two daughters before his death in 1915.

Son George William died on December 12, 1862, and was buried beside his mother and sister at Old Tinkling Springs Church. Russie, Imboden's daughter, remained a spinster and died in Roanoke on May 15, 1930. His youngest daughter Helen married John Trout of Roanoke on July 12, 1895, but died five months later at the age of eighteen.[3]

Imboden spent a considerable amount of time during the last several years of his life writing about his wartime exploits. His first published work on the war appeared in *Galaxy Magazine* in November 1871. In this two-part article entitled "Reminiscences of Lee and Jackson," he shared personal recollections of the two great Confederate commanders.[4] He then wrote an article concerning the battle of Piedmont and Hunter's raid on the Valley entitled "Fire, Sword, and the Halter" for the *Philadelphia Weekly Times*, later published as a chapter in *The Annals of the War* in 1879.[5]

In 1876 the *Southern Historical Society Papers* published a piece he authored on Maj. Henry Wirtz and the treatment of prisoners of war at Andersonville.[6] Imboden also penned five articles for the *Century Magazine* in their "The Century War Series," later published as the four volume *Battles and Leaders of the Civil War* in 1883. On July 13, 1894, the Staunton *Vindicator* contained his article by the title of "An Augusta Battlefield," a piece about the battle of Piedmont. The *Confederate Veteran* magazine also published a two-part piece entitled "The Battle of Piedmont."[7] Other articles written by the general included "Stonewall Jackson at Harpers Ferry in 1861"; "Incidents of First Bull Run"; "Stonewall Jackson in the Shenandoah"; "Confederates Retreat from Gettysburg"; and "Battle of New Market, Va."[8]

Active in erecting the famous Lee statue on Monument Boulevard in Richmond, Imboden was one of twenty-two Confederate generals present at the organizational meeting. In a pouring rain on October 27, 1887, Imboden rode in a parade with twenty-four former Confederate generals, members of the Lee family, Virginia military units, the governor and dignitaries from all over the South to the cornerstone-laying ceremony.

At the unveiling of the statue on May 29, 1890, he rode as an honored guest in an open carriage with other Confederate generals.[9]

Imboden's wife Annie had by this time contracted a heart condition and demanded constant attention. On July 5, 1888, she died and was buried in Richmond.

In the fall of 1889, at age sixty-seven, Imboden met Florence Johnson Crockett (1852–1908) of Chattanooga, the daughter of Lafayette Johnson and Harriet Moosman of Lynchburg and a widow with two sons. They were married on May 22, 1890. Imboden thoroughly enjoyed the two boys, Wirt Johnson Crockett and Cory Ingram Crockett, and treated them as his own sons.[10]

On August 15, 1895, suddenly and unexpectedly, with his brother Jim at his side, the seventy-two-year-old general died. Initially buried in a small family service in a local plot in Damascus, his body was later reinterred at Hollywood Cemetery in Richmond in the finest aristocratic military tradition of the South.[11]

There, in a virtual Confederate memorial among the ancient oaks and wrought iron fences, Brig. Gen. John D. Imboden rests with more than eighteen thousand Confederate soldiers.[12] His daughters Helen, Rebecca, Martha Russell and Jane Crawford; his grandson Hunter Imboden Snyder; and his fourth wife, Annie Harper, share the little Imboden family plot in the Confederate officers' section, where he lies beneath a simple granite stone emblazoned with the Confederate battle flag.

Notes

Introduction

1. William Couper, *History of Shenandoah Valley*, Vol.1 (New York: Simon & Schuster, 1952), 139.

The Son of Immigrants

1. Imboden Family Genealogy, University of Virginia Library, compiled by Helen McGuire Imboden Trout, 1948 (Hereafter Genealogy). Eleanor Diller Imboden was of French Huguenot descent.
2. Imboden Family Papers, Genealogical Department of the Church of Jesus Christ of Latter-day Saints.
3. Virginius Dabney, *Virginia: The New Dominion* (Garden City, NJ: Doubleday, 1971), 91-94.
4. John Walter Wayland, *The German Element of the Shenandoah Valley of Virginia* (Harrisonburg, VA: Shenandoah Press, 1978), 104.
5. Augusta County, Virginia, Deed Book No. 29, 194 (Hereafter Deed Book).
6. William D. Hager, "The Civilian Life and Accomplishments of J. D. Imboden." History thesis, James Madison University, 1988, 9 (Hereafter Hager).
7. Ibid., 11.
8. Genealogy.

Childhood on the Farm

1. Genealogy.
2. Deed Book, 194.
3. The Imboden home was razed in 1993.
4. Joseph A. Waddell, *Annals of Augusta County, Virginia, from 1726-1871* (Harrisonburg, VA: Shenandoah Press, 1902), 443.
5. Census of 1820, Augusta County, Virginia.
6. Imboden papers, Virginia Military Institute, Lexington, VA. Boutwell Dunlap to Col. Joseph R. Anderson, 1 January 1916 (Hereafter VMI papers).
7. Genealogy.

The Learning Years

1. "Catalogue at Washington College, Lexington, Virginia, for the Session 1841-2." Archives of Washington and Lee University Library, Lexington, VA.
2. Ibid.
3. Journal of the Virginia House of Delegates 1839-40, 18.
4. The author has also written a biography of James Lawson Kemper, published by Rockbridge Publishing Co.
5. "Washington and Lee University Catalog of Officials and Alumni 1749-1888." Archives of Washington and Lee University Library, Lexington, VA.

Choosing a Career

1. Imboden papers, Library of Congress, Washington, DC. John D. Imboden to John

Boyd Thatcher, 31 July 1894 (Hereafter L of C papers).
2. Ibid.
3. Genealogy.
4. Augusta County Court Records.
5. Records of the Grand Lodge of Virginia A.F. & A.M., Richmond, VA.
6. Hager, 21.
7. Imboden papers, University of Kentucky, Lexington, Kentucky (Hereafter U of KY papers).

The Young Lawyer Settles Down

1. Imboden Family Papers, from Mrs. Katherine G. Bushman, Staunton, Virginia (Hereafter Bushman).
2. Genealogy.
3. John N. McCue, *The McCues of the Old Dominion* (Mexico, MO: Self-published, 1912), 39 (Hereafter McCue).
4. Bushman.

Entrance into Politics

1. R. McKinley Ormsley, *A History of the Whig Party*, 2nd ed. (Boston: 1860), 185.
2. Hager, 60.
3. Genealogy.
4. Augusta County Will Book No. 28, 148.
5. F. N. Boney, *John Letcher of Virginia: The Story of Virginia's War Governor* (Montgomery, AL: Univ. of Alabama, 1966), 42 (Hereafter Boney).
6. Hager, 66.

Political Career

1. Imboden papers, University of Virginia, Charlottesville, VA. 27 January 1851 (Hereafter U of VA papers).
2. Ibid., 9 March 1851.
3. Arthur Charles Cole, *The Whig Party in the South* (Washington, DC: 1913), 316 (Hereafter Cole).
4. U of VA papers, 7 August 1852.
5. Hager, 69-70.
6. Cole, 325.
7. Ibid.
8. Staunton *Spectator*, 4 May 1857.
9. Boney, 70.
10. Augusta County Common Law Book No. 46, 162.
11. Genealogy.

Militia Service

1. McCue, 39.
2. James Blythe Anderson papers, Archives of Wilson Library, University of Kentucky, Lexington, KY. 11 January 1848.
3. Genealogy.
4. Harold R. Woodward, Jr., *The Confederacy's Forgotten Son: Major General James*

Lawson Kemper, C.S.A. (Berryville, VA: Rockbridge Publishing Co., 1993), 25-26.
5. U of VA papers, militia commission.
6. Ibid., William H. Baylor to Imboden, 25 August 1858.
7. Robert J. Driver, Jr., *The Staunton Artillery and McClanahan's Battery* (Lynchburg, VA: H.E. Howard, 1988), 1 (Hereafter *Staunton*).
8. Staunton *Spectator*, 10 January 1860.
9. *Staunton*, 1.
10. VMI papers, 12 December 1859.
11. *Staunton*, 1.
12. Ibid.
13. Staunton *Spectator*, 10 January 1860.
14. Ibid., 28 February 1860.
15. Ibid., 24 May 1860.
16. *Staunton*, 2.
17. U of VA papers, John B. Floyd to Imboden, 16 January 1860.

The Secession Crisis

1. U of VA papers, Executive Committee of the Union Club to Imboden, 9 September 1860.
2. J. Lewis Peyton, *History of Augusta County, Virginia* (Bridgewater, VA: Self-published, 1953), 226-27 (Hereafter Peyton).
3. Robert Underwood Johnson and Clarence Clough Buell, eds., *Battles and Leaders of the Civil War*, Vol. 1 of 4 (New York: Thomas Yoseloff, 1956), 111 (Hereafter *Battles and Leaders*).
4. Ibid.
5. Virginia's Ordinance of Secession.
6. L of C papers, Imboden to John R. Kilby, Esq., 25 February 1861.
7. *Staunton*, 2.
8. Ibid.

Raid on Harpers Ferry

1. *Battles and Leaders*, Vol. 1, 111.
2. *Staunton*, 2.
3. Ibid.
4. *Battles and Leaders*, Vol. 1, 111.
5. Richard Patterson, "Schemes and Treachery." *Civil War Times Illustrated*, April 1989, 38 (Hereafter "Schemes").
6. "The Confederacy Mounts Its Iron Horse." *Ties: The Southern Railway System Magazine*, Vol. XV, 16 (Hereafter "Iron Horse").
7. *Battles and Leaders*, Vol. 1, 112.
8. *Staunton*, 3.
9. *Battles and Leaders*, Vol. 1, 112.
10. *Staunton*, 3.
11. "Schemes," 40.
12. *Battles and Leaders*, Vol. 1, 112.
13. Ibid.
14. Ibid., 113.
15. Ibid., 114.

16. *Staunton*, 3.

The Secession of Virginia & Capture of Harpers Ferry

1. Charles C. Osborne, *Jubal: The Life and Times of General Jubal A. Early, C.S.A., Defender of the Lost Cause* (Chapel Hill, NC: Univ. of North Carolina Press, 1992), 49-50 (Hereafter Osborne).
2. Ibid.
3. *Battles and Leaders*, Vol. 1, 115.
4. "Iron Horse," 16.
5. "Schemes," 41.
6. "Iron Horse," 16.
7. *Battles and Leaders*, Vol. 1, 115.
8. Ibid., 117.
9. Richmond *Enquirer*, 23 April 1861.
10. Millard K. Bushong, *General Turner Ashby and Stonewall Jackson's Valley Campaign* (Waynesboro, VA: Self-published, 1992), 33 (Hereafter Bushong).
11. *Battles and Leaders*, Vol. 1, 118.
12. Bushong, 32.
13. *Battles and Leaders*, Vol. 1, 118.
14. "Schemes," 44.
15. *Battles and Leaders*, Vol. 1, 118.

Soldiering at Harpers Ferry

1. *Battles and Leaders*, Vol. 1, 118.
2. Ibid., 119.
3. Ibid.
4. Ibid., 120.
5. Ibid.
6. Russell Allen Osmianski, "Dress and Undress: A Sketch of Stonewall Jackson." *Confederate Veteran*. January-February 1992, 12.
7. *Battles and Leaders*, Vol. 1, 121.
8. Ibid.
9. Ibid., 122.
10. Ibid.

The Great Train Heist

1. Arthur Candenquist, "The Great Train Robbery: Stonewall Jackson Helps Himself to a Railroad." *Civil War*, Vol. IX, No. 6, 42 (Hereafter "Robbery").
2. *Battles and Leaders*, Vol. 1, 123.
3. "Robbery," 42.
4. *Battles and Leaders*, Vol. 1, 123.
5. "Robbery," 42.
6. Ibid., 42-43.
7. *Battles and Leaders*, Vol. 1, 124.
8. Bushong, 34.
9. R. L. Dabney, *Life and Campaigns of Lt. Gen. T. J. (Stonewall) Jackson* (Harrisonburg, VA: 1983), 195-96.

10. *Battles and Leaders*, Vol. 1, 124-25.

The March to Manassas

1. *Battles and Leaders*, Vol. 1, 124-25.
2. *Staunton*, 6.
3. Ibid., 6-7.
4. *Battles and Leaders*, Vol. 1, 229.
5. *Staunton*, 7.
6. *Battles and Leaders*, Vol. 1, 229.
7. John W. Thomason, Jr., *J.E.B. Stuart* (New York: C. Scribner's Sons, 1930), 39 (Hereafter Thomason).
8. *Staunton*, 7.
9. *Battles and Leaders*, Vol. 1, 230.
10. *Staunton*, 7.
11. "War of the Rebellion: A Compilation of the Official Records of the Union and Confederate Armies." Series I, Vol. II. U.S. War Department, Washington, DC, 1880-1891, 43 (Hereafter O.R.).
12. *Battles and Leaders*, Vol. 1, 230.

The Battle of Manassas

1. *Battles and Leaders*, Vol. 1, 230.
2. *Staunton*, 7-8.
3. *Battles and Leaders*, Vol. 1, 95.
4. Ibid., 232.
5. Ibid.
6. *Staunton*, 8.
7. *Battles and Leaders*, Vol. 1, 232.
8. *Staunton*, 8
9. Ibid., 8-9.
10. *Battles and Leaders*, Vol. 1, 233.
11. *Staunton*, 9.
12. *Battles and Leaders*, Vol. 1, 233.
13. *Staunton*, 9.
14. *Battles and Leaders*, Vol. 1, 234.
15. *Staunton*, 9.
16. Ibid.
17. *Battles and Leaders*, Vol. 1, 234.
18. *Staunton*, 9.
19. Ibid.
20. *Battles and Leaders*, Vol. 1, 235.
21. Ibid.
22. *Staunton*, 2.
23. *Battles and Leaders*, Vol. 1, 236.
24. Ibid.
25. Ibid., 237.

Aftermath of Manassas

1. Battles and Leaders, Vol. 1, 237.
2. Ibid.
3. Ibid., 238.
4. Ibid.
5. Staunton Vindicator, 20 February 1863.
6. Staunton, 13.
7. O.R., Series I, Vol. II, 490-91.
8. General Joseph E. Johnston, Narrative of Military Operations During the Civil War (New York: Da Capo, 1959), 46.
9. Clayton Malcolm Thomas, III, "The Military Career of John D. Imboden." Master of Arts thesis, University of Virginia, 1965, 62-63 (Hereafter Thomas).
10. Staunton, 13.
11. Battles and Leaders, Vol. 1, 239.
12. Staunton, 14.
13. Ibid.
14. Ibid.
15. Ibid., 14-15.
16. Ibid, 15.
17. Ibid.
18. Richmond Dispatch, 3 December 1861.
19. Staunton, 16.

Partisan Service

1. Staunton, 16.
2. Burke Davis, They Called Him Stonewall: A Life of Lt. Gen. T. J. Jackson, C.S.A. (New York: Rinehart, 1954), 138.
3. Virgil Carrington Jones, Gray Ghosts and Rebel Raiders (McLean, VA: EPM Publications, Inc., 1956), 76 (Hereafter Jones).
4. O.R., Series 4, Vol. 1, 395.
5. Jones, 76.
6. Staunton, 18.
7. VMI papers, letter of Francis Marion Imboden.
8. O.R., Series II, Vol. 3, 869.
9. Staunton, 18.
10. Albert Casteel, "The Guerilla War." Civil War Times Illustrated, October 1974, 9 (Hereafter "Guerilla War").
11. Jones, 80.
12. U of VA papers, Imboden to Francis M. Imboden, 29 April 1862.
13. Ibid.,George W. Randolph to Imboden, 7 May 1862.
14. Roger U. Delauter, Jr., 62nd Virginia Infantry (Lynchburg, VA: H.E. Howard, 1988), 3 (Hereafter 62nd VA).
15. "Guerilla War," 9.
16. Ibid.
17. Richmond Dispatch, 8 May 1862.
18. Jones, 83.
19. 62nd VA, 2.

The First Virginia Partisan Rangers

1. U of VA papers, Hiram L. Opie to Imboden, 11 May 1862.
2. Ibid, John Alexander Ruff Imboden to Imboden, 13 May 1862.
3. *Battles and Leaders*, Vol. 2, 286-87.
4. O.R., Series I, Vol. XII, Pt. III, 883.
5. *Battles and Leaders*, Vol. 2, 286-87.
6. Ibid., 287-88.
7. Ibid., 288-90.
8. Ibid., 290-91.
9. Ibid., 291-92.
10. Ibid., 293.
11. Ibid.
12. *Staunton*, 68.
13. *Battles and Leaders*, Vol. 2, 293-95.
14. Ibid.
15. Peter Svenson, *Battlefield: Farming a Civil War Battleground* (Boston: Faber & Faber, 1992), 41.
16. *Staunton*, 70.
17. U of VA papers, Capt. John F. Harding to Imboden, 7 July 1862.
18. Roger U. Delauter, Jr., *McNeill's Rangers* (Lynchburg, VA: H.E. Howard, 1986), 1-18 (Hereafter *McNeill's*).

Independent Command

1. Clifford Dowdey and Louis Manarin, *The Wartime Papers of R. E. Lee* (Boston: Fairfax Press, 1961), 257 (Hereafter Dowdey & Manairn).
2. O.R., Vol. XII, Pt. III, 949-50.
3. Thomas, 78.
4. Jones, 117.
5. Thomas, 80. A.J. Borman to Gov. Peirpoint, 4 September 1862.
6. *Staunton*, 70.
7. *McNeill's*, 22.
8. Ibid., 23.
9. Ibid.
10. U of VA papers, R. E. Lee to Imboden, 6 October 1862.
11. *62nd VA*, 4.
12. Thomas, 82.
13. *62nd VA*, 5.
14. *McNeill's*, 25.
15. Roger U. Delauter, Jr., *18th Virginia Cavalry* (Lynchburg, VA: H.E. Howard, 1985), 1 (Hereafter *18th VA*).
16. Ibid., 1-3.
17. Ibid.
18. Jones, 129.
19. Ibid.

Winter of 1862-1863

1. *McNeill's*, 25.

2. Jones, 130.
3. Ibid., 131.
4. Ibid.
5. Dowdey & Manarin, 338. 11 November 1962.
6. Jones, 131.
7. McNeill's, 28.
8. By Constance Fenimore Woolson of Tucker County, W.Va. Provided by John L. Heatwole.
9. O.R., Vol. IV, 913.

Reorganization

1. Thomas, 88.
2. Ibid., 89.
3. Ibid.
4. Jones, 144.
5. John O. Casler, Four Years in the Stonewall Brigade (Dayton, OH: Morningside Books, 1971), 126-34 (Hereafter Casler).
6. O.R., Vol. XXI, 1076.
7. Jones, 137.
8. National Archives, Compiled Service Records.
9. Staunton Vindicator, 20 February 1863.
10. 62nd VA, 7.
11. Jones, 137.
12. 62nd VA, 7-8.

The Jones-Imboden Raid

1. Edward G. Longacre, Mounted Raids of the Civil War (New York: Bison Books, 1975), 123 (Hereafter Longacre).
2. 62nd VA, 12.
3. Festus P. Summers, "The Jones-Imboden Raid." West Virginia History, Vol. I, 15.
4. Thomas, 95.
5. Staunton, 72.
6. John A. McNeill, "The Imboden Raid and Its Effects." Southern Historical Society Papers, Vol. XXXIV, 294 (Hereafter "Effects").
7. O.R., Series I, Vol. XXV, Pt. 1, 99.
8. Ibid., 114.
9. Thomas, 97.
10. O.R., Vol. XXV, Pt. 1, 94.
11. Longacre, 131.
12. O.R., Vol. XXV, Pt. 1, 100.
13. Longacre, 131.
14. O.R., Vol. XXV, Pt. 1, 101.
15. Longacre, 132.
16. Thomas, 101.
17. Longacre, 132-33.
18. "Effects," 294.
19. Dowdey & Manarin, 450-51.
20. O.R., Vol. XXV, Pt. 1, 115.

21. *Staunton*, 74.
22. Longacre, 142.
23. Thomas, 103-4.
24. Longacre, 143.
25. Thomas, 105.
26. Longacre, 145.
27. O.R., Vol. XXV, Pt. 1, 102-4.

The High Tide

1. *Staunton*, 74.
2. *62nd VA*, 16.
3. Ibid., 16-17.
4. Dowdey & Manarin, 510.
5. *62nd VA*, 17.
6. Thomas, 111.
7. Thomas Nelson Page, *Robert E. Lee, Man and Soldier* (New York: Scribners, 1923), 707. Lee's Report to Adj. Gen. Samuel Cooper, 31 July 1863.
8. Rual Purcell Anderson, *Genealogy Spaid, Anderson, Whitacre, and a Number of Allied Families Also Historical Facts and Memories* (Strasburg, VA: Shenandoah Press, 1975), 447 (Hereafter Anderson).
9. Dowdey & Manarin, 536.
10. *18th VA*, 7.
11. Dowdey & Manarin, 536-37.
12. Anderson, 449.

The Retreat

1. *Battles and Leaders*, Vol. III, 420.
2. Ibid., 420-21.
3. Ibid., 421.
4. Ibid.
5. Ibid., 422.
6. Ibid.
7. Ibid.
8. John W. Schildt, *Roads from Gettysburg, PA* (Chewsville, MD: Self-published, 1979), 19 (Hereafter Schildt).
9. John Punifoy, "A Night of Horror." *Confederate Veteran*, Vol. 33, 95.
10. *Battles and Leaders*, Vol. III, 423.
11. Schildt, 28.
12. Schildt, 41.
13. *Battles and Leaders*, Vol. III, 424.
14. Anderson, 449.
15. *Battles and Leaders*, Vol. III, 423.
16. Ibid., 424.
17. Ibid., 425.
18. Thomas, 115.

Williamsport

1. *Battles and Leaders*, Vol. III, 425.
2. Schildt, 47.
3. Ibid., 80.
4. *Battles and Leaders*, Vol. III, 426-27.
5. Schildt, 83.
6. *Battles and Leaders*, Vol. III, 427.
7. Anderson, 450.
8. *Battles and Leaders*, Vol. III, 428.
9. Anderson, 450.
10. Casler, 179.
11. *Battles and Leaders*, Vol. III, 428-29.

District Command

1. *Battles and Leaders*, Vol. III, 432-33.
2. Anderson, 451.
3. *Battles and Leaders*, Vol. IV, 480.
4. Anderson, 451.
5. *Battles and Leaders*, Vol. IV, 480.
6. Dowdey & Manarin, 556-57, 587.
7. O.R., Series I, Vol. XXIX, Pt. 1, 105.
8. Ibid., Series I, Vol. XXIX, Pt. 2, 650-739.
9. Anderson, 452.
10. Thomas, 121.
11. O.R., Series I, Vol. XXIX, Pt. 1, 106.
12. Thomas, 122.
13. Hager, 88-89.

The Dash on Charles Town

1. O.R., Series I, Vol. XXIX, Pt. 2, 709.
2. *62nd VA*, 21.
3. Ibid.
4. Ibid., 22.
5. Anderson, 454-55.
6. *Staunton*, 81.
7. Jefferson County Historical Society, Vol. LIV, December 1988, 15-16.
8. *McNeill's*, 55.
9. *Staunton*, 81.
10. Ibid.
11. Ibid.
12. Capt. F. M. Berkley, "Imboden's Dash into Charles Town." *Southern Historical Society Papers*, Vol. XXXI, 12-16 (Hereafter "Dash").
13. Ibid., 15.
14. *Staunton*, 82.
15. Ibid.
16. "Dash," 15.
17. Thomas, 124.

18. Dowdey & Manarin, 614.
19. Stan Cohen, *The Civil War in West Virginia: A Pictorial History* (Charleston, WV: Pictorial Histories Publishing, 1976), 101.

Averell's Raids

1. *62nd VA*, 22.
2. O.R., Series I, Vol. XXIX, Pt. 2, 411.
3. Jack L. Dickinson, *Jenkins of Greenbottom: A Civil War Saga* (Charleston, WV: Pictorial Histories Publishing, 1988), 68 (Hereafter Dickinson).
4. Anderson, 454.
5. *Staunton*, 82.
6. Dickinson, 68.
7. *18th VA*, 12.
8. Dowdey & Manarin, 617-18.
9. *McNeill's*, 55-56.
10. Robert J. Driver, Jr., *Lexington and Rockbridge County in the Civil War* (Lynchburg, VA: H.E. Howard, 1989), 50 (Hereafter *Lexington*).
11. *McNeill's*, 56.
12. *Lexington*, 50.
13. Ibid., 51.
14. Beverly Stanard, *Letters of a New Market Cadet.* Edited by John G. Barrett and Robert K. Turner, Jr. (Chapel Hill, NC: Univ. of North Carolina Press, 1961), 20.
15. *McNeill's*, 56-57.
16. *62nd VA*, 23.
17. Ibid., 24.
18. Eric Miller, "Civil War Letters Show Personal Struggles." *Rural Living*, March 1991, 10 (Hereafter Miller).
19. *Lexington*, 52.
20. Ibid., 53.
21. Osborne, 217.
22. Ibid., 219-20.
23. *Lexington*, 55.
24. *18th VA*, 12.

The Start of a New Year

1. *McNeill's*, 60-61.
2. *62nd VA*, 25.
3. Osborne, 221.
4. Douglas Southall Freeman, *Lee's Lieutenants: A Study in Command*, Vol. III (New York: Charles Scribner's Sons, 1942), 328 (Hereafter Freeman).
5. *62nd VA*, 25.
6. *Staunton*, 84.
7. *62nd VA*, 25-26.
8. *McNeill's*, 61-63.
9. *62nd VA*, 26.
10. *18th VA*, 15.
11. *McNeill's*, 64.
12. Robert E. Denney, *Civil War Prisons and Escapes: A Day to Day Chronicle* (New

York: Sterling Publishing Co., 1993), 144-45 (Hereafter Denney).
13. *62nd VA*, 27.
14. *McNeill's*, 65.

Against Sigel in the Valley

1. Joseph W. A. Whitehorne, "The Long Road to New Market." *Civil War*, Vol. XX, 9-17.
2. William C. Davis, *The Battle of New Market* (Baton Rouge: Louisiana State Univ. Press, 1975), 195-97 (Hereafter *New Market*).
3. Dowdey & Manarin, 709.
4. *New Market*, 15-17.
5. *Battles and Leaders*, Vol. IV, 480.
6. O.R., Series I, Vol. XXXVII, Pt. 1, 710-16.
7. *Battles and Leaders*, Vol. IV, 480-81.
8. *McNeill's*, 66.
9. O.R., Series I, Vol. XXXVII, Pt. 1, 726.
10. *18th VA*, 17.
11. Ibid.
12. *McNeill's*, 68-69.
13. *18th VA*, 17-18.
14. Robert Louis Crabill and Patricia Louise Crabill, *How We Came to Be* (Baltimore: Self-published, 1983), 68-69.
15. Thomas A. Lewis, *The Shenandoah in Flames* (Alexandria, VA: Time-Life Publ., 1987), 28 (Hereafter Lewis).
16. *18th VA*, 19.
17. Lewis, 28.

The Battle of New Market

1. O.R., Series I, Vol. XXXVII, Pt. 1, 731-33.
2. *18th VA*, 19.
3. *Battles and Leaders*, Vol. IV, 481-82.
4. Ibid., 482.
5. Ibid., 482-83.
6. *New Market*, 482-83.
7. *18th VA*, 21.
8. *Battles and Leaders*, Vol. IV, 483.
9. Lewis, 30-31.
10. *Battles and Leaders*, Vol. IV, 483.
11. Ibid., 484.
12. *62nd VA*, 30.
13. Ibid., 31.
14. *Battles and Leaders*, Vol. IV, 484.
15. Ibid., 484-85.
16. Ibid., 491.
17. Eliza Clinedist Crim, "New Market: When Boys Became Men." *The Virginian*, May-June 1989, 40-41.
18. Robert Grier Stephens, Jr., ed., *Intrepid Warrior, Clement Anselon Evans, Confederate General from Georgia: Life, Letters, and Diaries of the War Years* (Dayton, OH:

Morningside Books, 1992), 417.

Guarding the Valley

1. *Battles and Leaders*, Vol. IV, 485.
2. O.R., Series I, Vol. XXXVII, Pt. 1, 739.
3. Ibid., 742-43.
4. Marshall Moore Brice, *Conquest of a Valley* (Charlottesville, VA: Univ. of Virginia Press, 1965), 14-15 (Hereafter Brice).
5. Ibid., 10.
6. Ibid., 16.
7. John D. Imboden, "The Battle of Piedmont." *Confederate Veteran*, Vol. 31, 459, and Vol. 32, 18 (Hereafter "Piedmont").

Facing Hunter in the Valley

1. Brice, 17.
2. Gary C. Walker, *Hunter's Fiery Raid Through Virginia's Valleys* (Roanoke: A&W Enterprise, 1989), 34 (Hereafter Walker).
3. O.R., Series I, Vol. XXXVII, Pt. 1, 161.
4. Col. Harry Gilmor, *Four Years in the Saddle* (New York: Harper & Brothers, 1866), 161-162.
5. Walker, 35.
6. Richard B. Kleese, *Shenandoah County in the Civil War: The Turbulent Years* (Lynchburg, VA: H.E. Howard, 1992), 68.
7. Walker, 59.
8. Brice, 20.
9. Walker, 62.
10. Brice, 20.
11. Ibid., 21.
12. John D. Imboden, "Fire, Sword, and Halter." *The Annals of the War Written by Leading Participants North and South*, by Alexander K. McClure. (Philadelphia: Times Publ. Co., 1878), 172-73 (Hereafter McClure).

Preparing for Battle

1. Brice, 24.
2. Staunton *Vindicator*, 27 May 1864.
3. O.R., Vol. XXXVII, Pt. 1, 744.
4. Brice, 26.
5. O.R., Vol. XXXVII, Pt. 1, 748.
6. Brice, 26.
7. O.R., Vol. XXXVII, Pt. 1, 748.
8. Brice, 27.
9. O.R., Vol. XXXVII, Pt. 1, 749.
10. Brice, 28-29.
11. Ibid., 29-30.
12. Ibid., 31.
13. O.R., Vol. LI, Pt. 2, 981-2.
14. Brice, 33.

180

15. Walker, 64.
16. Brice, 34-35.
17. Ibid., 36-37.
18. Walker, 66.

The Battle of Piedmont

1. Walker, 85.
2. Brice, 39.
3. McClure, 173.
4. Brice, 40-41.
5. Ibid., 42.
6. McClure, 174.
7. Brice, 43-45.
8. Ibid., 47.
9. Ibid., 48-49.
10. Staunton *Vindicator*, 13 July 1894.
11. Ibid.
12. Ibid.
13. Brice, 51.
14. Staunton *Vindicator*, 13 July 1894.
15. Brice, 51.
16. Staunton *Vindicator*, 13 July 1894.

Confederate Defeat

1. Brice, 52.
2. Ibid., 55-56.
3. Ibid., 61-62.
4. Ibid., 63-70.
5. Ibid., 70-74.
6. Walker, 102-3.
7. Brice, 75-79.
8. Ibid., 85.

The Fall of Staunton

1. Brice, 82-84.
2. Ibid., 86-88.
3. O.R., Vol. LI, Pt. 2, 990.
4. Brice, 89.
5. Ibid., 89-90.
6. Ibid., 93-95.
7. Charles Culbertson, "Mary Julia and the General." *The Mary Baldwin Magazine*, Vol. 5, No. 1, August 1991, 4-5 (Hereafter "Mary Julia").
8. Peyton, 237.
9. "Mary Julia," 5.
10. Ibid., 6.
11. Peyton, 237.
12. "Mary Julia," 6.

13. Ibid.
14. Milton W. Humphreys, *A History of the Lynchburg Campaign* (Charlottesville, VA: Univ. of Virginia Press, 1924), 53 (Hereafter Humphreys).
15. "Mary Julia," 6.

Slowing Hunter's Advance

1. McClure, 175.
2. Humphreys, 54.
3. George Morris and Susan Foutz, *Lynchburg in the Civil War: The City—The People—The Battle* (Lynchburg, VA: H.E. Howard, 1984), 39 (Hereafter Morris & Foutz).
4. Thomas, 142.
5. Morris & Foutz, 39.
6. Humphreys, 55.
7. Morris & Foutz, 39-40.
8. McClure, 177.
9. Ibid., 177-79.
10. Miller, 14.
11. McClure, 179.

The Battle of Lynchburg

1. Morris & Foutz, 42.
2. Ibid., 41-42.
3. Ibid., 42.
4. Ibid., 43.
5. Ibid.
6. Ibid., 44.
7. The Old Quaker Meeting House is still standing. Built in 1798, it is now open to the public. Next door to it is the Quaker Memorial Presbyterian Church.
8. Humphreys, 62.
9. Ibid., 63.
10. Osborne, 257.
11. Morris & Foutz, 44-45.
12. Ibid., 46-47.
13. Humphreys, 70.
14. Osborne, 265.

With Early in the Valley

1. *62nd VA*, 36.
2. *Staunton*, 99.
3. *18th VA*, 27.
4. *62nd VA*, 37.
5. Ibid.
6. *Staunton*, 99.
7. *18th VA*, 27.
8. *62nd VA*, 37.
9. John D. Imboden, "Statement of General John D. Imboden to General D.H. Murray

on January 12, 1876, Regarding the Treatment of Prisoners at Andersonville."
Southern Historical Society Papers, Vol. 1, 187 (Hereafter "Treatment").

10. Shelby Foote, *The Civil War, A Narrative: Red River to Appamattox* (New York: Random House, 1974), 448.
11. O.R., Series I, Vol. XXXVII, 116.
12. *Washington Times*, 11 January 1992.
13. *Washington Post*, 14 July 1989.
14. Ibid.
15. Ibid., 14 July 1992.
16. *18th VA*, 28.
17. Ibid., 28-29.

Against Sheridan in the Shenandoah

1. *The Grolier Encyclopedia.*
2. Bell Irvin Wiley, *The Life of Johnny Reb: The Common Soldier of the Confederacy* (Baton Rouge: Louisiana State Univ. Press, 1943), 253.
3. *18th VA*, 29.
4. Greater Chambersburg Chamber of Commerce, *Southern Revenge* (Shippensburg, PA: White Mane, 1989).
5. Anderson, 461.
6. Jubal A. Early, *Lt. Gen. Jubal A. Early: Narrative of the War Between the States* (New York: Da Capo Press, 1989), 402 (Hereafter Early).
7. *18th VA*, 30.
8. Ibid.
9. Anderson, 455.
10. *Proceedings of the Clarke County Historical Association*, Vol. XV, 13.
11. Early, 406.
12. Anderson, 459.
13. Freeman, Vol. III, 568.
14. *Washington Times*, 30 November 1991.
15. *18th VA*, 32-33.

From Fisher's Hill to Cedar Creek

1. *18th VA*, 33.
2. Ibid., 33-34.
3. *62nd VA*, 42.
4. *Washington Times*, 30 November 1991.
5. *62nd VA*, 43.
6. Ibid.
7. *18th VA*, 35.
8. *62nd VA*, 43.
9. *18th VA*, 36.

Reassignment

1. *62nd VA*, 44.
2. Ibid., 44-45.
3. *18th VA*, 36-37.

4. "Treatment," 187.
5. Confederate War Records, National Archives, Washington, DC. Imboden to Robert E. Lee, 4 January 1865.
6. Ibid.
7. "Treatment," 187.
8. Arch Frederic Blakey, *General John H. Winder, C.S.A.* (Gainesville, FL: Univ. of Florida Press, 1991), 2 (Hereafter Blakey).
9. "Treatment," 187.

The Confederate Prison System

1. James West Thomason, "Controversy: Partisan Comment on Andersonville." *Blue and Gray*, Vol. III, No. 3, 34 (Hereafter Thomason).
2. Blakey, 2.
3. Thomason, 35.
4. Blakey, 182.
5. James R. Clarke, "The Cost of Capture." *Civil War Times Illustrated*, Vol. XXXI, No. 1, 26.
6. Denney, 367.
7. Blakey, 197.

Tackling the Abyss

1. "Treatment," 187.
2. Blakey, 5.
3. "Treatment," 187.
4. O.R., Series II, Vol. 8, 117-22.
5. "Treatment," 187.
6. Ibid.
7. Ibid.

The Collapse of the Confederacy

1. "Treatment," 187. Taylor surrendered the last sizeable, organized Confederate Army east of the Mississippi River on May 4, 1865.
2. Ibid.
3. U of VA papers, parole pass, 3 May 1865.
4. O.R., Series II, Vol. 8, 535.
5. "Treatment," 187.

The Trial of Henry Wirtz

1. "Treatment," 187.
2. Denney, 370.
3. "Treatment," 187.
4. Denney, 370.

Getting on with His Life

1. Hager, 1.
2. Woodward, 124.

3. Lynchburg *Virginian*, 14 November 1865.
4. Company Charter, Virginia State Library & Archives, Richmond, Va.
5. Ibid.
6. Lynchburg *Virginian*, 30 January 1866.
7. Ibid., 2 October 1866.
8. Ibid.
9. Imboden papers, Washington & Lee University. Imboden to John Letcher, 16 August 1869 (Hereafter W & L papers).
10. Hager, 145.
11. U of VA papers, 8 December 1870.

Natural Resources and Railroads

1. U of VA papers, Virginia Central Railroad to Imboden, 27 March 1860.
2. Hager, 102-3.
3. Bruce S. Greenwalt, ed., "Virginians Face Reconstruction: Correspondence from the James Dorman Davidson Papers 1865-1880." *The Virginia Magazine of History and Biography*, Vol. 78, No. 4, October 1979, 458.
4. Hager, 103.
5. Ibid., 104-5.
6. U of VA papers, 19 October 1875.
7. Ibid., 13 December 1875.
8. Ibid., 23 October 1875.
9. Ibid., Imboden to Annie, 27 November 1875.
10. Ibid., A.D. Goshom to Imboden, 27 August 1874.
11. Hager, 107.
12. U of VA papers, 22 April 1876.
13. U of KY papers, Imboden to McCue, 6 August 1876.
14. U of VA papers, 4 October 1876.
15. Ibid., 10 November 1876.
16. Ibid., Lee Crandall to Imboden, 10 September 1877.
17. Hager, 113.
18. U of VA papers, Imboden to McCue, 18 November 1881.
19. Ibid., 19 July 1883.
20. Ibid., 30 July 1883.
21. Hager, 199.
22. Ibid., 120-23.

The Imboden Family

1. Genealogy.
2. Imboden Family Papers, T. Gibson Hobbs, Lynchburg, VA (Hereafter Hobbs).
3. Genealogy.
4. John D. Imboden, "Reminiscences of Lee and Jackson." *The Galaxy Magazine*, Vol. 12, No. 5, November 1871, 41.
5. McClure.

6. "Treatment," 187.
7. "Piedmont," Vol. 31, 459, and Vol. 32, 18.
8. *Battles and Leaders*, Vol. 1, 111, 129; Vol. 2, 286; Vol. 3, 420; and Vol. 4, 480.
9. *Southern Historical Society Papers*, Vol. XVII, 190-266.
10. Genealogy.
11. Hobbs.
12. Phillip Burnham, "Hollywood: A Changing Legend." *Richmond Surroundings*, Vol. 8, No. 3, April/May 1993, 56.

Bibliography and Sources

Books

Anderson, Rual Purcell. *Genealogy Spaid, Anderson, Whitacre, and a Number of Allied Families Also Historical Facts and Memories*. Strasburg, VA: Shenandoah Press, 1975.

Ashby, Thomas A. *The Valley Campaign: Being the Reminiscences of a Non-Combatant While Between the Lines in the Shenandoah Valley During the War Between the States*. New York: Neale Publ. Co., 1914.

Beck, Brandon H. and Charles S. Grunder. *The Second Battle of Winchester, June 12-15, 1863*. Lynchburg, VA: H.E. Howard, 1989.

Blakey, Arch Frederic. *General John H. Winder, C.S.A.*, Gainesville, FL: University of Florida Press, 1991.

Boatner Mark Mayo, III. *The Civil War Dictionary*. New York: Vintage Books, 1959.

Boney, F. N. *John Letcher of Virginia: The Story of Virginia's Civil War Governor*. Montgomery, AL: Univ. of Alabama, 1966.

Bowers, John. *Stonewall Jackson: Portrait of a Soldier*. New York: William Morrow & Co., 1989.

Brice, Marshall Moore. *Conquest of a Valley*. Charlottesville, VA: Univ. of Virginia Press, 1965.

Brookshear, William R. and David K. Snider. *Glory at a Gallop: Tales of the Confederate Cavalry*. Washington, DC: Brassey's, 1993.

Bushong, Millard K. *General Turner Ashby and Stonewall Jackson's Valley Campaign*. Waynesboro, VA: Self-published, 1992.

_____. *Old Jube: A Biography of General Jubal A. Early*. Shippensburg, PA: White Mane Publishing, 1990.

Casler, John O. *Four Years in the Stonewall Brigade*. Dayton, OH: Morningside Books, 1971.

Clark, Champ. *Decoying the Yanks*. Alexandria, VA: Time-Life Publ., 1984.

_____. *Gettysburg*. Alexandria, VA: Time-Life Publ., 1985.

Cohen, Stan, *The Civil War in West Virginia: A Pictorial History*. Charleston, WV: Pictorial Histories Publishing, 1976.

Cole, Arthur Charles. *The Whig Party in the South*. Washington, DC: 1913.

Commager, Henry Steele. *The Blue and the Gray*. Two Vol. in one. Indianapolis: Bobbs-Merrill, 1950.

Couper, William. *History of Shenandoah Valley*. 3 vols. New York: Simon & Schuster, 1952.

Crabill, Robert Louis and Patricia Louise. *How We Came to Be*. Baltimore: Self-published, 1983.

Current, Richard N., ed. *Encyclopedia of the Confederacy*. 4 Vol. New York: Simon & Schuster, 1993.

Dabney, R.L. *Life and Campaigns of Lt. Gen. T. J. (Stonewall) Jackson*. Harrisonburg, VA: Sprinkle Publications, 1983.

Dabney, Virginius. *Virginia: The New Dominion*. Garden City, NJ: Doubleday, 1971.

Davis, Burke. *The Gray Fox: Robert E. Lee and the Civil War*. New York: Holt, Rinehart & Winston, 1956.

_____. *They Called Him Stonewall: A Life of Lt. Gen. T. J. Jackson, C.S.A.* New York: Rinehart, 1954.

Davis, Jefferson. *The Rise and Fall of the Confederate Government*. New York: D. Appleton & Co., 1881.

Davis, William C. *Battle at Bull Run: A History of the First Major Campaign of the Civil War*. Baton Rouge: Louisiana State Univ. Press, 1977.

_____. *First Blood*. Alexandria, VA: Time-Life, 1983.

_____. *The Battle of New Market*. Baton Rouge: Louisiana State Univ. Press, 1975.

_____, ed. *The Confederate General*. Vol. 3. Harrisburg, PA: National Historical Society, 1991.

Delauter, Roger U., Jr. *McNeill's Rangers*. Lynchburg, VA: H.E. Howard, 1986.

_____. *18th Virginia Cavalry*. Lynchburg, VA: H.E. Howard, 1985.

_____. *62nd Virginia Infantry*. Lynchburg, VA: H.E. Howard, 1988.

Denney, Robert E. *Civil War Prisons and Escapes: A Day to Day Chronicle*. New York: Sterling Pub. Co., 1993.

Dickinson, Jack L. *Jenkins of Greenbottom: A Civil War Saga*. Charleston, WV: Pictorial Histories Publishing, 1988.

Douglas, Henry Kyd. *I Rode With Stonewall*. Chapel Hill, NC: Univ. of North Carolina Press, 1940.

Dowdey, Clifford. *Death of a Nation: The Story of Lee and His Men at Gettysburg*. New York: Knopf, 1958.

_____. *Lee's Last Campaign: The Story of Lee and His Men Against Grant - 1864*. Wilmington, NC: Broadfoot, 1988.

Dowdey, Clifford and Louis H. Manarin. *The Wartime Papers of R. E. Lee*. Boston: Fairfax Press, 1961.

Driver, Robert J., Jr. *Lexington and Rockbridge County in the Civil War*. Lynchburg, VA: H.E. Howard, 1989.

_____. *The Staunton Artillery and McClanahan's Battery*. Lynchburg, VA: H.E. Howard, 1988.

Du Pont, Henry A. *The Campaign of 1864 in the Valley of Virginia and the Expedition to Lynchburg*. New York: Simon & Schuster, 1925.

Early, Jubal A. *Lt. Gen. Jubal A. Early: Narrative of the War Between the States*. New York: Da Capo Press, 1989.

Faust, Patrica L., ed. *Historical Times Illustrated Encyclopedia of the Civil War*. New York: Harper & Row, 1986.

Fieberger, Colonel G. J. *The Campaign and Battle of Gettysburg*. West Point, NY: U.S. Army Military Academy, 1915.

Foote, Shelby. *The Civil War, A Narrative: Red River to Appomattox*. New York: Random House, 1974.

Freeman, Douglas Southall. *Lee's Lieutenants: A Study in Command*. 3 vols. New York: Charles Scribner's Sons, 1942.

Gallagher, Gary W. *Fighting For the Confederacy: The Personal Recollections of General Edward Porter Alexander*. Chapel Hill, NC: Univ. of North Carolina Press, 1989.

_____, ed. *Struggle for the Shenandoah: Essays on Confederate & Union Leadership*. Kent, OH: Kent State Univ. Press, 1991.

Gilmor, Harry. *Four Years in the Saddle*. New York: Harper & Brothers, 1866.

Greater Chambersburg Chamber of Commerce. *Southern Revenge*. Shippensburg, PA: White Mane, 1989.

Hale, Laura Virginia. *Four Valiant Years in the Lower Shenandoah Valley 1861-1865*. Strasburg, VA: Shenandoah Publishing House, 1986.

Henderson, George F. R. *Stonewall Jackson and the American Civil War*. New York: Book Sales, Inc., 1988.

Hennessy, John. *The First Battle of Manassas: An End to Innocence July 18-21, 1861.*
Lynchburg, VA: H.E. Howard, 1989.

Henry, Robert Selph. *The Story of the Confederacy.* Indianapolis: Bobbs-Merrill, Co.,
1931.

Hotchkiss, Jedediah. *Confederate Military History: Extended Edition, Vol. IV, Virginia.*
Edited by Clement A. Evans. Wilmington, NC: Broadfoot, 1987.

Humphreys, Milton W. *A History of the Lynchburg Campaign.* Charlottesville, VA:
Univ. of Virginia Press, 1924.

Imboden, John D. *Coal and Iron Resources of Virginia.* 1872.

Johnson, Robert Underwood and Clarence Clough Buell, eds. *Battles and Leaders of the
Civil War.* 4 Vol. New York: Thomas Yoseloff, 1956.

Johnson, Rossiter. *Campfire and Battlefield.* New York: Simon & Schuster, 1894.

Johnston, Gen. Joseph E. *Narrative of Military Operations During the Civil War,* New
York: Da Capo Press, 1959.

Jones, Virgil Carrington. *Gray Ghosts and Rebel Raiders.* McLean, VA: EPM
Publications, Inc., 1956.

_____. *Ranger Mosby.* Chapel Hill, NC: Univ. of North Carolina Press, 1944.

Kennedy, Frances, H., ed. *The Civil War Battlefield Guide.* Boston: Houghton-Mifflin,
1990.

Kleese, Richard B. *Shenandoah County in the Civil War: The Turbulent Years.*
Lynchburg, VA: H.E. Howard, 1992.

Lambert, Dobbie Edward. *Grumble: The W.E. Jones' Brigade of 1863-1864.* Wahiawa,
HI: Lambert Enterprises, 1992.

Lewis, Thomas A. *The Shenandoah in Flames.* Alexandria, VA: Time-Life Publ., 1987.

Longacre, Edward G. *Mounted Raids of the Civil War.* New York: Bison Books, 1975.

Loth, Calder, ed. *The Virginia Landmarks Register.* 3rd ed. Charlottesville, VA: Univ. of
Virginia Press, 1986.

McClure, Alexander K. *The Annals of the War Written by Leading Participants North and
South.* Philadelphia: Times Publ. Co., 1878.

McCue, John N. *The McCues of the Old Dominion.* Mexico, MO: Self-published, 1912.

Mills, Joseph. *Bull Run Remembers.* Manassas, VA: U.S. National Park Service, 1953.

Morris, George and Susan Foutz. *Lynchburg in the Civil War: The City—The
People—The Battle.* Lynchburg, VA: H.E. Howard, 1984.

Osborne, Charles C. *Jubal: The Life and Times of General Jubal A. Early, C.S.A.,
Defender of the Lost Cause.* Chapel Hill, NC: Univ. of North Carolina Press, 1992.

Ormsley, R. McKinley. *A History of the Whig Party.* 2nd ed. Boston: 1860.

Page, Thomas Nelson. *Robert E. Lee, Man and Soldier.* New York: Scribners, 1923.

Pauley, Michael J. *Unreconstructed Rebel: The Life of General John McCausland, C.S.A.*
Charleston, WV: Pictorial Histories Publishing, 1992.

Peyton, J. Lewis. *History of Augusta County, Virginia.* Bridgewater, VA: Self-published,
1953.

Pond, George E. *The Shenandoah Valley in 1864.* New York: Scribners, 1883.

Robertson, James I., Jr. *The Stonewall Brigade.* Baton Rouge: Louisiana State Univ.
Press, 1963.

Russell, Charles Wells. *Gray Ghost: the Memoirs of Colonel John S. Mosby.* Reprint.
Gaithersburg, MD: Olde Soldier Books, 1992.

Schildt, John W. *Roads from Gettysburg, PA.* Chewsville, MD: Self-published, 1979.

Stackpole, Edward J. *Sheridan in the Shenandoah.* Harrisburg, PA: Stackpole Books,
1992.

_____. *They Met at Gettysburg.* Harrisburg, PA: Stackpole Books, 1956.

Stanard, Beverly. *Letters of a New Market Cadet*. Edited by John G. Barrett and Robert K. Turner, Jr. Chapel Hill, NC: Univ. of North Carolina Press, 1961.

Stephens, Robert Grier, Jr., ed. *Intrepid Warrior, Clement Anselon Evans, Confederate General from Georgia: Life, Letters, and Diaries of the War Years*. Dayton, OH: Morningside Books, 1992.

Strickler, Harry M. *Forerunners: Strickler and Allied Families*. Harrisonburg, VA: Shenandoah Press, 1977.

Summers, Festus P. *A Borderland Confederate*. Pittsburgh: Univ. of Pittsburgh Press, 1962.

Svenson, Peter. *Battlefield: Farming a Civil War Battleground*. Boston: Faber & Faber, 1992.

Tanner, Robert G. *Stonewall in the Valley*. Garden City, NY: Doubleday & Co., 1976.

Thomason, John W., Jr. *J.E.B. Stuart*. New York: C. Scribners Sons, 1930.

Tucker, Glenn. *High Tide at Gettysburg: The Campaign in Pennsylvania*. Dayton, OH: Morningside Books, 1983.

Turner, Charles W., ed. *Ted Barclay, Liberty Hall Volunteers: Letters from the Stonewall Brigade*. Berryville, VA: Rockbridge Publ. Co., 1992.

Waddell, Joseph A. *Annals of Augusta County, Virginia from 1726-1871*. Harrisonburg, VA: Shenandoah Press, 1902.

Walker, Gary C. *Yankee Soldiers in Virginia Valleys: Hunter's Raid*. Roanoke: A&W Enterprise, 1989.

Wallace, Lee A., Jr. *Guide to Virginia Military Organizations 1861-65*. Lynchburg, VA: H.E. Howard, 1986.

Walters, Mary. *History of Mary Baldwin College, 1842-1942*. Staunton, VA: Mary Baldwin College, 1942.

Warner, Ezra J. *Generals in Gray: The Lives of the Confederate Commanders*. Baton Rouge: Louisiana State Univ. Press, 1959.

Wayland, John Walter. *The German Element of the Shenandoah Valley of Virginia*. Harrisonburg, VA: Shenandoah Press, 1978.

Wert, Jeffrey D. *From Winchester to Cedar Creek: The Shenandoah Campaign of 1864*. Carlisle, PA: South Mountain Press, 1987.

Wiley, Bell Irvin. *The Life of Johnny Reb: The Common Soldier of the Confederacy*. Baton Rouge: Louisiana State Univ. Press, 1943.

Woodward, Harold R., Jr. *The Confederacy's Forgotten Son: Major General James Lawson Kemper, C.S.A.* Berryville, VA: Rockbridge Publ. Co., 1993.

Letters and Papers

Diary of Francis M. Imboden, West Virginia Univ. Library, Charleston, WV.

Imboden Family Genealogy, Univ. of Virginia Library, compiled by Helen McGuire Imboden Trout, 1948.

Imboden Family Papers, Genealogical Department, Church of Jesus Christ of Latter-day Saints.

Imboden Family Papers, Mr. T. Gibson Hobbs, Jr., Lynchburg, VA.

Imboden Family Papers, Mrs. Katherine G. Bushman, Staunton, VA.

Papers of James Blythe Anderson, Univ. of Kentucky, Lexington, KY.

Papers of John D. Imboden, Library of Congress, Washington, DC.

Papers of John D. Imboden, Univ. of Kentucky, Lexington, KY.

Papers of John D. Imboden, Univ. of Virginia Library, Charlottesville, VA.

Papers of John D. Imboden, Virginia Military Institute, Lexington, VA.
Papers of John D. Imboden, Washington and Lee Univ., Lexington, VA.

Official Manuscripts

Augusta County Common Law Book No. 46.
Augusta County Court Records.
Augusta County, VA, Deed Book No. 29.
Augusta County Will Book No. 28 (1847).
"Catalogue at Washington College, Lexington, Virginia, for the Session 1841-2."
    Archives of Washington and Lee Univ. Library, Lexington, VA.
Census of 1820, Augusta County, VA.
Census of 1850, Augusta County, VA.
National Archives Compiled Service Records.
Journal of the Virginia House of Delegates, 1839-40.
Records of the Grand Lodge of Virginia A.F. & A.M., Richmond, VA.
Records of the War Department: Collection of Confederate War Records, National
    Archives, Washington, DC.
Virginia's Ordinance of Secession.
"War of the Rebellion: A Compilation of the Official Records of the Union and
    Confederate Armies" 128 Vol., U.S. War Department, Washington, DC, 1880-1891.
"Washington and Lee University Catalog of Officials and Alumni 1749-1888."
    Archives of Washington and Lee Univ. Library, Lexington, VA.

Theses

Hager, William D. "The Civilian Life and Accomplishments of J. D. Imboden." History
    thesis, James Madison Univ., 1988.
Thomas, Clayton Malcolm, III. "The Military Career of John D. Imboden." Master of
    arts thesis, Univ. of Virginia, 1965.

Pamphlets

A Diary Depicting the Experiences of DeWitt Clinton Gallaher in the War Between the
    States While Serving in the Confederate Army. Charleston, WV: DeWitt C. Gallaher,
    Jr., 1945.
Civil War Battles in Winchester and Frederick County, Virginia, 1861-1865. Winchester
    and Frederick County Civil War Centennial Commission, 1960.
Proceedings of the Clarke County Historical Association, Vol. XV 1963-1964, Containing:
    Accounts of Ten Memorable Engagements Which Took Place in Clarke County During
    the War Between the States July 18, 1864-Feb. 19, 1865. Clarke County Historical
    Association, 1964.

Newspaper Articles

Harrisonburg Daily News Record, September 14, 1991.
Lynchburg Virginian, November 14, 1865; January 30, 1866; October 2, 1866.
Richmond Dispatch, December 3, 1861; May 8, 1862.
Richmond Enquirer, May 4, 1857; April 23, 1861.

Staunton *Spectator*, May 4, 1857; January 10, 1860; February 28, 1860; May 24, 1860; September 3, 1878.

Staunton *Vindicator*, May 28, 1859; February 20, 1863; July 6, 1894; July 13, 1894; July 29, 1894; August 23, 1895; May 27, 1964; November 30, 1991.

Washington Post, July 14, 1989; July 14, 1992; January 24, 1993.

Washington Times, November 30, 1991; January 11, 1992; September 12, 1992.

Magazine Articles

Abbot, Haviland Harris. "General John D. Imboden." *West Virginia History*, Vol. XXI, 88.

Albto, Walter. "Forgotten Battle for the Capitol." *Civil War Times Illustrated*, Vol. XXXI, No. 6, 40.

Bakeles, John. "Catching Harry Gilmor." *Civil War Times Illustrated*, Vol. X, No. 1, 34.

Berkley, Captain F.M. "Imboden's Dash into Charles Town." *Southern Historical Society Papers*, Vol. XXXI, 12-16.

Burnham, Phili "Hollywood: A Changing Legend." *Richmond Surroundings*, Vol. 8, No. 3, April/May 1993, 56.

Candenquist, Arthur. "The Great Train Robbery: Stonewall Jackson Helps Himself to a Railroad." *Civil War*, Vol. IX, No. 6, 40-42.

Casteel, Albert. "The Guerilla War." *Civil War Times Illustrated*, October 1974, 9.

Clarke, James R. "The Cost of Capture." *Civil War Times Illustrated*, Vol. XXXI, No. 1, 26.

Cochour, Darrell. "Confederates' Brilliant Exploits." *America's Civil War*, September 1991, 40.

"The Confederacy Mounts Its Iron Horse." *Ties: The Southern Railway System Magazine*, Vol. XV, 16.

Crellen, Joseph. "Sheridan Wins at Winchester." *Civil War Times Illustrated*, Vol. II, 5.

Crim, Eliza Clinedist. "New Market: When Boys Became Men." *The Virginian*, May-June 1989, 40-41.

Culbertson, Charles. "Mary Julia and the General." *The Mary Baldwin Magazine*, Vol. 5, No. 1, August 1991, 4-5.

Curtis, Shawn. "Stonewall in the Valley." *America's Civil War*, Vol. 5, No. 6, 34.

Davis, William C. "The Day at New Market." *Civil War Times Illustrated*, Vol. X, No. 4, 4.

_____. "Jubilee: General Jubal A. Early." *Civil War Times Illustrated*, Vol. IX, No. 8, 4.

Franklin, Donald. "The V.M.I. Cadets at New Market." *Virginia Country's Civil War*, Vol. II, 49.

Greenwalt, Bruce S., ed. "Virginians Face Reconstruction: Correspondence from the James Dorman Davidson Papers 1865-1880." *The Virginia Magazine of History and Biography*, Vol. 78, No. 4, October 1979, 458.

Hughes, George McQuinton, Jr., and K. Jeffrey Donald. "Capture at Cumberland." *Confederate Veteran*, March-April 1990, 22.

Imboden, John D. "The Battle of Piedmont." *Confederate Veteran*, Vol. 31, 459 and Vol. 32, 18.

_____. "Reminiscences of Lee and Jackson." *Galaxy Magazine*, Vol. 12, No. 5, November 1871, 41.

_____. "Statement of General John D. Imboden to General D.H. Murray." *Southern Historical Society Papers*, Vol. I, 187.

"Lee's High Estimate of General Imboden." *Confederate Veteran*, Vol. 29, 421.

Mallinson, David L. "The Andersonville Raiders." *Civil War Times Illustrated*, Vol. X, No. 4, 24.

McNeill, John A. "The Imboden Raid and Its Effects." *Southern Historical Society Papers*, Vol. XXXIV, 294.

Miller, Eric. "Civil War Letters Show Personal Struggles." *Rural Living*, March 1991, 10-14.

Murray, Frances J. "Yes, Dixie, West Virginia is Southern Too." *United Daughters of the Confederacy Magazine*, Vol. LII, No. 4, 20.

Osmianski, Russell Allen. "Dress and Undress: A Sketch of Stonewall Jackson." *Confederate Veteran*, January-February 1992.

Patterson, Richard. "Schemes and Treachery." *Civil War Times Illustrated*, April 1989, 38-44.

Prichard, Arthur C. "A World 'First': An Army moved by Rail." *Wonderful West Virginia*, August 1984, 18.

Punifoy, John. "A Night of Horror." *Confederate Veteran*, Vol. 33, 95.

_____. "A Unique Battle." *Confederate Veteran*, Vol. 33, 132.

Reed, Thomas J. "Valley in Flames." *America's Civil War*, July 1889, 42.

Robertson, James I., Jr. "Stonewall in the Shenandoah Valley Campaign of 1862." *Civil War Times Illustrated*, Vol. XI, No. 2, 3.

Summers, Festus. "The Jones-Imboden Raid." *West Virginia History*, Vol. I, 15.

"'They Are Coming!' Testimony of the Court of Inquiry on Imboden's Capture of Charles Town." *Magazine of the Jefferson County Historical Society*, Vol. LIV, December 1988, 15-16.

Thompson, James West. "Controversy—Partisan Comment on Andersonville." *Blue and Gray Magazine*, Vol. III, issue 3, 22, 34-35.

Turner, Edward Raymond. "The Battle of New Market." *Confederate Veteran*, Vol. 29, 71.

Wert, Jeffrey. "First Fair Chance." *Civil War Times Illustrated*, Vol. XVII, No. 5, 1.

Whitaker, B.W. "Hunter's Coming! A Rebel's Experiences in Hunter's Raid on Lynchburg." *Virginia Country's Civil War Quarterly*, Vol. VI, 30.

Whitehorne, Joseph W. A. "The Long Road to New Market." *Civil War*, Vol. XX, 9-17.

Index